THE BEDFORD SERIES IN HISTORY AND CULTURE

The Era of Franklin D. Roosevelt, 1933–1945

A Brief History with Documents

Related Titles in
THE BEDFORD SERIES IN HISTORY AND CULTURE
Advisory Editors: Natalie Zemon Davis, Princeton University
Ernest R. May, Harvard University

Confronting Southern Poverty in the Great Depression: THE REPORT ON
ECONOMIC CONDITIONS OF THE SOUTH *with Related Documents*
Edited with an Introduction by David L. Carlton, *Vanderbilt University,* and
Peter A. Coclanis, *University of North Carolina at Chapel Hill*

America Views the Holocaust, 1933–1945: A Brief Documentary History
Robert H. Abzug, *University of Texas at Austin*

*Pearl Harbor and the Coming of the Pacific War: A Brief History with
Documents and Essays*
Akira Iriye, *Harvard University*

The Nuremberg War Crimes Trial, 1945–46: A Documentary History
Michael R. Marrus, *University of Toronto*

*Lyndon B. Johnson and American Liberalism: A Brief Biography with
Documents*
Bruce J. Schulman, *Boston University*

The Era of Franklin D. Roosevelt, 1933–1945

A Brief History with Documents

Richard Polenberg

Cornell University

BEDFORD/ST. MARTIN'S   Boston • New York

E
806
.P64
2000

For Joni and Jesse

For Bedford/St. Martin's
Executive Editor for History and Political Science: Katherine E. Kurzman
Developmental Editor: Charisse Kiino
Editorial Assistant: Chip Turner
Production Supervisor: Cheryl Mamaril
Marketing Manager: Charles Cavaliere
Project Management: Books By Design, Inc.
Text Design: Claire Seng-Niemoeller
Indexer: Books By Design, Inc.
Cover Design: Richard Emery Design, Inc.
Cover Photo: Copyright American Stock. Courtesy of Picture Network International Ltd.
Composition: G&S Typesetters, Inc.
Printing and Binding: Haddon Craftsmen, an R. R. Donnelley & Sons Company

President: Charles H. Christensen
Editorial Director: Joan E. Feinberg
Director of Marketing: Karen R. Melton
Director of Editing, Design, and Production: Marcia Cohen
Manager, Publishing Services: Emily Berleth

Library of Congress Catalog Card Number: 99-62437

For information, write: Bedford/St. Martin's, 75 Arlington Street, Boston, MA 02116 (617-399-4000)

ISBN: 0-312-13310-3 (paperback)
ISBN: 0-312-22764-7 (hardcover)

Acknowledgments

Acknowledgments and copyrights appear at the back of the book on page 243, which constitutes an extension of the copyright page.

Foreword

The Bedford Series in History and Culture is designed so that readers can study the past as historians do.

The historian's first task is finding the evidence. Documents, letters, memoirs, interviews, pictures, movies, novels, or poems can provide facts and clues. Then the historian questions and compares the sources. There is more to do than in a courtroom, for hearsay evidence is welcome, and the historian is usually looking for answers beyond act and motive. Different views of an event may be as important as a single verdict. How a story is told may yield as much information as what it says.

Along the way the historian seeks help from other historians and perhaps from specialists in other disciplines. Finally, it is time to write, to decide on an interpretation and how to arrange the evidence for readers.

Each book in this series contains an important historical document or group of documents, each document a witness from the past and open to interpretation in different ways. The documents are combined with some element of historical narrative — an introduction or a biographical essay, for example — that provides students with an analysis of the primary source material and important background information about the world in which it was produced.

Each book in the series focuses on a specific topic within a specific historical period. Each provides a basis for lively thought and discussion about several aspects of the topic and the historian's role. Each is short enough (and inexpensive enough) to be a reasonable one-week assignment in a college course. Whether as classroom or personal reading, each book in the series provides firsthand experience of the challenge — and fun — of discovering, recreating, and interpreting the past.

Natalie Zemon Davis
Ernest R. May

Preface

On May 2, 1997, the Franklin D. Roosevelt Memorial was dedicated and opened to the public. More than forty years in the planning, the memorial is located in the nation's capital, not far from the Washington Monument, the Jefferson Memorial, and the Lincoln Memorial. Designed by architect Lawrence Halprin, it covers seven and a half acres along the Tidal Basin and is divided into four outdoor galleries, each representing one of FDR's terms in office and each containing some of his best-known quotations carved in granite. It is the first presidential memorial built to be wheelchair accessible, and the first to honor a first lady, for it has a bronze statue of Eleanor Roosevelt standing in front of the symbol of the United Nations. At the opening ceremony, attended by many of the Roosevelts' grandchildren, President Bill Clinton said that FDR was "the greatest president of this great American century."

The design of the memorial raised issues that were emblematic of the 1990s. To mollify animal-rights advocates, the statue of Eleanor Roosevelt did not include the fox-fur boa she often wore around her shoulders. To satisfy antismoking activists, FDR's trademark cigarette holder was not displayed. And in response to protests by the National Organization on Disability, a last-minute decision was made to include a depiction of FDR in a wheelchair, thereby reversing the original plan. This decision resulted from a demand by people with disabilities for a truthful depiction of the president, a demand that was echoed by former presidents Gerald Ford, Jimmy Carter, and George Bush, as well as by many New Deal historians.

Although the manner in which Franklin D. Roosevelt was to be represented remained controversial, the policies he championed no longer were. After more than half a century, FDR's achievements had gained widespread acceptance. President Clinton suggested as much in his homily, which, summing up those achievements, praised Roosevelt for having forged a strong and unapologetic government, determined to tame the savage cycles of boom and bust, able to meet the national challenges too big for families and individuals to meet on their own. And when he restored dignity to old age, when he helped millions to keep their farms or own their homes, when he provided the simple opportunity to go to work in the morning, to millions, he was proving that the American dream was not a distant glimmer, but something every American could grasp.

During the Roosevelt era, however, virtually everything that the government attempted to do, whether successful or not, sparked intense controversy. If FDR was the most loved president in modern times, he was also the most hated. His policies, lavishly praised by some, were bitterly condemned by others. Seldom in our history has the pace of economic, political, and social change been more rapid, or the changes more far-reaching, than during the years 1933 to 1945. This book attempts to recapture the turbulence of those years, when modern America emerged from the cauldron of the Great Depression and World War II.

The documents I have chosen include statements by Franklin D. Roosevelt and Eleanor Roosevelt, as well as by their supporters and critics, which offer an ideal way to understand the profound changes — political, economic, social, and constitutional — that occurred in American life during the era. I have also selected documents to represent the views of women, African Americans, Native Americans, Mexican Americans, and Asian Americans, groups whose diverse experiences illustrate some of the strengths and many of the limitations of the reform impulse. Because the 1930s and 1940s saw an unprecedented government-backed effort to depict American life visually, I have included representative photographs and posters that reflect the sensibility of the times. A final group of documents is designed to appraise the impact of World War II on American society.

ACKNOWLEDGMENTS

My thanks go to Niels Aaboe, who first proposed a book of this nature to me. I am grateful to the many individuals at Bedford/St. Martin's who have been extraordinarily helpful and supportive: Charles H. Christensen, Joan E. Feinberg, Katherine Kurzman, Chip Turner, Emily Berleth, and Charisse Kiino. I am indebted to David Oshinsky, David Steigerwald, Allan Winkler, and Nan Elizabeth Woodruff for their critical reading of the manuscript and for their many valuable suggestions. Marc Whitman and Lauren Eisenberg, superb research assistants, helped me locate hard-to-find material. I received indispensable help from Nancy Benjamin of Books By Design, Inc. I am also grateful for the superb copyediting by Barbara Jatkola. Above all, I thank the Cornell students who have taken my seminar on the era of Franklin D. Roosevelt and with whom I have discussed many of the documents in this book.

Richard Polenberg

Contents

THE BEDFORD SERIES IN HISTORY AND CULTURE

The Era of Franklin D. Roosevelt, 1933–1945

A Brief History with Documents

PART ONE

Introduction:
Franklin D. Roosevelt
and American Liberalism

FDR: THE PARADOX

Franklin D. Roosevelt's political career is a paradox. Although he was conservative in outlook and disposition, he never feared change or experimentation. He was genuinely committed to certain moral principles and yet was the most pragmatic of leaders. The historian Richard Hofstadter went so far as to dub him "the patrician as opportunist."[1] Born on a country estate and raised in affluent surroundings, he was loved by the common people as no other president in modern times. Biographer James MacGregor Burns said that he was "democracy's aristocrat."[2] He was supremely self-confident, but at the same time he sought to avoid unpleasant personal confrontations.

The complexities of his character baffled relatives and friends alike. On the one hand, he projected extraordinary warmth: the ready smile, the enjoyment of good company, the ability to address a nationwide

---

[1] Richard Hofstadter, *The American Political Tradition* (New York: Alfred A. Knopf, 1948), 315.
[2] James MacGregor Burns, *Roosevelt: The Lion and the Fox* (New York: Harcourt Brace, 1956), 472.

radio audience as "my friends" and sound as if he meant it. On the other hand, he possessed a remote quality. His wife, Eleanor, would term it an "innate kind of reticence."[3] One of his speechwriters, Robert E. Sherwood, spoke of his "thickly forested interior."[4] Secretary of Labor Frances Perkins said that FDR was "the most complicated human being I have ever known."[5]

Roosevelt once told Secretary of the Treasury Henry Morgenthau, his former Dutchess County neighbor and close friend for nearly thirty years, "You know, I am a juggler, and I never let my right hand know what my left hand does." Later, when he half-jokingly advised Morgenthau, "Never let your left hand know what your right is doing," Morgenthau asked, "Which hand am I, Mr. President?"

"My right hand," the president replied, "but I keep my left hand under the table."[6]

Not surprisingly, Morgenthau termed Roosevelt "a man of bewildering complexity of moods and motives."[7]

This most enigmatic of men became the most influential American political leader of the twentieth century. Although he did not achieve all of his goals, his accomplishments are nevertheless impressive: He founded the modern welfare state based on the concept that the federal government has a responsibility to guarantee a minimum standard of living; he transformed the institution of the presidency, becoming, as the historian William E. Leuchtenburg has said, "the first modern President";[8] he changed forever the way politicians use mass media to present their messages, and themselves, to the electorate; he helped engineer a constitutional revolution, converting the Supreme Court into a body that would sanction social reform; and he fashioned an electoral coalition based on a convergence of class, ethnic, and racial interests that would dominate national politics long after his death.

Critics correctly pointed out that Roosevelt left much undone, that he lacked a coherent economic philosophy, and that many New Deal programs benefited privileged and powerful groups, not the weak and dispossessed. A fair appraisal of the Roosevelt presidency surely must take

---

[3] Geoffrey C. Ward, *A First-Class Temperament: The Emergence of Franklin Roosevelt* (New York: Harper & Row, 1989), 18.

[4] Robert E. Sherwood, *Roosevelt and Hopkins: An Intimate History* (New York: Harper, 1948), 9.

[5] Frances Perkins, *The Roosevelt I Knew* (New York: Viking Press, 1946), 3.

[6] John Morton Blum, *Roosevelt and Morgenthau* (Boston: Little, Brown, 1970), 136.

[7] Sherwood, *Roosevelt and Hopkins*, 9.

[8] William E. Leuchtenburg, *The FDR Years: On Roosevelt and His Legacy* (New York: Columbia University Press, 1995), 1.

into account his failures: his unwillingness to advance the cause of racial justice; his inability to convert the Democratic party, at the grassroots level, into a vehicle of social reform; his disregard for civil liberties during the wartime emergency; and his readiness to use that emergency as an excuse to jettison social reform programs. Roosevelt frequently used the presidency to educate his fellow citizens about the real issues before them, but he occasionally resorted to shrill demagogic appeals. In some respects, the Roosevelt record is as paradoxical as the man himself.

HYDE PARK TO WASHINGTON

Franklin Delano Roosevelt was born on January 30, 1882. His father, James Roosevelt, was a graduate of Harvard Law School. James's inherited wealth, combined with successful high-risk business ventures, provided a comfortable life for his family. Residing chiefly at a Hudson River estate in Hyde Park, New York, James also maintained an apartment in lower Manhattan, since his work required that he spend some time in New York City. Left a widower in 1876 after the death of his first wife, Rebecca, James soon met Sara Delano, and the two fell in love. They were married in 1880, when he was fifty-two years of age and she was twenty-six. So Franklin grew up in unusual family circumstances: His father was about the same age as his maternal grandfather; his half brother, James Roosevelt, Jr. ("Rosy") — the son of James and Rebecca — was about the same age as his mother; and his half nephew and half niece, Rosy's children, were both older than he was.

Sara Delano Roosevelt lavished all her attention on Franklin, her only child, keeping him, after the fashion of the day, in dresses and long curls until he was nearly six years old. Seeing to all of Franklin's needs, Sara also sought to control his behavior. As FDR biographer Geoffrey Ward has said, "No moment of Franklin's day was unscheduled or unsupervised. . . . There was no such thing as privacy."[9] In 1890, when Franklin was eight years old, his father suffered a heart attack, which left him in precarious health and increased even further Sara's influence over her son. For Franklin, the advantages of a privileged upbringing included summers at Campobello, an island off the coast of Maine; leisurely trips to European spas; and private tutors. Not until he turned fourteen could Sara bring herself to send him off to school. In 1896 he entered Groton,

[9] Geoffrey C. Ward, *Before the Trumpet: Young Franklin Roosevelt* (New York: Harper & Row, 1985), 125.

a fashionable preparatory school in Massachusetts founded by the Reverend Endicott Peabody. FDR arrived two years later than most other students; Sara wrote, "It is hard to leave my darling boy."[10]

Franklin spent four years at Groton, where nine out of ten students came from families listed in the social register of New York City, Boston, Philadelphia, or Newport, Rhode Island. Similarity of class background did not make it any easier for Franklin, who had always been the center of attention, to adjust to his new environment. Other students appear to have regarded him as charming but snobbish and insincere. In 1900 he entered Harvard, where he did well enough in his studies and served as editor of the *Crimson,* the school newspaper. Chiefly concerned with athletics and social standing, he was most disappointed by his failure to make the football team (because he was too light) and his rejection by Porcellian, the most exclusive social club on campus.

Franklin's father died during his first winter at Harvard, and Sara thereafter tried to spend as much time as possible in Boston to be near her son. To guard against her intrusiveness, Franklin developed what biographer Ted Morgan terms "a core of inner armor"— an ability to dissemble, to mask his feelings by resorting to "protective ambiguity."[11] There was nothing ambiguous, however, about the feelings he developed for his distant cousin, Eleanor Roosevelt, after they began seeing each other socially in 1903, while he was still an undergraduate. Eleanor was Theodore Roosevelt's niece; her father, Elliott, was the president's younger brother. At Thanksgiving in 1903, Franklin shocked his mother by announcing that he was in love with Eleanor and she with him, and that they planned to be married. After graduating from Harvard in June 1904, FDR moved to New York City to attend Columbia Law School. He and Eleanor were married in March 1905, and in June they left for a three-month European honeymoon.

FDR returned for a second year of law school but elected not to enroll for the required third year. He did not complete the degree but decided to take the bar examination anyway, a rather common course at the time. After passing the exam, he went to work for a Wall Street law firm. He and Eleanor also began raising a family. They lived in midtown Manhattan near Sara Roosevelt, who in 1908 arranged for them to reside in a house adjoining hers on East 65th Street. Not very pleased with his work, FDR decided to run for political office. He planned to seek the Democratic nomination for a seat in the state assembly in 1910, but

---

[10] Ibid., 177.
[11] Ted Morgan, *FDR: A Biography* (New York: Simon & Schuster, 1985), 50.

when the Democratic incumbent decided not to retire, FDR set his sights on the state senate seat for Dutchess County, which no Democrat had held for a quarter of a century. After conducting a vigorous campaign, he won a narrow victory. FDR compiled a moderately progressive record as a state senator, opposing Tammany Hall's nominee for the U.S. Senate (at a time when the election was still in the hands of the state legislature) and lending his support to a bill establishing a fifty-four-hour workweek for women and children. His most thoughtful statement in support of reform came in a speech in Troy, New York, in March 1912. Advocating the conservation of natural resources, FDR maintained that the time had come to replace competition with cooperation. The "liberty of the community," he asserted, must sometimes take precedence over "the liberty of the individual to do as he pleased with his own property." The role of government was to protect the general welfare, to guard against the disastrous social consequences that would result "if the individuals are allowed to do as they please with the natural resources to line their own pockets during their life." [12]

Roosevelt was reelected in 1912 but soon accepted the post of undersecretary of the Navy in Woodrow Wilson's administration. In so doing, he was following the career path of his fifth cousin, Theodore Roosevelt, whom he greatly admired. Moving from Albany to Washington, FDR assumed responsibility for the Navy's procurement, supply, and civilian personnel policies. With the outbreak of World War I, he pressed for preparedness and naval expansion. After the United States entered the conflict in April 1917, he sought an officer's commission but had to settle for various civilian missions to inspect naval stations in the European theater of war. When the armistice was signed, he was at once relieved that the war was over and dismayed that he had missed the chance to lead men into battle.

In September 1918, a profoundly disturbing event shook the foundations of Roosevelt's personal life and might have led him to renounce politics. Returning from a trip abroad, Roosevelt came down with a severe case of double pneumonia and was confined to bed. While Eleanor was unpacking his things, she discovered a packet of love letters he had received from Lucy Mercer, a young woman whom Eleanor had hired as her social secretary four years earlier. In the summer of 1917, perhaps suspecting her husband's infidelity, Eleanor had fired Mercer, who had

---

[12] Basil Rauch, ed., *The Roosevelt Reader* (New York: Holt, Rinehart and Winston, 1957), 12–16.

then taken a job with the Navy Department and so remained in close touch with FDR. Meanwhile, to escape Washington's oppressively hot weather, Eleanor was spending long summer vacations with the five Roosevelt children at Campobello, allowing FDR and Lucy to spend considerable time together. When Eleanor came across the letters, her worst suspicions were confirmed. She was ready to file for a divorce. But FDR knew that the scandal of a divorce would ruin his political career, and his mother also threatened to cut off his inheritance if he went ahead with it. So he promised Eleanor that he would never see Lucy Mercer again (a promise he would later break), and the couple remained together, although their marriage would never again be based on intimacy and mutual trust.

In 1920 the Democratic party nominated Roosevelt for vice president on the ticket headed by James M. Cox. Although the Republicans, led by Warren G. Harding, won the election, Roosevelt gained valuable national exposure. He appeared to have a bright political future, but another tragic event nearly destroyed his prospects. In August 1921, while vacationing at Campobello, FDR was stricken with poliomyelitis, a dread disease also known as infantile paralysis because it affected children more often than adults. Despite years of physical therapy and treatment, FDR never regained the use of his legs. He could stand only with the use of heavy steel braces and when he could lean on something; he could walk only by using crutches or by leaning on someone's arm. His battle against polio was as much psychological as physical, as much an effort to defeat depression as to regain the strength in his ravaged limbs. As Geoffrey Ward notes, FDR's struggle changed him for the better, for it required "patience, application, recognition of his own limitations, a willingness to fail in front of others and try again." [13]

Although his mother wanted him to retreat into a cloistered life, FDR refused to permit his disability to end his political career. By 1924 he had recovered sufficiently to make a dramatic appearance at the Democratic National Convention to nominate New York governor Alfred E. Smith, whom he praised as "the 'Happy Warrior' of the political battlefield." [14] Smith failed to gain the nomination, but in 1928, when he became the Democratic candidate for president, he convinced FDR to run for governor of New York. During the campaign, Roosevelt defended his party's record of support for protective labor legislation and criticized Republicans who, he said, belonged to

[13] Ward, *First-Class Temperament,* 600.
[14] Ibid., 691–99.

the old school of thought, which held to the theory that when an employer hired working men or working women, that employer became the master of the fate of his employees; that when a worker entered the factory doors it was nobody's business as to how he worked, how long he was worked, or how much he was paid.[15]

Smith lost to Herbert Hoover, but Roosevelt won a narrow victory and in 1930 easily gained reelection.

From the start, he proved himself a capable, energetic governor. The Great Depression, which began in the fall of 1929 and worsened by the month, brought out the best in Roosevelt: his talent for administration and his ability to persuade large numbers of people that he was the right person to manage a crisis. In 1931 he created the Temporary Emergency Relief Administration, the first agency of its kind in any state, to provide food, clothing, and housing for the unemployed and to find them jobs if possible. He also elaborated on the argument he had first made in his Troy speech about the need for social interests to take precedence over individual concerns. People created government "for their mutual protection and well-being," he said in 1931, and consequently "the duty of the State toward the citizens is the duty of the servant to its master." One of those duties

> is that of caring for those of its citizens who find themselves the victims of such adverse circumstances as makes them unable to obtain even the necessities for mere existence without the aid of others. . . .
> In broad terms I assert that modern society, acting through its Government, owes the definite obligation to prevent the starvation or the dire want of any of its fellow men and women who try to maintain themselves but cannot.

It was not a matter of charity, he concluded, but "a matter of social duty."[16]

By 1932 FDR was a leading contender for the Democratic presidential nomination. In a radio address in April, called "the forgotten man" speech, he put a new twist on what he had been saying for twenty years. The Republicans favored top-down policies, FDR claimed, while he wanted lasting economic recovery, which required new initiatives that "put their faith once more in the forgotten man at the bottom of the economic pyramid." He compared the economic crisis to a war and demanded that the nation "mobilize" to meet it. He defined what he

[15] Rauch, *Roosevelt Reader,* 55–59.
[16] Ibid., 62–64.

thought were a "few essentials of a planned program": restoring agricultural purchasing power, protecting homeowners from the threat of mortgage foreclosures, and obtaining foreign markets for American goods by lowering tariff barriers. Above all, Roosevelt insisted, people and their leaders had to face facts squarely and admit "that we are in the midst of an emergency."[17]

On July 2, 1932, appearing at the Democratic convention in Chicago to accept the party's presidential nomination, FDR promised "a new deal for the American people." His speech painted in broad outline the policies he had in mind. "What do the people of America want more than anything else?" he asked, and then he answered, "Two things; Work; work with all the moral and spiritual values that go with work. And with work, a reasonable measure of security — security for themselves and for their wives and children." He rejected the notion that inviolable economic laws make depressions inevitable. The fact was that "men and women are starving," that "economic laws are not made by nature. They are made by human beings." The states had the primary responsibility for relieving distress, he said, "yet the Federal Government has always had and still has a continuing responsibility for the broader public welfare."[18] In a real sense, the history of FDR's presidency was the history of the government's efforts — often halting, always controversial — to shoulder that responsibility.

THE NEW DEAL, 1933–1936

In November 1932, Roosevelt received a resounding popular mandate, obtaining 22.8 million votes to Hoover's 15.8 million, and the Democrats won substantial majorities in Congress, where they outnumbered Republicans 59 to 36 in the Senate and 313 to 117 in the House of Representatives. Moreover, FDR took office at a time when the nation was facing a crisis of such magnitude that he could count on an extraordinary amount of cooperation. As a midwestern congressman told him, "I will do anything you ask. You are my leader."[19] From FDR's perspective, the stakes could not have been higher. He feared that a revolution was likely if he failed, as Hoover had, to solve the nation's problems.[20]

---

[17] Samuel I. Rosenman, ed., *The Public Papers and Addresses of Franklin D. Roosevelt,* 13 vols. (New York: Random House; Harper and Bros., 1938–1950), 1:624–27.

[18] Ibid., 647–49.

[19] Burns, *Roosevelt: The Lion and the Fox,* 168.

[20] On the fear of revolution, see Robert S. McElvaine, *The Great Depression: America 1929–1941,* 2nd ed. (New York: Times Books, 1993), 90–94.

During the campaign, FDR had asserted in his Commonwealth Club address that everyone had "a right to make a comfortable living," that the government "owes to every one an avenue to possess himself of a portion of that plenty sufficient for his needs, through his own work." [21] Early New Deal programs were designed not so much to promote reform as to produce recovery, so they often benefited big business and big agriculture — well-organized and influential groups on whose fate an upturn, it was believed, depended. Weaker, more marginal groups — such as small businesses, blue-collar workers, and landless farmers — found themselves on the outside looking in. Yet even the earliest New Deal measures clearly indicated that the Roosevelt administration intended to move the country in a dramatically new direction.

That direction depended largely, but not entirely, on Roosevelt's own outlook. The New Deal ultimately drew on many sources: the recommendations of the president's "brain trust" (Columbia University professors Rexford G. Tugwell, Raymond Moley, and Adolf A. Berle); the advice of influential cabinet members such as Secretary of the Interior Harold L. Ickes, Secretary of Agriculture Henry A. Wallace, and Secretary of Labor Frances Perkins; the initiatives taken by Democratic congressional leaders such as Senator Robert F. Wagner of New York; and grassroots political ferment that made itself felt in the nation's capital. FDR's function, by no means an easy one, was to reconcile the sharply conflicting views of his reform-minded supporters — some of whom favored a highly competitive economy, others of whom preferred a corporatist, or collectivist, approach. The New Deal, as historian Michael Parrish says, "bore the stamp of many authors, arose from no master plan, and did not fit neatly into a single ideological box." [22]

The most important early New Deal initiative was the National Industrial Recovery Act (NIRA), passed in June 1933, which created the National Recovery Administration (NRA). Based on the ideal of a business-government partnership, the NRA permitted business executives to draft codes of fair competition, subject to presidential approval, that regulated prices and wages with the goal of keeping both high enough to ensure reasonable profits and decent wages. Moreover, the codes forbade or restricted a broad range of cutthroat competitive practices, such as below-cost sales, trade-in allowances, and the use of child labor. In addition, the NRA supposedly guaranteed labor the right to organize and

[21] Rosenman, *Public Papers,* 1:754.
[22] Michael Parrish, *Anxious Decades: America in Prosperity and Depression* (New York: W. W. Norton, 1992), 299.

funded a public works program to pump money into the economy. Industries that participated in these agreements were exempt from the antitrust laws.

When one of Roosevelt's advisers, Raymond Moley, suggested that the NRA represented a giant step away from the philosophy of laissez-faire individualism, the president replied, "If that philosophy hadn't proved to be bankrupt, Herbert Hoover would be sitting here right now. I never felt surer of anything in my life than I do of the soundness of this passage."[23] FDR defended the new approach as creating a "partnership in planning" between government and business. "Government ought to have the right and will have the right, after surveying and planning for an industry, to prevent, with the assistance of the overwhelming majority of that industry, all unfair practices and to enforce that agreement by the authority of government," he maintained.[24]

In September 1934, more than a year after its inception, FDR defended the NRA in a fireside chat. Conceding that "there is no magic formula" for achieving recovery, and admitting that the economy had not yet been restored to its pre-Depression levels, Roosevelt still claimed that the NRA had chalked up major victories in eliminating child labor, shortening the workday, and establishing a minimum wage. The American people, he added, must never return "to that definition of liberty under which for many years a free people were being gradually regimented into the service of the privileged few."[25]

By May 1935, when the Supreme Court unanimously declared the NIRA unconstitutional in *A. L. A. Schechter Poultry Corp. v. United States,* it was already apparent that the agency had failed to accomplish its broader purposes. Big business had used its domination of the code-drafting process to consolidate control over the market, in part by inserting provisions that kept production low and prices high. Consequently, the agency had come under attack from consumers and small business operators, as well as from labor leaders dissatisfied because Section 7(a), which was intended to protect the right to organize, was proving ineffectual. Although Section 7(a) prohibited employers from interfering with workers' rights to join unions and choose bargaining officials, it did not create adequate enforcement machinery or require employers to bargain in good faith. The NRA's initials, said the disenchanted, stood for "No Recovery Allowed."

---

[23] Arthur M. Schlesinger, Jr., *The Coming of the New Deal* (Boston: Houghton Mifflin, 1959), 98.
[24] Russell D. Buhite and David W. Levy, eds., *FDR's Fireside Chats* (Norman: University of Oklahoma Press, 1992), 24.
[25] Ibid., 62.

In *Schechter,* known colloquially as the "sick chicken" case, the Supreme Court declared that the Schechter brothers, who purchased, slaughtered, and sold chickens, were engaged only in intrastate commerce; their enterprise was, therefore, outside the scope of federal regulation under the Constitution's commerce clause. Roosevelt reacted angrily to the ruling because he recognized that the justices' reasoning struck directly at his conception of government as a guarantor of social welfare. The Court's narrow construction of the commerce clause, he realized, would doom many reform proposals. Privately, he commented that the justices would probably find that only 10 percent of all business transactions were directly involved in interstate commerce. Publicly, he assailed the ruling at a press conference, permitting reporters to quote this remark: "We have been relegated to the horse-and-buggy definition of interstate commerce."[26]

On May 14, 1935, less than two weeks before the Supreme Court's ruling in *Schechter,* FDR spoke informally to a delegation of farmers who were visiting the capital. He used the occasion to defend the Agricultural Adjustment Act (AAA), which had for two years served as the foundation of New Deal farm policy. The government had attempted, he explained, to balance agricultural production and consumption so as to avoid surpluses and ensure that farmers got a fair price. Because a powerful elite no longer dictated agricultural policy, FDR said, "a great many of the high and mighty — with special axes to grind — have been deliberately trying to mislead people who know nothing of farming by misrepresenting — no, why use a pussyfoot word — by lying, about the kind of a farm program under which this nation is operating today." Despite "the crocodile tears shed by the professional mourners of an old and obsolete order," the president declared, his administration had successfully boosted agricultural income.[27]

The AAA was based on a "domestic allotment" plan under which farmers agreed to reduce the acreage they cultivated or otherwise limit production. The plan affected the major commodities: wheat, cotton, tobacco, corn, rice, hogs, and milk. In return for curbing output, farmers received government subsidies, which, in turn, were funded by a tax on the processors of agricultural goods. The new policy, as Arthur M. Schlesinger said, "assigned the federal government the decisive role in protecting farm income."[28] According to Secretary of Agriculture Henry A. Wallace, the plan was "a contrivance as new in the field of

[26] Rosenman, *Public Papers,* 4:221.
[27] Ibid., 175–80.
[28] Schlesinger, *Coming of the New Deal,* 38.

social relations as the first gasoline engine was new in the field of mechanics."[29]

Federal payments under the AAA greatly benefited farmers who owned their own land, but as they reduced their acreage, they naturally had less need for farm laborers, and the domestic allotment program led to the eviction of tenant farmers and other agricultural laborers. In 1935 the Roosevelt administration created the Resettlement Administration to assist displaced farmers by helping them acquire their own land and tools. Meanwhile, the AAA accomplished a good deal: By 1936 gross farm income was up by 50 percent, commodity prices had risen by 66 percent, and farm indebtedness was down by $1 billion. In January 1936, however, the Supreme Court declared the AAA unconstitutional in *United States v. Butler.* "The decision virtually prohibits the President and Congress from the right, under modern conditions, to intervene reasonably in the regulation of nation-wide commerce and nation-wide agriculture," FDR wrote angrily in a confidential memorandum. The people's will, he added, was being subverted by "the private, social philosophy of a majority of nine appointed members of the Supreme Court."[30]

In addition to helping business and agriculture cope with the ravages of the Depression, Roosevelt recognized the government's obligation to provide relief to the destitute. Funds to aid the jobless were dispensed first through the Federal Emergency Relief Administration and then, during the winter of 1933–34, through the Civil Works Administration, and eventually through the Works Progress Administration. By providing outright federal grants, the New Deal broke decisively with past practice and provided millions of Americans with the necessities of life. The historian James Patterson has pointed out that "during the 1930s, some 46 million people, 35% of the population, received public aid or social insurance at one time or another."[31]

His administration's relief policies rested on "elementary principles of justice and fairness," FDR explained, and he further asserted, "The primary concern of any government dominated by the humane ideals of democracy is the simple principle that in a land of vast resources no one should be permitted to starve." The goal was not merely to offer grants, he said, but to provide the unemployed with "useful and remunerative

---

[29]Ibid., 39.
[30]William E. Leuchtenburg, *The Supreme Court Reborn: The Constitutional Revolution in the Age of Roosevelt* (New York: Oxford University Press, 1995), 99.
[31]James T. Patterson, *America's Struggle against Poverty, 1900–1994* (Cambridge: Harvard University Press, 1994), 76.

work." Addressing Congress in 1938, FDR summed up the New Deal's social philosophy:

> Government has a final responsibility for the well-being of its citizenship. If private co-operative endeavor fails to provide work for willing hands and relief for the unfortunate, those suffering hardship from no fault of their own have a right to call upon the Government for aid; and a government worthy of its name must make fitting response.[32]

No cause was nearer Roosevelt's heart than conservation, and in no area did his administration come up with more innovative measures. "The forests are the 'lungs' of our land," he once said, "purifying our air and giving fresh strength to our people."[33] The Civilian Conservation Corps, which enrolled half a million young men, combined the functions of relief and forestry. The volunteers fought forest fires and reseeded grazing lands; they constructed roads, bridges, water-storage basins, and camping facilities; they built wildlife refuges, fish-rearing ponds, and animal shelters. The Tennessee Valley Authority (TVA) transformed social and economic conditions in a 40,000-square-mile region. It not only provided cheap electric power but also helped prevent soil erosion and control floods. FDR wanted the TVA to have broad authority to plan "for the proper use, conservation and development of the natural resources of the Tennessee River drainage basin and its adjoining territory for the general social and economic welfare of the nation."[34]

By 1935, within two years of taking office, Roosevelt had transformed Americans' expectations by demonstrating that they could reasonably look to government for assistance when faced with economic distress. In the process, he effectively disarmed conservative critics who asserted that New Deal programs were subverting personal freedom. In a fireside chat in June 1934, the president rebutted those "plausible self-seekers and theoretical diehards [who] will tell you of the loss of individual liberty." He advised his listeners, "Answer this question out of the facts of your own life. Have you lost any of your rights or liberty or constitutional freedom of action and choice?" All anyone had to do, he added, was read the Bill of Rights "and ask yourself whether you personally have suffered the impairment of a single jot of these great assurances." He was confident of the answer: "The record is written in the experiences of your own personal lives."[35]

[32] Rosenman, *Public Papers,* 7:14.
[33] Schlesinger, *Coming of the New Deal,* 336.
[34] Rosenman, *Public Papers,* 2:122.
[35] Buhite and Levy, *FDR's Fireside Chats,* 49.

To counter critics on the left, Roosevelt adopted a different strategy: He incorporated essential aspects of their programs into his own legislative agenda. This was certainly the case with the Social Security Act, which FDR signed in August 1935. Ever since 1912, reformers had been advocating old-age pensions, and in 1932 Wisconsin became the first state to adopt an unemployment compensation plan. The Great Depression provided a further stimulus to these efforts. Generous old-age pensions amounting to fifty dollars a month were a key feature of Upton Sinclair's rousing, if unsuccessful, California gubernatorial campaign in 1934. Moreover, Dr. Francis E. Townsend was advocating the still more generous, and more popular, Old Age Revolving Pension Plan, under which all persons over the age of sixty would receive two hundred dollars a month on the condition that they spend the full amount each month and retire if still employed. The plan was to be financed by a national sales tax. Millions of elderly Americans joined Townsend clubs and helped crystallize popular sentiment in favor of old-age pensions, a sentiment that helped move Social Security (a considerably scaled-down version of Townsendism) through Congress.

In June 1935, partly as a way of responding to Louisiana senator Huey P. Long's immensely popular Share Our Wealth movement, FDR called on Congress to impose high taxes on inherited wealth, corporate profits, and "very great individual incomes." In proposing the Wealth Tax Act, FDR used rhetoric similar to that used by Long: "Wealth in the modern world does not come merely from individual effort; it comes from a combination of individual effort and of the manifold uses to which the community puts that effort. . . . The people in the mass have inevitably helped to make large fortunes possible." FDR maintained that "vast personal incomes come not only through the effort or ability or luck of those who receive them, but also because of the opportunities for advantage which government itself contributes. Therefore, the duty rests upon the government to restrict such incomes by very high taxes." [36] In its final form, the Wealth Tax Act did not set rates at the level FDR proposed, much less as high as Long would have liked, but the measure nevertheless symbolized the president's belief that the national interest took priority over individual gains.

By the end of his first term in office, Franklin D. Roosevelt had expanded the role of government in people's lives and, in so doing, had permanently altered their assumptions about what government could and should do to protect them against economic adversity. Nothing better

[36] Rosenman, *Public Papers,* 4:270–76.

illustrates the New Deal's repudiation of the older laissez-faire outlook than the 1936 Democratic party platform. Drafted chiefly by one of FDR's advisers, Samuel I. Rosenman, it incorporated many of the president's own suggestions, including a line based on the Declaration of Independence: "We hold this truth to be self-evident — that government in a modern civilization has certain inescapable obligations to its citizens, among which are: (1) Protection of the family and the home; (2) Establishment of a democracy of opportunity for all the people; (3) Aid to those overtaken by disaster."[37]

During the 1936 presidential campaign, FDR took dead aim at those he termed "economic royalists." His frank appeal to class resentments was unprecedented for a major party candidate. Denouncing the "new economic royalty," which had once dominated economic life, Roosevelt claimed that the rich and powerful opposed the New Deal because it had destroyed their dictatorial power. The "privileged princes of these new economic dynasties," FDR said, "thirsting for power, reached out for control over government itself. They created a new despotism and wrapped it in the robes of legal sanction." The Great Depression, however, "showed up the despotism for what it was," and people turned to government for salvation. Roosevelt defended his programs without apology:

> Governments can err — Presidents do make mistakes, but the immortal Dante tells us that divine justice weighs the sins of the cold-blooded and the sins of the warm-hearted in different scales. Better the occasional faults of a government that lives in a spirit of charity than the consistent omissions of a government frozen in the ice of its own indifference.[38]

Election Day returns confirmed Roosevelt's decision to make the campaign a referendum on the welfare state. He received 27,750,000 votes; the Republican candidate, Governor Alf M. Landon of Kansas, received only 16,679,000 votes. William Lemke, running on the Union party ticket, received 900,000 votes. FDR carried every state but Maine and Vermont and won a lopsided 523–8 electoral college victory. The Democrats, moreover, won enormous majorities in the House of Representatives (331–89) and the Senate (76–16). FDR received 60.8 percent of the popular vote. Even more significant was the electorate's class alignment: 42 percent of upper-income voters backed FDR, compared to 60 percent of middle-income and 76 percent of lower-income voters. A

[37] Leuchtenburg, *FDR Years,* 125–26.
[38] Rosenman, *Public Papers,* 5:232–36.

whopping 80 percent of union members voted for FDR, as did 84 percent of relief recipients. A letter FDR received from a furniture worker in Texas expressed a widely felt sentiment: "You are the one & only President that ever helped a Working Class of People."[39]

In winning reelection, Roosevelt forged a coalition that would dominate American politics for nearly fifty years. The coalition embraced southern whites as well as northern blacks, rural folks as well as urban immigrants, farmers as well as blue-collar workers, middle-class homeowners and jobless men and women — all attracted by economic policies that benefited them and sometimes saved their very lives, and by a recognition that the Democratic party, having introduced the welfare state, could be trusted to expand it. The coalition also had an ethnic-religious dimension, for the New Deal gave Jews and Catholics a greater voice in policymaking than they had ever had before and consequently cemented the Democratic loyalties of those groups. But FDR's electoral base was built on pocketbook issues. In the decades that followed, whenever economic concerns were foremost in the public mind, the Roosevelt coalition reasserted itself. Only when social issues, cultural conflicts, or foreign policy debates became centrally important did the tensions inherent in the coalition lead to its fragmentation.

THE WANING OF REFORM, 1937–1940

On January 20, 1937, FDR delivered his second inaugural address. Speaking from the Capitol rotunda on a cold, rainy day, the president declared that although the nation had made great strides toward economic recovery, much more remained to be done. Tens of millions of Americans, he said, "are denied the greater part of what the very lowest standards of today call the necessities of life"; are "trying to live on incomes so meager that the pall of family disaster hangs over them day by day"; and are "denied education, recreation, and the opportunity to better their lot and the lot of their children." Then came one of his most famous utterances: "I see one-third of a nation ill-housed, ill-clad, ill-nourished." FDR said that he painted this grim picture not in despair but in hope, "because the Nation, seeing and understanding the injustice in it, proposes to paint it out."[40]

Ten days earlier, meeting with congressional leaders, FDR had unveiled a bold, far-reaching plan of administrative reform based on the report of a committee he had appointed in March 1936. The committee's

---

[39] Leuchtenburg, *FDR Years,* 153.
[40] Rosenman, *Public Papers,* 6:1–6.

goal, according to its chairman, Louis Brownlow, was "to discover and invent ways and means to give the President effective managerial direction and control over all departments and agencies of the Executive Branch of the Federal government commensurate with his responsibility."[41] The committee proposed to strengthen the president by furnishing him with six executive assistants with "a passion for anonymity"; by expanding the merit system and replacing the three-member Civil Service Commission with a single administrator; by encouraging budget planning and restoring control of accounts to the executive; by making the National Resources Planning Board a permanent agency to coordinate government programs; and, finally, by creating two new cabinet-level departments (Public Works and Welfare), changing the name of the Department of the Interior to the Department of Conservation, and bringing every executive agency, including the nonjudicial functions of the independent regulatory commissions, under one of the cabinet departments.

Having presided over the creation of the welfare state, Roosevelt was now attempting to give order to the structure of that state. Reforming governmental administration, he understood, would also aid in achieving the broad social purposes of the New Deal. "The gains of civilization are essentially mass gains," the Brownlow report declared. "They should be distributed as fairly as possible among those who created them." In language that surely reflected the president's own views, the report noted that executive reorganization would benefit all segments of society, especially the underprivileged: "For they need the help of government in their struggle for justice, security, steadier employment, better living and working conditions, and a growing share of the gains of civilization."[42]

"The great stake in efficient demōcracy," FDR said in his message to Congress, "is the stake of the common man."[43]

On February 5, before Congress had fully absorbed the implications of executive reorganization, FDR sprang another, even more shocking surprise: his plan to "pack" the Supreme Court by adding a new justice for each sitting justice who, having served at least ten years, did not resign or retire within six months after reaching the age of seventy (with a proviso that no more than six additional justices would be appointed). In proposing this plan, FDR reasoned correctly that conservative justices,

[41] Richard Polenberg, *Reorganizing Roosevelt's Government: The Controversy over Executive Reorganization, 1936–1939* (Cambridge: Harvard University Press, 1966), 15.
[42] Ibid., 26.
[43] Ibid., 43.

who objected to the growth of the welfare state, were permitting their personal preferences to influence their interpretation of congressional powers under the Constitution. One of the more liberal members of the Court, Justice Harlan Fiske Stone, later commented that the archconservative Justice Willis Van Devanter "conceived it his duty to declare unconstitutional any law which he particularly disliked."[44]

In seeking judicial approval for the New Deal, however, Roosevelt actually chose one of the more cautious routes available to him. Many of his critics complained that, rather than attempting to enlarge the Court, FDR should have sought to amend the Constitution so as to require a two-thirds vote by the justices to declare an act unconstitutional, to permit Congress to override a Court decision, or to broaden congressional power to regulate the economy. All of these proposals, Roosevelt believed, suffered from a common defect: They would never be approved — and would certainly never be approved quickly enough — by the necessary three-fourths of the state legislatures. More important, each of the proposed amendments would have meant tampering with the Constitution, when, in Roosevelt's view, the document's language, properly construed, could easily allow for the kind of economic regulation his administration supported.

Roosevelt's conservative critics, who had made little headway by denouncing the welfare state, found the public considerably more receptive to attacks on executive reorganization and Court reform. The president's initiatives in these areas, his opponents maintained, proved that he was dangerously power hungry and that he aspired to be a dictator. The charges, though wildly exaggerated, struck a responsive chord at a time when many Americans were troubled by the advance of dictatorships in Europe. Neither administrative nor judicial reform enjoyed the backing of any sizable constituency, for people did not associate either of them with immediate, tangible, or direct benefits, as they did earlier New Deal measures such as river valley development, agricultural price supports, old-age pensions, unemployment insurance, and relief programs.

Consequently, both Court packing and reorganization went down to defeat in Congress, the former in July 1937, when the Senate rejected the plan, and the latter in April 1938, when more than one hundred Democrats in the House of Representatives broke with the administration to kill it. Yet FDR did not come away empty-handed. In the spring of 1937,

[44]Richard Polenberg, "The Decline of the New Deal," in *The New Deal: The National Level,* ed. John Braeman et al. (Columbus: Ohio State University Press, 1975), 248.

partly because Justice Owen Roberts changed his position, giving the liberal faction a needed fifth vote, the Supreme Court upheld state minimum wage laws, the Social Security Act, and the National Labor Relations Act. In addition, Justice Van Devanter resigned, giving Roosevelt his first Court appointment. During his second term, he named five justices, and the Court thereafter posed no barrier to the expansion of the welfare state. In 1939 Congress passed a modified reorganization bill, which, while omitting the far-reaching provisions of the original measure, nevertheless permitted FDR to create the Executive Office of the President and to make a number of sensible interagency transfers in the interest of efficient administration.

Just as Roosevelt worked to reform the judiciary and the bureaucracy, he moved to effect political realignment by intervening in Democratic party primaries in the 1938 congressional elections. His chief targets were the southern Democrats, whose fundamental conservatism had become more evident as the administration had grown more responsive to its northern, urban constituency. Not only had many southerners opposed Court packing and executive reorganization, but they also had come close to eviscerating the United States Housing Act. That measure, enacted in September 1937, authorized expenditures of $500 million for the construction of low-cost housing. Southerners succeeded in limiting Federal Housing Authority expenditures to no more than $5,000 for any family unit, a figure that failed to take into account high construction costs in large cities. Even so, many southern Democratic senators, including Ellison D. ("Cotton Ed") Smith of South Carolina, Walter F. George of Georgia, and Millard Tydings of Maryland, voted against the bill.

Southern Democrats also attempted to block another reform in which FDR placed great hopes, the Fair Labor Standards Act, which was designed to outlaw child labor and establish minimum wage and maximum hour levels. On May 24, 1937, Roosevelt asked Congress to pass the bill, declaring, "The time has arrived for us to take further action to extend the frontiers of social progress." This action, he claimed, "is within the common sense framework and purpose of our Constitution and receives beyond doubt the approval of our electorate." Rejecting the view that the time had come for government to "take a holiday," FDR added, "A self-supporting and self-respecting democracy can plead no justification for the existence of child labor, no economic reason for chiseling workers' wages or stretching workers' hours."[45]

[45] Rosenman, *Public Papers,* 6:209–14.

From the standpoint of many southern Democrats, any measure that raised wages across the board threatened to deprive their region of its competitive advantage as a cheap labor market (and also threatened to overturn the prevailing system under which African Americans earned less than whites). In the spring of 1937, southern Democrats on the House Rules Committee joined with Republicans to prevent the bill from reaching the floor after it had passed the Senate. In the fall, when a discharge petition pried it loose from the committee, the House voted to recommit (send the bill back to the committee), with southern Democrats favoring recommittal by a margin of 74 to 17. The House eventually passed the bill in May 1938, but only after it had been amended to exempt domestic workers (chiefly African American women) and farm laborers, to allow for regional wage differentials, and to provide that the minimum wage rise gradually over three years, from 25 cents to 40 cents an hour.

Faced with this record of opposition to the extension of the New Deal, FDR decided on an attempt to defeat conservative Democrats in the 1938 primaries. Among those he wanted to oust were Senators Smith, George, and Tydings. In South Carolina, FDR helped persuade Governor Olin T. Johnston to run against Smith, a savage racist who had stalked out of the Democratic National Convention in 1936 when an African American minister was invited to give an invocation. (Smith later said that he had left when a "slew-footed, blue-gummed, kinky-headed Senegambian . . . started praying."[46]) In Georgia, on August 11, 1938, FDR asserted that the people of that state needed representatives in Congress who would fight for "laws with teeth in them that will go to the root of the problem; which remove the inequities, raise the standards and, over a period of years, give constant improvement to the conditions of human life in this State." His own goals, FDR said, were "to work for a wider distribution of national income, to improve the conditions of life, especially among those who need it most and, above all, to use every honest effort to keep America in the van of social and economic progress." On most questions, FDR said, he and Walter George — who was seated near him on the platform — "do not speak the same language."[47] A month later, speaking on the Eastern Shore of Maryland, Roosevelt suggested that the incumbent Millard Tydings was one of "those in public life who quote the Golden Rule and take no steps to bring it closer."[48]

[46] Page Smith, *Redeeming the Time: A People's History of the 1920s and the New Deal* (New York: McGraw-Hill, 1987), 75.
[47] Rosenman, *Public Papers,* 7:468–69.
[48] Ibid., 520.

FDR's attempt to "purge" the Democratic party was less successful than his efforts to reform the Supreme Court or to reorganize the executive branch of government. Of the ten conservative Democrats he opposed, all but one gained renomination, and, once reelected, they had even less reason to follow the president than they had before. (The purge's only victim was not a southerner but Congressman John O'Connor of New York City, chairman of the House Rules Committee.) Many southern Democrats resented the president's intrusion into local elections, and most of the incumbents, no matter how conservative their voting records, simply presented themselves as independent-minded. Those who benefited the most from New Deal relief programs and constituted the only likely constituency for the purge — poor African Americans and whites — either did not vote in the primaries or participated at very low levels.

Roosevelt's three-pronged effort to achieve administrative, judicial, and political reform occurred against a most inauspicious backdrop: an economic collapse that began in the fall of 1937 and lasted well into 1938. The rate of decline during the "Roosevelt recession" was sharper than that of 1929. Over a ten-month period, industrial production fell by 33 percent, industrial stock prices by 50 percent, and national income by 12 percent. Nearly 4 million people lost their jobs, boosting total unemployment to 11.5 million. The slump occurred largely because the administration, in attempting to balance the budget, had cut expenditures sharply. The government's contribution to consumer purchasing power dropped from $4.1 billion in 1936 to less than $1 billion in 1937. The president's conservative critics attributed the downturn to the business community's lack of confidence in the New Deal. To encourage investment or expansion, they argued, the government should cut spending still further, repeal burdensome taxes on business, and call a halt to reform.

Deeply troubled by the course of events, Roosevelt nevertheless resisted embarking on a new spending program. He did not want to admit that his earlier policies had failed, and he was too traditional in his thinking to accept planned budget deficits during an economic downturn. He believed that pump priming had been appropriate "when the water had receded to the bottom of the well," but he doubted its worth in 1938 "with the water within twenty-five or thirty per cent of the top."[49] For several months, the president let things slide, as conditions worsened, factories shut down, and the stock market tumbled. In March 1938, Secretary of the Treasury Henry Morgenthau, Jr., noted that Roosevelt was "just

---

[49] Harold Ickes, *The Secret Diary of Harold Ickes* (New York: Simon & Schuster, 1954), 2:317.

treading water . . . to wait to see what happens this spring."[50] Only in April, when it was apparent that the recession could spell disaster for the Democrats in the fall elections, did the president reject Morgenthau's fiscal conservatism and turn to Harry Hopkins and other advisers who, influenced by the views of British economist John Maynard Keynes, favored additional spending even at the risk of creating a larger budget deficit. He then asked Congress to authorize a $3.75 billion relief appropriation. "We have been travelling fast this last week," he told Morgenthau, "and we have covered a lot of ground and you will have to hurry to catch up."[51]

Roosevelt's hesitant behavior contrasted sharply with the impression of energy and purpose he had conveyed in 1933. Moreover, his decision to adopt a spending policy to combat the recession marked an important turning point in the New Deal. The administration became less committed to restructuring the economy and more interested in stabilizing it and producing growth. Historian Alan Brinkley maintains that by 1938 New Dealers

> were no longer much concerned about controlling or punishing "plutocrats" and "economic royalists," an impulse central to New Deal rhetoric in the mid-1930s. Instead, they spoke of their commitment to providing a healthy environment in which the corporate world could flourish and in which the economy could sustain "full employment."[52]

Liberals pinned their hopes on Keynesian fiscal policy, which appeared to provide the quickest fix for economic problems.

The widespread distress resulting from the recession badly hurt Democrats in the 1938 midterm elections. Republicans won a smashing victory, gaining 81 seats in the House and 8 in the Senate. The Congress that assembled in January 1939 was more conservative than any Roosevelt had so far faced. Since all the Democratic losses had taken place in the North and West, particularly in states such as Ohio and Pennsylvania, southerners were in a relatively strong position. The House contained 169 nonsouthern Democrats, 93 southern Democrats, 169 Republicans, and 4 third-party representatives. For the first time, Roosevelt could not form a majority without the help of some southerners or Republicans. Most observers agreed that the president could at best hope to consolidate, but certainly not to extend, the New Deal. FDR admitted

---

[50]John M. Blum, *From the Morgenthau Diaries: Years of Crisis* (Boston: Little, Brown, 1957), 415.

[51]Ibid., 420.

[52]Alan Brinkley, *The End of Reform: New Deal Liberalism in Recession and War* (New York: Alfred A. Knopf, 1995), 7.

as much when he delivered his annual message in January: "We have now passed the period of internal conflict in the launching of our program of social reform. Our full energies may now be released to invigorate the processes of recovery in order to preserve our reforms."[53]

Yet even the effort to preserve reforms proved difficult in the vastly changed political climate of 1939. Congress demonstrated its resentment at what it judged to have been an attempted politicization of relief by passing the Hatch Act, which prohibited all federal employees, except high-ranking members of the executive branch, from engaging in political campaigns. The House abruptly cut off funds for the Federal Theatre Project, one of the most popular and controversial efforts by the Works Progress Administration to provide relief for unemployed creative artists. Congress repealed the tax on undistributed corporate profits, killed a request to increase expenditures for public housing, and rejected a $3.86 billion appropriation for self-liquidating public works projects. Roosevelt dodged a hopeless battle by withholding support from Senator Robert Wagner's national health bill, which would have established a program of medical insurance and authorized federal aid for child and maternity care, public health services, and hospital construction. FDR also blocked a move to offset the imbalance in old-age benefits between rich and poor states by expanding the federal contribution to Social Security. "Not one nickel more," he said. "Not one solitary nickel. Once you get off the 50-50 matching basis the sky's the limit, and before you know it, we'll be paying the whole bill."[54]

As the president became preoccupied with issues of national defense and foreign policy, he became more reluctant to press for reform. He turned his attention instead to obtaining a revision of the neutrality laws. Enacted between 1935 and 1937, these measures barred the sale of munitions to nations at war and prohibited private loans to them. FDR wanted the authority, in the event of war, to provide arms on a cash-and-carry basis to England and France. Since southern Democrats were generally willing to support him in this effort, FDR had every reason to avoid alienating them by pressing his domestic reform agenda. Despite his efforts, the House on June 30, 1939, voted to maintain the embargo on arms and ammunition, and shortly thereafter the Senate Foreign Relations Committee, by a vote of 12 to 11, decided to postpone neutrality revision. Not until September, when Germany invaded Poland and the world was plunged into war, did Congress lift the arms embargo. By

[53] Rosenman, *Public Papers,* 8:7.

[54] Arthur J. Altmeyer, *The Formative Years of Social Security* (Madison: University of Wisconsin Press, 1966), 112.

then the president was, according to one southern conservative, "culti-vating us in a very nice way."[55]

By mid-1940, as German forces swept through the Low Countries and into France, Roosevelt readied the American people for a policy of ex-tending economic and military aid to the Allies. Private industry would have to manufacture airplanes, tanks, munitions, and ships, he declared, and the government was prepared to fund this expansion of productive capacity for national defense. Then he listed the most important achieve-ments of the New Deal, those he was most determined to protect: mini-mum wages and maximum hours, old-age pensions and unemployment insurance, conservation of natural resources, assistance to agriculture and housing, "help to the under-privileged," collective bargaining, and the protection of consumer purchasing power. Together, they amounted to "an offensive on a broad front against social inequalities and abuses." As his second term was drawing to an end, Roosevelt said, "We must make sure that there be no breakdown or cancellation of any of the great social gains which we have made in these past years."[56]

LIBERALS AT WAR, 1941–1945

As the United States moved toward involvement in World War II and then entered the conflict after Japan attacked Pearl Harbor on Decem-ber 7, 1941, Roosevelt continued to advocate an enhanced role for gov-ernment in making a better life. In his January 1941 State of the Union message, FDR included "freedom from want" on his list of the "Four Freedoms" (along with freedom of speech, freedom of religion, and free-dom from fear) and reiterated his belief in equality of opportunity, "jobs for those who can work," "security for those who need it," "the ending of special privilege for the few," and the widening of "opportunities for ad-equate medical care."[57] His 1944 message to Congress went even further in calling for "a second Bill of Rights under which a new basis of security and prosperity can be established for all." As FDR envisioned this "Eco-nomic Bill of Rights," Americans should be guaranteed useful and re-munerative employment; earnings adequate for the necessities of life and recreation; freedom from monopolies for business; decent housing; a good education; and protection from the hazards of old age, sickness, accident, and unemployment. "All of these rights spell security," FDR

---

[55] Polenberg, "Decline of the New Deal," 262.
[56] Buhite and Levy, *FDR's Fireside Chats,* 159.
[57] Rosenman, *Public Papers,* 9:671.

declared. "And after this war is won we must be prepared to move forward, in the implementation of these rights, to new goals of happiness and well-being."[58]

The operative phrase, of course, was "after this war is won." FDR's rhetoric may have remained staunchly reformist, but as historian John Morton Blum has observed, "He made no convincing effort to give substance to his oratory."[59] As long as the nation was engaged in all-out war, FDR did not consider it desirable — or necessary — to press for additional reforms. In early 1942, for example, he approved a plan to postpone, for the duration of the war, any antitrust prosecutions that might hamper military production. "The war effort must come first and everything else must wait," he said.[60] He made the point more graphically at a press conference in December 1943 when he announced that "Dr. New Deal" had outlived his usefulness and should step aside for "Dr. Win-the-War." That statement, Alan Brinkley claims, amounted to "a belated public acknowledgement of an already well-advanced abandonment of the liberal agenda."[61]

If the president was willing to abandon that agenda, it was largely because significant portions of it were being realized as a result of the wartime economic boom. The war produced virtually full employment and a higher standard of living. It strengthened trade unions, membership in which climbed from 10.5 million to 14.75 million. It drove farm income to new heights and reduced tenancy as landless farmers found jobs in factories. It led Congress to pass the GI Bill of Rights, a wide-ranging reform measure providing veterans with generous education benefits, readjustment allowances during the transition to civilian life, and guarantees of mortgage loans. By 1943 one reformer would note, "The honest-minded liberal will admit that the common man is getting a better break than ever he did under the New Deal."[62]

So FDR was only stating an obvious truth when he informed an adviser that "the weaknesses and many of the social inequalities as of 1932 have been repaired or removed and the job now is, first and foremost, to win the war."[63] That conviction led him to agree to liquidate the Civilian Conservation Corps and to terminate the Works Progress

[58] Ibid., 13:40–42.

[59] John Morton Blum, *V Was for Victory: Politics and American Culture during World War II* (New York: Harcourt Brace Jovanovich, 1976), 249.

[60] Richard Polenberg, *War and Society: The United States, 1941–1945* (Philadelphia: J. B. Lippincott, 1972), 78.

[61] Brinkley, *End of Reform*, 144.

[62] Polenberg, *War and Society*, 93.

[63] Ibid., 76.

Administration, an agency that, he said, deserved an "honorable discharge." More important, the president refused to back a wartime expansion of Social Security and unemployment insurance as proposed in the Wagner–Murray-Dingell bill. Introduced in Congress in 1943, the measure endeavored to create a national unemployment insurance system to replace the existing federal-state arrangement, to extend coverage to 15 million agricultural and domestic workers, and to increase benefits. In addition, it proposed a federal system of health insurance with provisions for medical and hospital care. Recognizing that powerful groups opposed these reforms — and that the 1942 midterm elections had produced a more conservative Congress (Republicans had captured forty-four additional seats in the House and nine in the Senate) — FDR ducked a losing battle. "We can't go up against the State Medical Societies," he concluded, "we just can't do it."[64]

Although the war solved many long-standing economic problems, it also created new ones, particularly in the area of civil liberties. The cardinal assumption of the New Deal — the belief that government could be trusted with broad-ranging powers to regulate the economy in the national interest — also shaped Roosevelt's view of First Amendment freedoms. In time of peace, FDR was genuinely committed to protecting individual liberty and freedom of expression. In time of war, however, he was prepared to impose harsh restrictions. As Attorney General Francis Biddle later remarked, Roosevelt believed that "it was all very well to be liberal . . . but you must not be soft."[65]

The president exhibited his hard side in the spring of 1940, when he began to fear that immigrants and aliens might be doing undercover work for foreign powers. "Of course we have got this fifth column thing, which is altogether too widespread through the country," FDR told the Council on National Defense on May 30. "In the bringing in of new people we have got to be pretty darned careful."[66] Accordingly, Roosevelt approved Secretary of State Cordell Hull's recommendation that aliens who applied for visas as temporary visitors should be fingerprinted, and he signed the Smith Act, which obliged all aliens to register. The president also authorized the use of wiretaps against anyone "suspected of subversive activities." He later explained that "wire tapping should be used against those persons, not citizens of the United

[64] Ibid., 87.
[65] Francis Biddle, *In Brief Authority* (Garden City, N.Y.: Doubleday, 1962), 108.
[66] Richard Polenberg, "Franklin D. Roosevelt and Civil Liberties: The Case of the Dies Committee," *The Historian* 30 (February 1968): 176.

States, and those few citizens who are traitors to their country, who to-day are engaged in espionage or sabotage."[67]

After the attack on Pearl Harbor, FDR remarked that "some degree of censorship is essential in wartime, and we are at war."[68] The censorship he had in mind involved suppressing not only information that would be useful to the enemy — such as news concerning troop movements, ship landings, and battle casualties — but also criticism of the government that passed permissible bounds. In January 1942, FDR wrote to J. Edgar Hoover, director of the Federal Bureau of Investigation (FBI), calling his attention to a pro-fascist sheet and commenting, "Now that we are in the war, it looks like a good chance to clean up a number of these vile publications."[69] In May he suggested to Biddle that editorials in the *Chicago Tribune* and *New York Daily News* critical of the Allies might warrant action: "The tie-in between the attitude of these papers and the Rome-Berlin [Axis Powers] broadcasts is something far greater than mere coincidence." In October he noted, "I would raise the question as to whether freedom of the press is not essentially freedom to print correct news," and he added that freedom of the press meant freedom to criticize government policy on the basis of "factual truth. I think there is a big distinction between this and freedom to print untrue news."[70]

Throughout the first year of the war, the president urged Biddle and his aides in the Justice Department to act against far-right critics on the grounds that their speech was seditious. In April 1942, Biddle asked the postmaster general to suspend the second-class mailing privileges of Father Charles E. Coughlin's monthly, *Social Justice*. The "radio priest's" publication had grown more stridently anti-Semitic. According to Biddle, it echoed the enemy's line that the war was unnecessary, and therefore its distribution could damage troop morale. Ultimately, the administration persuaded the Catholic hierarchy to silence Coughlin, thereby avoiding the necessity of a trial. In July 1942, after more needling by the president, Biddle moved to indict twenty-eight "native fascists" for violating the 1917 Espionage Act. Their attacks on government policy, the Department of Justice maintained, amounted to a conspiracy to cause insubordination in the armed forces.

[67] Ibid., 177.
[68] Patrick S. Washburn, *A Question of Sedition* (New York: Oxford University Press, 1986), 41.
[69] Richard Polenberg, "World War II and the Bill of Rights," in *The Home-Front War*, ed. Kenneth Paul O'Brien and Lynn Hudson Parsons (Westport, Conn.: Greenwood Press, 1995), 16.
[70] Polenberg, *War and Society*, 45.

Roosevelt's belief in the overriding importance of national security led him to approve, unhesitatingly, the relocation of 110,000 West Coast Japanese Americans, two-thirds of whom were U.S. citizens. Troubled by allegations (however unfounded) that Japanese Americans were preparing to commit espionage, recognizing that public opinion in California strongly favored their removal, and preoccupied with matters of global military strategy, FDR simply accepted Secretary of War Henry L. Stimson's recommendation for evacuation. On February 11, 1942, Stimson reported that he raised the matter with FDR and "fortunately found that he was very vigorous about it and [he] told me to go ahead on the line that I had myself thought the best."[71] On February 19, 1942, the president issued Executive Order 9066, which gave the secretary of war the power to "prescribe military areas in such places and of such extent . . . from which any or all persons may be excluded." As historian Roger Daniels notes, this "strangely reticent" proclamation "mentions no ethnic or racial group by name, nor does it specify place."[72] Yet everyone knew it would be used to banish Japanese Americans from the West Coast, and so it was. "The country had never been in such peril, and Roosevelt shouldered an awesome burden of wartime responsibility," Peter Irons writes in *Justice at War*. "In this atmosphere of anxiety, the rights of an isolated racial minority had little claim on his sympathies."[73]

Having made the decision for relocation, FDR apparently never second-guessed himself. Nothing more clearly illustrates his lack of concern for the violation of civil liberties than his response when, in June 1944, Secretary of the Interior Harold L. Ickes urged closing of the camps. Since the policy toward Japanese Americans could no longer be justified on the grounds of military necessity, Ickes said, "the continued retention of these innocent people would be a blot upon the history of this country." Roosevelt did not wish to take any "drastic or sudden" action. "I think the whole problem, for the sake of internal quiet, should be handled gradually," he said.[74] Two things, he added, were preferable to allowing Japanese Americans to return to their homes: "seeing with great discretion, how many Japanese families would be acceptable to public opinion in definite localities on the West Coast" and "seeking to extend greatly the distribution of other families in many parts of the

---

[71] Ibid., 64.
[72] Roger Daniels, *Prisoners without Trial: Japanese Americans in World War II* (New York: Hill and Wang, 1993), 46.
[73] Peter Irons, *Justice at War: The Story of the Japanese American Internment Cases* (New York: Oxford University Press, 1983), 364.
[74] Ibid., 273.

U.S. . . . Dissemination and distribution constitute a great method of avoiding public outcry."[75] Most historians believe that FDR's reluctance to release internees was driven by a fear of angering whites on the West Coast before the 1944 presidential election.

This harsh policy contrasted sharply with FDR's leniency toward German Americans and Italian Americans, but the leniency, like the harshness, owed much to political calculation. Germans and Italians were numerous (there were approximately 264,000 German and 599,000 Italian aliens) and widely dispersed geographically. Many were influential and well assimilated, and FDR believed that it would be unwise to take action against them. Even as Japanese Americans were being rounded up on the West Coast, FDR told Stimson, "American citizens with German and Italian names are also worried [about evacuation]. I am inclined to think this may have a bad effect on morale."[76] His administration's policy was accordingly benign. In October 1942, Biddle ruled that Italian aliens would no longer be classified as aliens of "enemy nationality." No such concession was made to German Americans, since the political payoff seemed less certain, but FDR went out of his way to praise them, pointing out in 1944 "how many good men and women of German ancestry have proved loyal, freedom loving, and peace-loving citizens."[77]

The war forced Roosevelt to reconsider his administration's policies toward the nation's largest minority, African Americans. In 1940 three-fourths of the nation's thirteen million African Americans lived in southern states, which barred them from going to the polls, but African American voters in the North and West were among FDR's staunchest backers. Eleanor Roosevelt enjoyed a well-deserved reputation as a champion of racial equality. More important, New Deal relief and welfare programs had had a profoundly beneficial effect on a group that, before, during, and after the Great Depression, was the first to be fired and the last to be hired. The widely shared consensus during the 1930s that economic recovery was the priority had enabled FDR to sidestep civil rights issues without losing African American voters' support. When pressed to take a stand in behalf of racial justice, FDR's standard reply was that economic policy took precedence. To support civil rights legislation, he added, would jeopardize recovery by antagonizing powerful southern Democrats in Congress.

[75] Doris Kearns Goodwin, *No Ordinary Time: Franklin and Eleanor Roosevelt, the Home Front in World War II* (New York: Simon & Schuster, 1994), 514–15.

[76] Polenberg, *War and Society,* 61.

[77] Richard Polenberg, *One Nation Divisible: Class, Race, and Ethnicity in the United States since 1938* (New York: Viking Press, 1980), 60.

A classic statement of this rationalization came in the spring of 1935, when Walter White, head of the National Association for the Advancement of Colored People (NAACP), met with FDR to urge his support for a federal anti-lynching bill. White remembered FDR saying:

> I did not choose the tools with which I must work. I've got to get legislation passed by Congress to save America. The Southerners by reason of the seniority rule in Congress are chairmen or occupy strategic places on most of the Senate and House committees. If I come out for the anti-lynching bill now, they will block every bill I ask Congress to pass to keep America from collapsing. I just can't take that risk.[78]

White, a loyal FDR supporter, confessed that he was "very annoyed" at the president's failure, then and later, to take a more forthright stand. His disappointment paled beside that of another civil rights activist, Charles H. Houston, who told White, "All along I've been telling you that your President had no real courage and that he would chisel in a pinch."[79] Such criticism did not stop African Americans from voting overwhelmingly for FDR in the 1936 and 1940 elections.

The nation's entry into war intensified demands for racial equality. The theme most insistently sounded in the African American press was that the global conflict must not be allowed to divert attention from the struggle for civil rights. By ending racial oppression, editorial writers said, the government could ensure African American support for the war. Black leaders undertook a controversial "Double V" campaign, which stressed victory in the struggle for equality at home as well as victory on the battlefield. They believed, with some reason, that a militant posture would be most likely to extract concessions from the Roosevelt administration. "It is our duty to submit the injustices and hypocrisies of this nation to the conscience of the Republic," wrote a columnist in the *Pittsburgh Courier.* "We will remember Pearl Harbor and we will aid in avenging it, but we are not forgetting ourselves."[80]

One especially acute source of resentment was the policies of the armed forces, a wretched mixture of exclusion, discrimination, and segregation. African Americans could not enlist in the Marines or Air Corps; they could join the Navy but only to work in the mess halls; they were rigidly segregated in the Army. Yet FDR responded cautiously to critics of these restrictive practices, as was evident in September 1940

[78] Walter White, *A Man Called White* (New York: Viking Press, 1948), 169–70.
[79] Harvard Sitkoff, *A New Deal for Blacks: The Emergence of Civil Rights as a National Issue* (New York: Oxford University Press, 1978), 288.
[80] Washburn, *Question of Sedition,* 101.

when fifteen African American messmen serving on the USS *Philadelphia* made a public protest. In an open letter to the *Pittsburgh Courier,* they wrote, "We sincerely hope to discourage any other colored boys who might have planned to join the Navy and make the same mistake we did. All they would become is seagoing bell hops, chambermaids and dishwashers." The Navy threw the sailors into the brig, court-martialed them for insubordination, and gave them dishonorable discharges. When an outcry arose, Roosevelt, at his wife's urging, agreed to meet with African American leaders and the civilian heads of the armed services. Secretary of the Navy Frank Knox defended existing procedures by saying, "These men live aboard ship. And in our history we don't take Negroes into a ship's company." FDR's only suggestion, according to biographer Doris Kearns Goodwin, was "putting Negro bands on white ships to accustom white sailors to the presence of Negroes on ships."[81]

Yet Roosevelt was also capable of proposing a creative solution to the problem of discrimination in national defense industries. The impetus was provided when A. Philip Randolph, head of the Brotherhood of Sleeping Car Porters, called for one hundred thousand African Americans to march on Washington in July 1941. One of Randolph's goals was to integrate the armed forces, a demand FDR was not ready to meet, but another was to end discrimination in defense hiring, a demand FDR was quite prepared to grant. Late in May 1941, the president recommended to William Knudsen and Sidney Hillman, the codirectors of the Office of Production Management, that the government institute an employment quota system ordering contractors to hire African Americans "up to a certain percentage in factory order work." FDR urged the men to judge African American workers on "quality," noting that in many instances highly qualified black job applicants had been passed over in favor of less-qualified whites. Hillman and Knudsen demurred, preferring instead to "quietly get manufacturers to increase the number of Negroes for defense work. If we set a percentage it will immediately be open to dispute; quiet work with the contractors and the unions will bring better results."[82]

Fearing that the presence of a large number of African American protesters in the nation's capital might provoke violence and embarrass his administration, FDR tried to convince Randolph to call off the march. Through an emissary he sent word to the organizers that he was "much upset to hear that several negro organizations are planning to March

[81] Goodwin, *No Ordinary Time,* 168–72.
[82] Ibid., 249.

on Washington on July first, as he can imagine nothing that will stir up race hatred and slow up progress more than a march of that kind."[83] He prevailed on Eleanor Roosevelt and other whites with credibility in the African American community to press for cancellation. He issued a statement asserting that the United States must refute "at home the very theories which we are fighting abroad" and finally satisfied Randolph by issuing Executive Order 8802, which created the Committee on Fair Employment Practices and called on employers and unions "to provide for the full and equitable participation of all workers in defense industries, without discrimination because of race, creed, color or national origin."[84]

Roosevelt's concession undoubtedly expressed his genuine sympathy for victims of discrimination. But during the war, as before, that sympathy was tempered by the conviction that racial problems could best be solved by a gradual process of education, which hinged on the Democratic party's ability to win votes from southern whites as well as from northern African Americans. Other issues, such as economic recovery in the 1930s and military needs in the 1940s, took priority. When the cause of racial justice served the conduct of the war, as in adding African American workers to the labor force in defense industries, the president was supportive. When it seemed likely to disturb matters, as in provoking a congressional filibuster over a proposal to end poll taxes, he was unsympathetic. In December 1943, Roosevelt admitted, "I don't think, quite frankly, that we can bring about the millennium at this time."[85]

He made that remark at a press conference that, like all of Roosevelt's press conferences up to that point, was attended only by white reporters. FDR's press secretary, Steve Early, had excluded African American journalists since 1933 on the grounds that they did not represent dailies (specious grounds, indeed, since exceptions were made for influential white journalists who wrote for weekly papers). Only once, in May 1943, were African American reporters admitted to the White House press gallery, to cover a visit by the president of Liberia. On February 5, 1944, however, Roosevelt met with thirteen editors and publishers of African American newspapers. Percival Prattis of the *Pittsburgh Courier* read a prepared statement:

> We maintain that the Federal government should begin now to use its authority and powers of persuasion to end abridgement of the Negro's

[83] Polenberg, *War and Society,* 104.
[84] Ibid., 105.
[85] Ibid., 108.

citizenship, so as to bring about a more truly democratic America. Such action would support our claim that we fight for a world order in which economic equality, political self-determination, and social justice both prevail.

FDR replied, "I think it's an awfully good statement."[86] Three days later, Harry S. McAlpin attended a White House press conference as a representative of the National Negro Publishers Association and the *Atlanta Daily World*. FDR made a point of greeting him personally and shaking hands.

If this was token integration, it was integration nonetheless, and it indicated a growing if belated sensitivity on FDR's part and that of others to issues of racial injustice. During the war, as Eleanor Roosevelt's writings made abundantly clear, American liberals incorporated civil rights into the reform agenda. Their willingness to look to government, especially the federal government, to erase discrimination — as in the issuing of executive orders — was consistent with FDR's statist outlook. For if any element remained constant throughout his years as president, it was his conviction, eloquently stated in the Economic Bill of Rights, that government at the national level had an ongoing responsibility to ensure people's security and could be trusted to act in accord with their best interests. Evidence that governmental power could be abused — as when Japanese Americans were evacuated, relocated, and interned — was generally ignored in the heady atmosphere produced by fighting and winning a war.

FDR: THE LEGACY

When Franklin D. Roosevelt ran for a fourth term in 1944, he was already a very sick man. On August 3, while speaking to navy yard workers in Bremerton, Washington, he suffered an angina attack, which nearly prevented him from completing his remarks. To allay doubts about his health, he sometimes acted imprudently, as in late October when he insisted on riding for hours through the streets of New York City in an open car during a driving rainstorm. The strategy worked well enough for him to defeat the Republican candidate, Thomas E. Dewey, though by a relatively small margin: FDR received 53.4 percent of the popular vote, compared with 54.7 percent in his race against Wendell Willkie in 1940. By early 1945, FDR's relatives and friends were often commenting that he looked old, he tired easily, and he sometimes seemed distracted.

---

[86] Rauch, *Roosevelt Reader,* 350–55.

On January 23, 1945, three days after delivering his inaugural address, FDR left for Yalta, in the Crimea, where he met with Winston Churchill and Joseph Stalin to negotiate a postwar settlement. In all, the ocean voyages and the meeting took more than a month. On March 1, two days after returning to the United States, he addressed a joint session of Congress. He entered the chamber in a wheelchair rather than by supporting himself on someone's arm; he delivered his speech while seated rather than by bracing himself against a lectern; and for the first time, he mentioned his disability: "I hope you will pardon me for the unusual posture of sitting down during the presentation of what I want to say, but I know that you will realize that it makes it a lot easier for me in not having to carry about ten pounds of steel around on the bottom of my legs."[87]

On March 29, after spending a few days at Hyde Park, FDR left for a two-week vacation at his home in Warm Springs, Georgia, hoping the rest would enable him to regain his strength. On April 12, at one o'clock in the afternoon, while sitting for a portrait, he suddenly said, "I have a terrific pain in the back of my head," and slumped forward. He had suffered a massive cerebral hemorrhage and was pronounced dead at 3:35 P.M. That evening, Harry S. Truman was sworn in as president. Roosevelt's body was taken to Washington for a funeral service and then to Hyde Park for burial, as millions mourned in sadness and disbelief.

Just a day before he died, FDR had put the finishing touches on his Jefferson Day address. Thomas Jefferson had always occupied a special place in Roosevelt's pantheon of heroes. In 1932 FDR said that government, for Jefferson, "was a means to an end, not an end in itself; it might be either a refuge and a help or a threat and a danger, depending on the circumstances."[88] In 1938 Roosevelt made sure that Jefferson's visage would appear on the most commonly used (three-cent) postage stamp. In 1943 the president spoke at a dedication of the Jefferson Memorial; he had taken a personal interest in its design because he wanted it to reflect Jefferson's part in the nation's history. The speech he composed on April 11, 1945, emphasized that an enduring peace could be obtained only by removing the root causes of war — "the doubts and the fears, the ignorance and the greed." He concluded, characteristically, on a note of optimism: "The only limit to our realization of tomorrow will be our doubts of today. Let us move forward with strong and active faith."[89]

[87] Rosenman, *Public Papers,* 13:570.
[88] Ibid., 1:527–29.
[89] Ibid., 13:613–16.

Although Jefferson is properly identified with states' rights and limited government, there were reasonable grounds to assert, as one scholar did at the time, that New Deal philosophy was "essentially Jeffersonian": "It is merely selecting for emphasis the social rather than the individualistic side of the tradition. One emphasis is as necessary as the other if a working balance between liberty and equality, the basic concepts of democracy, is to be effected."[90] Franklin D. Roosevelt demonstrated that the tension between liberty and equality, though inevitably a source of social conflict, could be resolved creatively. Recognizing that freedom and security could be complementary, he knew that gaining one did not necessarily mean forfeiting the other.

To be sure, Roosevelt did not always succeed in striking an ideal balance between the two objectives, and he probably would not have claimed that he did. The New Deal demonstrated that individual freedom could be reconciled with governmental regulation designed to promote economic security. Just as clearly, however, the wartime experience demonstrated that basic liberties could be lost in the face of fears that they endangered national security. The theologian Reinhold Niebuhr once defined democracy as "a method of finding proximate solutions for insoluble problems."[91] If the problems the American people faced in the years 1933 to 1945 were in some measure insoluble, proximate solutions were found. That, in truth, was Franklin D. Roosevelt's ultimate legacy.

[90] Charles M. Wiltse, *The Jeffersonian Tradition in American Democracy* (1935; reprint New York: Hill and Wang, 1960), 266.

[91] Reinhold Niebuhr, *The Children of Light and the Children of Darkness* (New York: Charles Scribner's Sons, 1944), 118.

PART TWO

The Documents

1

FDR as President

In his twelve and one-half years as president, Franklin D. Roosevelt gave hundreds of speeches, held nearly one thousand press conferences, issued numerous executive orders, and wrote countless letters and memorandums. Like all modern presidents, FDR relied on ghostwriters, but he edited the final versions of his speeches himself and often departed somewhat from the prepared text, always with a view toward making the language simpler, more direct, and more persuasive. The documents in this section illustrate some of the different ways in which FDR made his views known to the Congress, the press, and the people.

FRANKLIN D. ROOSEVELT

First Inaugural Address

March 4, 1933

This is Franklin D. Roosevelt's most famous speech, not because it proposed concrete ways to combat the Depression but rather because it instilled new hope in the people. In effect, Roosevelt said that the problems the nation faced as a result of the Depression, dire though they might be, were quite solvable: All that was needed was a willingness to face them candidly, to act decisively, and to recognize that there were "social values more noble than mere monetary profit." The most famous assertion in the speech was based on a line of Henry David Thoreau's ("Nothing is so much to be feared as fear"). This line appeared in a book that Eleanor Roosevelt had given to her

The Public Papers and Addresses of Franklin D. Roosevelt (New York: Random House, 1938), 2:11–16.

husband and that he had with him when he was revising the speech. Although FDR asserted that he would not hesitate to seek "broad Executive power to wage a war against the emergency," the overwhelmingly enthusiastic response to the address derived as much from his ringing voice and self-assured bearing as from the words themselves.

I am certain that my fellow Americans expect that on my induction into the Presidency I will address them with a candor and a decision which the present situation of our Nation impels. This is preeminently the time to speak the truth, the whole truth, frankly and boldly. Nor need we shrink from honestly facing conditions in our country today. This great Nation will endure as it has endured, will revive and will prosper. So, first of all, let me assert my firm belief that the only thing we have to fear is fear itself—nameless, unreasoning, unjustified terror which paralyzes needed efforts to convert retreat into advance. In every dark hour of our national life a leadership of frankness and vigor has met with that understanding and support of the people themselves which is essential to victory. I am convinced that you will again give that support to leadership in these critical days.

In such a spirit on my part and on yours we face our common difficulties. They concern, thank God, only material things. Values have shrunken to fantastic levels; taxes have risen; our ability to pay has fallen; government of all kinds is faced by serious curtailment of income; the means of exchange are frozen in the currents of trade; the withered leaves of industrial enterprise lie on every side; farmers find no markets for their produce; the savings of many years in thousands of families are gone.

More important, a host of unemployed citizens face the grim problem of existence, and an equally great number toil with little return. Only a foolish optimist can deny the dark realities of the moment.

Yet our distress comes from no failure of substance. We are stricken by no plague of locusts. Compared with the perils which our forefathers conquered because they believed and were not afraid, we have still much to be thankful for. Nature still offers her bounty and human efforts have multiplied it. Plenty is at our doorstep, but a generous use of it languishes in the very sight of the supply. Primarily this is because rulers of the exchange of mankind's goods have failed through their own stubbornness and their own incompetence, have admitted their failure, and have abdicated. Practices of the unscrupulous money changers stand indicted in the court of public opinion, rejected by the hearts and minds of men.

True they have tried, but their efforts have been cast in the pattern of an outworn tradition. Faced by failure of credit they have proposed only the lending of more money. Stripped of the lure of profit by which to induce our people to follow their false leadership, they have resorted to exhortations, pleading tearfully for restored confidence. They know only the rules of a generation of self-seekers. They have no vision, and when there is no vision the people perish.

The money changers have fled from their high seats in the temple of our civilization. We may now restore that temple to the ancient truths. The measure of the restoration lies in the extent to which we apply social values more noble than mere monetary profit.

Happiness lies not in the mere possession of money; it lies in the joy of achievement, in the thrill of creative effort. The joy and moral stimulation of work no longer must be forgotten in the mad chase of evanescent profits. These dark days will be worth all they cost us if they teach us that our true destiny is not to be ministered unto but to minister to ourselves and to our fellow men.

Recognition of the falsity of material wealth as the standard of success goes hand in hand with the abandonment of the false belief that public office and high political position are to be valued only by the standards of pride of place and personal profit; and there must be an end to a conduct in banking and in business which too often has given to a sacred trust the likeness of callous and selfish wrongdoing. Small wonder that confidence languishes, for it thrives only on honesty, on honor, on the sacredness of obligations, on faithful protection, on unselfish performance; without them it cannot live.

Restoration calls, however, not for changes in ethics alone. This Nation asks for action, and action now.

Our greatest primary task is to put people to work. This is no unsolvable problem if we face it wisely and courageously. It can be accomplished in part by direct recruiting by the Government itself, treating the task as we would treat the emergency of a war, but at the same time, through this employment, accomplishing greatly needed projects to stimulate and reorganize the use of our natural resources.

Hand in hand with this we must frankly recognize the overbalance of population in our industrial centers and, by engaging on a national scale in a redistribution, endeavor to provide a better use of the land for those best fitted for the land. The task can be helped by definite efforts to raise the values of agricultural products and with this the power to purchase the output of our cities. It can be helped by preventing realistically the tragedy of the growing loss through foreclosure of our small homes and our farms. It can be helped by insistence that the Federal, State, and local governments act forthwith on the demand that their cost be drastically reduced. It can be helped by the unifying of relief activities which today are often scattered, uneconomical, and unequal. It can be helped by national planning for and supervision of all forms of transportation and of communications and other utilities which have a definitely public character. There are many ways in which it can be helped, but it can never be helped merely by talking about it. We must act and act quickly.

Finally, in our progress toward a resumption of work we require two safeguards against a return of the evils of the old order: there must be a strict supervision of all banking and credits and investments, so that there will be an end to speculation with other people's money; and there must be provision for an adequate but sound currency.

These are the lines of attack. I shall presently urge upon a new Congress, in special session, detailed measures for their fulfillment, and I shall seek the immediate assistance of the several States.

Through this program of action we address ourselves to putting our own national house in order and making income balance outgo. Our international trade relations, though vastly important, are in point of time and necessity secondary to the establishment of a sound national economy. I favor as a practical policy the putting of first things first. I shall spare no effort to restore world trade by international economic readjustment, but the emergency at home cannot wait on that accomplishment.

The basic thought that guides these specific means of national recovery is not narrowly nationalistic. It is the insistence, as a first consideration, upon the interdependence of the various elements in and parts of the United States—a recognition of the old and permanently important manifestation of the American spirit of the pioneer. It is the way to recovery. It is the immediate way. It is the strongest assurance that the recovery will endure.

In the field of world policy I would dedicate this Nation to the policy of the good neighbor—the neighbor who resolutely respects himself and, because he does so, respects the rights of others—the neighbor who respects his obligations and respects the sanctity of his agreements in and with a world of neighbors.

If I read the temper of our people correctly, we now realize as we have never realized before our interdependence on each other; that we cannot merely take but we must give as well; that if we are to go forward, we must move as a trained and loyal army willing to sacrifice for the good of a common discipline, because without such discipline no progress is made, no leadership becomes effective. We are, I know, ready and willing to submit our lives and property to such discipline, because it makes possible a leadership which aims at a larger good. This I propose to offer, pledging that the larger purposes will bind upon us all as a sacred obligation with a unity of duty hitherto evoked only in time of armed strife.

With this pledge taken, I assume unhesitatingly the leadership of this great army of our people dedicated to a disciplined attack upon our common problems.

Action in this image and to this end is feasible under the form of government which we have inherited from our ancestors. Our Constitution is so simple and practical that it is possible always to meet extraordinary needs by changes in emphasis and arrangement without loss of essential form. That is why our constitutional system has proved itself the most superbly enduring political mechanism the modern world has produced. It has met every stress of vast expansion of territory, of foreign wars, of bitter internal strife, of world relations.

It is to be hoped that the normal balance of Executive and legislative authority may be wholly adequate to meet the unprecedented task before us. But it may be that an unprecedented demand and need for undelayed action may call for temporary departure from that normal balance of public procedure.

I am prepared under my constitutional duty to recommend the measures that a stricken Nation in the midst of a stricken world may require. These measures, or such other measures as the Congress may build out of its experience and wisdom, I shall seek, within my constitutional authority, to bring to speedy adoption.

But in the event that the Congress shall fail to take one of these two courses, and in the event that the national emergency is still critical, I shall not evade the clear course of duty that will then confront me. I shall ask the Congress for the one remaining instrument to meet the crisis— broad Executive power to wage a war against the emergency, as great as the power that would be given to me if we were in fact invaded by a foreign foe.

For the trust reposed in me I will return the courage and the devotion that befit the time. I can do no less.

We face the arduous days that lie before us in the warm courage of national unity; with the clear consciousness of seeking old and precious moral values; with the clean satisfaction that comes from the stern performance of duty by old and young alike. We aim at the assurance of a rounded and permanent national life.

We do not distrust the future of essential democracy. The people of the United States have not failed. In their need they have registered a mandate that they want direct, vigorous action. They have asked for discipline and direction under leadership. They have made me the present instrument of their wishes. In the spirit of the gift I take it.

In this dedication of a Nation we humbly ask the blessing of God. May He protect each and every one of us. May He guide me in the days to come.

FRANKLIN D. ROOSEVELT

First Press Conference
March 8, 1933

After FDR's first press conference, a reporter wrote, "I rubbed my ears and opened my eyes when I heard hard-boiled veterans, men who had lived through so many administrations that there are calluses in their brain, talk glibly about the merits of the White House incumbent." Roosevelt made so favorable an impression on the working press largely because of his informal, colloquial manner. He abandoned the written-question format and simply called on reporters who raised their hands, with the understanding that he would never be quoted directly unless permission was granted. Behind the good-natured bantering—it was still a time when Roosevelt could speak of "the Ananias Club" and reporters would understand his reference to the biblical liar (Acts 5:1–3)—both the president and the press had essentially serious purposes in mind. As historian Graham White has explained, reporters "were plugged in to an inexhaustible news source" and were "in a unique position to gain early insights into presidential thinking," while FDR, for his part, had "a springboard for the launching of ideas, an effective means of shaping public opinion."

The Press Conferences of Franklin D. Roosevelt, Franklin D. Roosevelt Library.

The President: It is very good to see you all and my hope is that these conferences are going to be merely enlarged editions of the kind of very delightful family conferences I have been holding in Albany for the last four years.

I am told that what I am about to do will become impossible, but I am going to try it. We are not going to have any more written questions and of course while I cannot answer seventy-five or a hundred questions because I simply haven't got the physical time, I see no reason why I should not talk to you ladies and gentlemen off the record just the way I have been doing in Albany and the way I used to do it in the Navy Department down here. Quite a number of you, I am glad to see, date back to the days of the previous existence which I led in Washington.

(Interruption—"These two boys are off for Arizona." John and Franklin Roosevelt saying "good-bye.")

And so I think we will discontinue the practice of compelling the submitting of questions in writing before the conference in order to get an answer. There will be a great many questions, of course, that I won't answer, either because they are "if" questions—and I never answer them—and Brother Stephenson will tell you what an "if" question is—

Mr. Stephenson: I ask forty of them a day.

The President: And the others of course are the questions which for various reasons I don't want to discuss or I am not ready to discuss or I don't know anything about. There will be a great many questions you will ask about that I don't know enough about to answer.

Then, in regard to news announcements, Steve [press secretary Stephen T. Early] and I thought that it was best that street news for use out of here should be always without direct quotations. In other words, I don't want to be directly quoted, with the exception that direct quotations will be given out by Steve in writing. Of course that makes that perfectly clear.

Then there are two other matters we will talk about: The first is "background information," which means material which can be used by all of you on your own authority and responsibility and must not be attributed to the White House, because I don't want to have to revive the Ananias Club. (Laughter)

Then the second thing is the "off the record" information which means, of course, confidential information which is given only to those who attend the conference. Now there is one thing I want to say right now on which I think you will go along with me. I want to ask you not to repeat this "off the record" confidential information either to your own editors or associates who are not here because there is always the danger that while you people may not violate the rule, somebody may forget to say, "This is off the record and confidential," and the other party may use it in a story. That is to say, it is not to be used and not to be told to those fellows who happen not to come around to the conference. In other words, this is only for those present.

Now, as to news, I don't think there is any. (Laughter)

Steve reminds me that I have just signed the application for Associate Membership in the Press Club, which I am very happy to do. . . .

Q: In your inaugural address, in which you only touched upon things, you said you are for sound and adequate—

The President: I put it the other way around. I said "adequate but sound."

Q: Now that you have more time, can you define what that is?

The President: No. (Laughter) In other words—and I should call this "off the record" information—you cannot define the thing too closely one way or the other. On Friday afternoon last we undoubtedly didn't have adequate currency. No question about that. There wasn't enough circulating money to go around.

Q: I believe that. (Laughter)

The President: We hope that when the banks reopen a great deal of the currency that was withdrawn for one purpose or another will find its way back. We have got to provide an adequate currency. Last Friday we would have had to provide it in the form of scrip and probably some additional issues of Federal Bank notes. If things go along as we hope they will, the use of scrip can be very greatly curtailed and the amounts of new Federal Bank issues we hope can be also limited to a very great extent. In other words, what you are coming to now really is a managed currency, the adequateness of which will depend on the conditions of the moment. It may expand one week and it may contract another week. That part is all off the record.

Q: Can we use that part—managed?

The President: No, I think not.

Q: That is a pretty good substitute for "controlled."

The President: Go and ask [Secretary of the Treasury] Will Woodin about it.

Q: He's too busy. (Laughter)

Q: Now you came down to adequacy, but you haven't defined what you think is sound, or don't you want to define that now?

The President: I don't want to define "sound" now. In other words, in its essence—this is entirely off the record—in its essence we must not

put the Government any further in debt. Now, the real mark of deline-
ation between sound and unsound is when the government starts to
pay its bills by starting printing presses. That is about the size of it.
Q: Couldn't you take that out and give it to us. That's a very good thing
at this time.
The President: I don't think so. There may be some talk about it tomorrow. . . .

FRANKLIN D. ROOSEVELT

Annual Message to the Congress

January 4, 1935

*Roosevelt's January 1935 State of the Union message is one of his most im-
portant—and most misunderstood—speeches. After two years in office, he
maintained that recovery and reform were inextricably linked. FDR
defined the social objectives of the New Deal in remarkably broad terms and
looked toward the goal of providing all Americans with adequate jobs, security against the hazards of life, and decent homes. He proposed a vast program of public works that would provide 3.5 million jobs and would cost
nearly $5 billion, and he laid out some of the projects he had in mind, in-
cluding slum clearance, rural electrification, and reforestation. Yet even
while asserting that the government had a responsibility to jobless workers,
FDR maintained that home relief—as opposed to work relief—was "a narcotic, a subtle destroyer of the human spirit." This statement, taken out of
context, would later be cited by politicians to justify cutting back or eliminating federal welfare programs.*

Mr. President, Mr. Speaker, Members of the Senate and of the House of
Representatives:

The Constitution wisely provides that the Chief Executive shall report to
the Congress on the state of the Union, for through you, the chosen leg-

Samuel I. Rosenman, ed., *The Public Papers and Addresses of Franklin D. Roosevelt* (New
York: Random House, 1938), 4:15–25.

islative representatives, our citizens everywhere may fairly judge the progress of our governing. I am confident that today, in the light of the events of the past two years, you do not consider it merely a trite phrase when I tell you that I am truly glad to greet you and that I look forward to common counsel, to useful cooperation, and to genuine friendships between us.

We have undertaken a new order of things; yet we progress to it under the framework and in the spirit and intent of the American Constitution. We have proceeded throughout the Nation a measurable distance on the road toward this new order. Materially, I can report to you substantial benefits to our agricultural population, increased industrial activity, and profits to our merchants. Of equal moment, there is evident a restoration of that spirit of confidence and faith which marks the American character. Let him, who, for speculative profit or partisan purpose, without just warrant would seek to disturb or dispel this assurance, take heed before he assumes responsibility for any act which slows our onward steps.

Throughout the world, change is the order of the day. In every Nation economic problems, long in the making, have brought crises of many kinds for which the masters of old practice and theory were unprepared. In most Nations social justice, no longer a distant ideal, has become a definite goal, and ancient Governments are beginning to heed the call.

Thus, the American people do not stand alone in the world in their desire for change. We seek it through tested liberal traditions, through processes which retain all of the deep essentials of that republican form of representative government first given to a troubled world by the United States.

As the various parts in the program begun in the Extraordinary Session of the 73rd Congress shape themselves in practical administration, the unity of our program reveals itself to the Nation. The outlines of the new economic order, rising from the disintegration of the old, are apparent. We test what we have done as our measures take root in the living texture of life. We see where we have built wisely and where we can do still better.

The attempt to make a distinction between recovery and reform is a narrowly conceived effort to substitute the appearance of reality for reality itself. When a man is convalescing from illness, wisdom dictates not only cure of the symptoms, but also removal of their cause.

It is important to recognize that while we seek to outlaw specific abuses, the American objective of today has an infinitely deeper, finer and more lasting purpose than mere repression. Thinking people in almost every country of the world have come to realize certain fundamental difficulties with which civilization must reckon. Rapid changes—the machine age, the advent of universal and rapid communication and many other new factors—have brought new problems. Succeeding generations have attempted to keep pace by reforming in piecemeal fashion this or that attendant abuse. As a result, evils overlap and reform becomes confused and frustrated. We lose sight, from time to time, of our ultimate human objectives.

Let us, for a moment, strip from our simple purpose the confusion that results from a multiplicity of detail and from millions of written and spoken words.

We find our population suffering from old inequalities, little changed by past sporadic remedies. In spite of our efforts and in spite of our talk, we have not weeded out the overprivileged and we have not effectively lifted up the underprivileged. Both of these manifestations of injustice have retarded happiness. No wise man has any intention of destroying what is known as the profit motive; because by the profit motive we mean the right by work to earn a decent livelihood for ourselves and for our families.

We have, however, a clear mandate from the people, that Americans must forswear that conception of the acquisition of wealth which, through excessive profits, creates undue private power over private affairs and, to our misfortune, over public affairs as well. In building toward this end we do not destroy ambition, nor do we seek to divide our wealth into equal shares on stated occasions. We continue to recognize the greater ability of some to earn more than others. But we do assert that the ambition of the individual to obtain for him and his a proper security, a reasonable leisure, and a decent living throughout life, is an ambition to be preferred to the appetite for great wealth and great power.

I recall to your attention my message to the Congress last June in which I said: "among our objectives I place the security of the men, women and children of the Nation first." That remains our first and continuing task; and in a very real sense every major legislative enactment of this Congress could be a component part of it.

In defining immediate factors which enter into our quest, I have spoken to the Congress and the people of three great divisions:

1. The security of a livelihood through the better use of the national resources of the land in which we live.
2. The security against the major hazards and vicissitudes of life.
3. The security of decent homes.

I am now ready to submit to the Congress a broad program designed ultimately to establish all three of these factors of security—a program which because of many lost years will take many future years to fulfill.

A study of our national resources, more comprehensive than any previously made, shows the vast amount of necessary and practicable work which needs to be done for the development and preservation of our natural wealth for the enjoyment and advantage of our people in generations to come. The sound use of land and water is far more comprehensive than the mere planting of trees, building of dams, distributing of electricity or retirement of sub-marginal land. It recognizes that stranded populations, either in the country or the city, cannot have security under the conditions that now surround them.

To this end we are ready to begin to meet this problem—the intelligent care of population throughout our Nation, in accordance with an intelligent distribution of the means of livelihood for that population. A definite program for putting people to work, of which I shall speak in a moment, is a component part of this greater program of security of livelihood through the better use of our national resources.

Closely related to the broad problem of livelihood is that of security against the major hazards of life. Here also, a comprehensive survey of what has been attempted or accomplished in many Nations and in many States proves to me that the time has come for action by the national Government. I shall send to you, in a few days, definite recommendations based on these studies. These recommendations will cover the broad subjects of unemployment insurance and old age insurance, of benefits for children, for mothers, for the handicapped, for maternity care and for other aspects of dependency and illness where a beginning can now be made.

The third factor—better homes for our people—has also been the subject of experimentation and study. Here, too, the first practical steps can be made through the proposals which I shall suggest in relation to giving work to the unemployed.

Whatever we plan and whatever we do should be in the light of these three clear objectives of security. We cannot afford to lose valuable time in haphazard public policies which cannot find a place in the broad outlines of these major purposes. In that spirit I come to an immediate issue made for us by hard and inescapable circumstance—the task of putting people to work. . . . The stark fact before us is that great numbers still remain unemployed.

A large proportion of these unemployed and their dependents have been forced on the relief rolls. The burden on the Federal Government has grown with great rapidity. We have here a human as well as an economic problem. When humane considerations are concerned, Americans give them precedence. The lessons of history, confirmed by the evidence immediately before me, show conclusively that continued dependence upon relief induces a spiritual and moral disintegration fundamentally destructive to the national fibre. To dole out relief in this way is to administer a narcotic, a subtle destroyer of the human spirit. It is inimical to the dictates of sound policy. It is in violation of the traditions of America. Work must be found for able-bodied but destitute workers.

The Federal Government must and shall quit this business of relief.

I am not willing that the vitality of our people be further sapped by the giving of cash, of market baskets, of a few hours of weekly work cutting grass, raking leaves or picking up papers in the public parks. We must preserve not only the bodies of the unemployed from destitution but also their self-respect, their self-reliance and courage and determination. This decision brings me to the problem of what the Government should do with approximately five million unemployed now on the relief rolls.

About one million and a half of these belong to the group which in the past was dependent upon local welfare efforts. Most of them are unable for one reason or another to maintain themselves independently—for the most part, through no fault of their own. Such people, in the days before the great depression, were cared for by local efforts—by States, by counties, by towns, by cities, by churches and by private welfare agencies. It is my thought that in the future they must be cared for as they were before. I stand ready through my own personal efforts, and through the public influence of the office that I hold, to help these local agencies to get the means necessary to assume this burden.

The security legislation which I shall propose to the Congress will, I am confident, be of assistance to local effort in the care of this type of cases. Local responsibility can and will be resumed, for, after all, common sense tells us that the wealth necessary for this task existed and still exists in the local community, and the dictates of sound administration require that this responsibility be in the first instance a local one.

There are, however, an additional three and one half million employable people who are on relief. With them the problem is different and the responsibility is different. This group was the victim of a nation-wide depression caused by conditions which were not local but national. The Federal Government is the only governmental agency with sufficient power and credit to meet this situation. We have assumed this task and we shall not shrink from it in the future. It is a duty dictated by every intelligent consideration of national policy to ask you to make it possible for the United States to give employment to all of these three and one half million employable people now on relief, pending their absorption in a rising tide of private employment.

It is my thought that with the exception of certain of the normal public building operations of the Government, all emergency public works shall be united in a single new and greatly enlarged plan.

With the establishment of this new system we can supersede the Federal Emergency Relief Administration with a coordinated authority which will be charged with the orderly liquidation of our present relief activities and the substitution of a national chart for the giving of work. . . .

The work itself will cover a wide field including clearance of slums, which for adequate reasons cannot be undertaken by private capital; in rural housing of several kinds, where, again, private capital is unable to function; in rural electrification; in the reforestation of the great watersheds of the Nation; in an intensified program to prevent soil erosion and to reclaim blighted areas; in improving existing road systems and in constructing national highways designed to handle modern traffic; in the elimination of grade crossings; in the extension and enlargement of the successful work of the Civilian Conservation Corps; in non-Federal works, mostly self-liquidating and highly useful to local divisions of Government; and on many other projects which the Nation needs and cannot afford to neglect.

This is the method which I propose to you in order that we may better meet this present-day problem of unemployment. Its greatest advantage is that it fits logically and usefully into the long-range permanent policy of providing the three types of security which constitute as a whole an American plan for the betterment of the future of the American people. . . .

FRANKLIN D. ROOSEVELT

Campaign Address at Madison Square Garden

October 31, 1936

*The printed version of Roosevelt's 1936 campaign address at New York's
Madison Square Garden hardly conveys the flavor of the event: the pas-
sionately enthusiastic audience; the blaring horns, ringing cowbells, and
roars of approval; the icy tone of the president's voice as he excoriated the
forces of "organized money." It was the most radical speech any American
president has ever given. Responding to the crowd's fervor, Roosevelt improvised, amending the prepared text as he went along. For example, he
said "our Nation" rather than "this Nation was afflicted with hear-nothing,
see-nothing, do-nothing Government," and he added the phrase "to mankind" after the line "that Government is best which is most indifferent."
When FDR asserted, "I should like to have it said of my first Administration that in it the forces of selfishness and of lust for power met their match,"
the noise became deafening; so he shouted, "I should like to have it said—
wait a minute!—I should like to have it said of my second Administration
that in it these forces met their master." The* New York Times *reported that
the crowd's applause came in "roars which rose and fell like the sound of
waves pounding in the surf."*

Senator Wagner, Governor Lehman, ladies and gentlemen:

On the eve of a national election, it is well for us to stop for a moment and
analyze calmly and without prejudice the effect on our Nation of a victory
by either of the major political parties.

The problem of the electorate is far deeper, far more vital than the
continuance in the Presidency of any individual. For the greater issue
goes beyond units of humanity—it goes to humanity itself.

In 1932 the issue was the restoration of American democracy; and the
American people were in a mood to win. They did win. In 1936 the issue
is the preservation of their victory. Again they are in a mood to win.
Again they will win.

Samuel I. Rosenman, ed., *The Public Papers and Addresses of Franklin D. Roosevelt* (New
York: Random House, 1938), 5:566–73.

More than four years ago in accepting the Democratic nomination in Chicago, I said: "Give me your help not to win votes alone, but to win in this crusade to restore America to its own people."

The banners of that crusade still fly in the van of a Nation that is on the march.

It is needless to repeat the details of the program which this Administration has been hammering out on the anvils of experience. No amount of misrepresentation or statistical contortion can conceal or blur or smear that record. Neither the attacks of unscrupulous enemies nor the exaggerations of over-zealous friends will serve to mislead the American people.

What was our hope in 1932? Above all other things the American people wanted peace. They wanted peace of mind instead of gnawing fear.

First, they sought escape from the personal terror which had stalked them for three years. They wanted the peace that comes from security in their homes: safety for their savings, permanence in their jobs, a fair profit from their enterprise.

Next, they wanted peace in the community, the peace that springs from the ability to meet the needs of community life: schools, playgrounds, parks, sanitation, highways—those things which are expected of solvent local government. They sought escape from disintegration and bankruptcy in local and state affairs.

They also sought peace within the Nation: protection of their currency, fairer wages, the ending of long hours of toil, the abolition of child labor, the elimination of wild-cat speculation, the safety of their children from kidnappers.

And, finally, they sought peace with other Nations—peace in a world of unrest. The Nation knows that I hate war, and I know that the Nation hates war.

I submit to you a record of peace; and on that record a well-founded expectation for future peace—peace for the individual, peace for the community, peace for the Nation, and peace with the world.

Tonight I call the roll—the roll of honor of those who stood with us in 1932 and still stand with us today.

Written on it are the names of millions who never had a chance—men at starvation wages, women in sweatshops, children at looms.

Written on it are the names of those who despaired, young men and young women for whom opportunity had become a will-o'-the-wisp.

Written on it are the names of farmers whose acres yielded only bitterness, business men whose books were portents of disaster, home owners who were faced with eviction, frugal citizens whose savings were insecure.

Written there in large letters are the names of countless other Americans of all parties and all faiths, Americans who had eyes to see and hearts to understand, whose consciences were burdened because too many of their fellows were burdened, who looked on these things four years ago and said, "This can be changed. We will change it."

We still lead that army in 1936. They stood with us then because in 1932 they believed. They stand with us today because in 1936 they know. And with them stand millions of new recruits who have come to know.

Their hopes have become our record.

We have not come this far without a struggle and I assure you we cannot go further without a struggle.

For twelve years this Nation was afflicted with hear-nothing, see-nothing, do-nothing Government. The Nation looked to Government but the Government looked away. Nine mocking years with the golden calf and three long years of the scourge! Nine crazy years at the ticker and three long years in the breadlines! Nine mad years of mirage and three long years of despair! Powerful influences strive today to restore that kind of government with its doctrine that that Government is best which is most indifferent.

For nearly four years you have had an Administration which instead of twirling its thumbs has rolled up its sleeves. We will keep our sleeves rolled up.

We had to struggle with the old enemies of peace—business and financial monopoly, speculation, reckless banking, class antagonism, sectionalism, war profiteering.

They had begun to consider the Government of the United States as a mere appendage to their own affairs. We know now that Government by organized money is just as dangerous as Government by organized mob.

Never before in all our history have these forces been so united against one candidate as they stand today. They are unanimous in their hate for me—and I welcome their hatred.

I should like to have it said of my first Administration that in it the forces of selfishness and of lust for power met their match. I should like to have it said of my second Administration that in it these forces met their master.

The American people know from a four-year record that today there is only one entrance to the White House—by the front door. Since March 4, 1933, there has been only one pass-key to the White House. I

have carried that key in my pocket. It is there tonight. So long as I am
President, it will remain in my pocket. . . .

I prefer to remember this campaign not as bitter but only as hard-
fought. There should be no bitterness or hate where the sole thought is
the welfare of the United States of America. No man can occupy the
office of President without realizing that he is President of all the people.

It is because I have sought to think in terms of the whole Nation that
I am confident that today, just as four years ago, the people want more
than promises.

Our vision for the future contains more than promises.

This is our answer to those who, silent about their own plans, ask us
to state our objectives.

Of course we will continue to seek to improve working conditions for
the workers of America—to reduce hours over-long, to increase wages
that spell starvation, to end the labor of children, to wipe out sweatshops.
Of course we will continue every effort to end monopoly in business, to
support collective bargaining, to stop unfair competition, to abolish dishonorable trade practices. For all these we have only just begun to fight.

Of course we will continue to work for cheaper electricity in the
homes and on the farms of America, for better and cheaper transportation, for low interest rates, for sounder home financing, for better banking, for the regulation of security issues, for reciprocal trade among nations, for the wiping out of slums. For all these we have only just begun
to fight.

Of course we will continue our efforts in behalf of the farmers of
America. With their continued cooperation we will do all in our power to
end the piling up of huge surpluses which spelled ruinous prices for
their crops. We will persist in successful action for better land use, for reforestation, for the conservation of water all the way from its source to
the sea, for drought and flood control, for better marketing facilities for
farm commodities, for a definite reduction of farm tenancy, for encour-
agement of farmer cooperatives, for crop insurance and a stable food
supply. For all these we have only just begun to fight.

Of course we will provide useful work for the needy unemployed; we
prefer useful work to the pauperism of a dole.

Here and now I want to make myself clear about those who disparage
their fellow citizens on the relief rolls. They say that those on relief are
not merely jobless—that they are worthless. Their solution for the relief
problem is to end relief—to purge the rolls by starvation. To use the language of the stock broker, our needy unemployed would be cared for
when, as, and if some fairy godmother should happen on the scene.

You and I will continue to refuse to accept that estimate of our unemployed fellow Americans. Your Government is still on the same side of the street with the Good Samaritan and not with those who pass by on the other side.

Again—what of our objectives?

Of course we will continue our efforts for young men and women so that they may obtain an education and an opportunity to put it to use. Of course we will continue our help for the crippled, for the blind, for the mothers, our insurance for the unemployed, our security for the aged. Of course we will continue to protect the consumer against unnecessary price spreads, against the costs that are added by monopoly and speculation. We will continue our successful efforts to increase his purchasing power and to keep it constant.

For these things, too, and for a multitude of others like them, we have only just begun to fight.

All this—all these objectives—spell peace at home. All our actions, all our ideals, spell also peace with other nations.

Today there is war and rumor of war. We want none of it. But while we guard our shores against threats of war, we will continue to remove the causes of unrest and antagonism at home which might make our people easier victims to those for whom foreign war is profitable. You know well that those who stand to profit by war are not on our side in this campaign.

"Peace on earth, good will toward men"—democracy must cling to that message. For it is my deep conviction that democracy cannot live without that true religion which gives a nation a sense of justice and of moral purpose. Above our political forums, above our market places stand the altars of our faith—altars on which burn the fires of devotion that maintain all that is best in us and all that is best in our Nation.

We have need of that devotion today. It is that which makes it possible for government to persuade those who are mentally prepared to fight each other to go on instead, to work for and to sacrifice for each other. That is why we need to say with the Prophet: "What doth the Lord require of thee—but to do justly, to love mercy and to walk humbly with thy God." That is why the recovery we seek, the recovery we are winning, is more than economic. In it are included justice and love and humility, not for ourselves as individuals alone, but for our Nation.

That is the road to peace.

FRANKLIN D. ROOSEVELT

Fireside Chat on Reorganization of the Judiciary
March 9, 1937

On February 5, 1937, FDR announced his plan to reform the Supreme Court. He claimed that the justices—six of whom were over the age of seventy—were too old to conduct the Court's work effectively. But everyone understood that it was the conservative outlook of a majority of the justices, not their ages, that moved the president to take action. In his March 9, 1937, fireside chat, FDR squarely addressed the issue of judicial ideology. Supreme Court rulings, he maintained, had all too often been based on the justices' personal convictions. The Court, he added, had made itself into a "super-legislature." His statement that action was needed "to save the Constitution from the Court and the Court from itself" was taken from a letter written to him by a supporter, Felix Frankfurter, a professor at Harvard Law School and an advocate of judicial restraint (whom FDR would appoint to the Supreme Court in 1939). Frankfurter advised Roosevelt to "take the country to school" on the subject of judicial review—that is, to explain why the Court should always exercise extreme caution in overturning legislative enactments. This fireside chat was Roosevelt's effort to do just that.

. . . I want to talk with you very simply about the need for present action in this crisis—the need to meet the unanswered challenge of one-third of a Nation ill-nourished, ill-clad, ill-housed.

Last Thursday I described the American form of Government as a three horse team provided by the Constitution to the American people so that their field might be plowed. The three horses are, of course, the three branches of government—the Congress, the Executive and the Courts. Two of the horses are pulling in unison today; the third is not. Those who have intimated that the President of the United States is trying to drive that team, overlook the simple fact that the President, as Chief Executive, is himself one of the three horses.

Samuel I. Rosenman, ed., *The Public Papers and Addresses of Franklin D. Roosevelt* (New York: Macmillan, 1941), 6:122–33.

It is the American people themselves who are in the driver's seat. It is the American people themselves who want the furrow plowed. It is the American people themselves who expect the third horse to pull in unison with the other two.

I hope that you have re-read the Constitution of the United States in these past few weeks. Like the Bible, it ought to be read again and again. It is an easy document to understand when you remember that it was called into being because the Articles of Confederation under which the original thirteen States tried to operate after the Revolution showed the need of a National Government with power enough to handle national problems. In its Preamble, the Constitution states that it was intended to form a more perfect Union and promote the general welfare; and the powers given to the Congress to carry out those purposes can be best described by saying that they were all the powers needed to meet each and every problem which then had a national character and which could not be met by merely local action.

But the framers went further. Having in mind that in succeeding generations many other problems then undreamed of would become national problems, they gave to the Congress the ample broad powers "to levy taxes . . . and provide for the common defense and general welfare of the United States."

That, my friends, is what I honestly believe to have been the clear and underlying purpose of the patriots who wrote a Federal Constitution to create a National Government with national power, intended as they said, "to form a more perfect union . . . for ourselves and our posterity."

For nearly twenty years there was no conflict between the Congress and the Court. Then Congress passed a statute which, in 1803, the Court said violated an express provision of the Constitution. The Court claimed the power to declare it unconstitutional and did so declare it. But a little later the Court itself admitted that it was an extraordinary power to exercise and through Mr. Justice Washington laid down this limitation upon it: "It is but a decent respect due to the wisdom, the integrity and the patriotism of the legislative body, by which any law is passed, to presume in favor of its validity until its violation of the Constitution is proved beyond all reasonable doubt."

But since the rise of the modern movement for social and economic progress through legislation, the Court has more and more often and more and more boldly asserted a power to veto laws passed by the Congress and State Legislatures in complete disregard of this original limitation.

In the last four years the sound rule of giving statutes the benefit of all reasonable doubt has been cast aside. The Court has been acting not as a judicial body, but as a policy-making body.

When the Congress has sought to stabilize national agriculture, to improve the conditions of labor, to safeguard business against unfair competition, to protect our national resources, and in many other ways, to serve our clearly national needs, the majority of the Court has been assuming the power to pass on the wisdom of these Acts of the Congress—and to approve or disapprove the public policy written into these laws.

That is not only my accusation. It is the accusation of most distinguished Justices of the present Supreme Court. I have not the time to quote to you all the language used by dissenting Justices in many of these cases. But in the case holding the Railroad Retirement Act unconstitutional, for instance, Chief Justice Hughes said in a dissenting opinion that the majority opinion was "a departure from sound principles," and placed "an unwarranted limitation upon the commerce clause." And three other Justices agreed with him.

In the case holding the A.A.A. unconstitutional, Justice Stone said of the majority opinion that it was a "tortured construction of the Constitution." And two other Justices agreed with him.

In the case holding the New York Minimum Wage Law unconstitutional, Justice Stone said that the majority were actually reading into the Constitution their own "personal economic predilections," and that if the legislative power is not left free to choose the methods of solving the problems of poverty, subsistence and health of large numbers in the community, then "government is to be rendered impotent." And two other Justices agreed with him.

In the face of these dissenting opinions, there is no basis for the claim made by some members of the Court that something in the Constitution has compelled them regretfully to thwart the will of the people.

In the face of such dissenting opinions, it is perfectly clear, that as Chief Justice Hughes has said: "We are under a Constitution, but the Constitution is what the Judges say it is."

The Court in addition to the proper use of its judicial functions has improperly set itself up as a third House of the Congress—a super-legislature, as one of the justices has called it—reading into the Constitution words and implications which are not there, and which were never intended to be there.

We have, therefore, reached the point as a Nation where we must take action to save the Constitution from the Court and the Court from itself.

We must find a way to take an appeal from the Supreme Court to the Constitution itself. We want a Supreme Court which will do justice under the Constitution—not over it. In our Courts we want a government of laws and not of men.

I want—as all Americans want—an independent judiciary as proposed by the framers of the Constitution. That means a Supreme Court that will enforce the Constitution as written—that will refuse to amend the Constitution by the arbitrary exercise of judicial power—amendment by judicial say-so. It does not mean a judiciary so independent that it can deny the existence of facts universally recognized.

How then could we proceed to perform the mandate given us? It was said in last year's Democratic platform, "If these problems cannot be effectively solved within the Constitution, we shall seek such clarifying amendment as will assure the power to enact those laws, adequately to regulate commerce, protect public health and safety, and safeguard economic security." In other words, we said we would seek an amendment only if every other possible means by legislation were to fail.

When I commenced to review the situation with the problem squarely before me, I came by a process of elimination to the conclusion that, short of amendments, the only method which was clearly constitutional, and would at the same time carry out other much needed reforms, was to infuse new blood into all our Courts. We must have men worthy and equipped to carry out impartial justice. But, at the same time, we must have Judges who will bring to the Courts a present-day sense of the Constitution—Judges who will retain in the Courts the judicial functions of a court, and reject the legislative powers which the courts have today assumed.

In forty-five out of the forty-eight States of the Union, Judges are chosen not for life but for a period of years. In many States Judges must retire at the age of seventy. Congress has provided financial security by offering life pensions at full pay for Federal Judges on all Courts who are willing to retire at seventy. In the case of Supreme Court Justices, that pension is $20,000 a year. But all Federal Judges, once appointed, can, if they choose, hold office for life, no matter how old they may get to be.

What is my proposal? It is simply this: whenever a Judge or Justice of any Federal Court has reached the age of seventy and does not avail himself of the opportunity to retire on a pension, a new member shall be appointed by the President then in office, with the approval, as required by the Constitution, of the Senate of the United States.

That plan has two chief purposes. By bringing into the judicial system a steady and continuing stream of new and younger blood, I hope, first, to make the administration of all Federal justice speedier and, therefore, less costly; secondly, to bring to the decision of social and economic problems younger men who have had personal experience and contact with modern facts and circumstances under which average men have to live and work. This plan will save our national Constitution from hardening of the judicial arteries.

The number of Judges to be appointed would depend wholly on the decision of present Judges now over seventy, or those who would subsequently reach the age of seventy.

If, for instance, any one of the six Justices of the Supreme Court now over the age of seventy should retire as provided under the plan, no additional place would be created. Consequently, although there never can be more than fifteen, there may be only fourteen, or thirteen, or twelve. And there may be only nine.

There is nothing novel or radical about this idea. It seeks to maintain the Federal bench in full vigor. It has been discussed and approved by many persons of high authority ever since a similar proposal passed the House of Representatives in 1869.

Why was the age fixed at seventy? Because the laws of many States, the practice of the Civil Service, the regulations of the Army and Navy, and the rules of many of our Universities and of almost every great private business enterprise, commonly fix the retirement age at seventy years or less.

The statute would apply to all the courts in the Federal system. There is general approval so far as the lower Federal courts are concerned. The plan has met opposition only so far as the Supreme Court of the United States itself is concerned. If such a plan is good for the lower courts it certainly ought to be equally good for the highest Court from which there is no appeal.

Those opposing this plan have sought to arouse prejudice and fear by crying that I am seeking to "pack" the Supreme Court and that a baneful precedent will be established.

What do they mean by the words "packing the Court"?

Let me answer this question with a bluntness that will end all *honest* misunderstanding of my purposes.

If by that phrase "packing the Court" it is charged that I wish to place on the bench spineless puppets who would disregard the law and would decide specific cases as I wished them to be decided, I make this answer: that no President fit for his office would appoint, and no Senate of honorable men fit for their office would confirm, that kind of appointees to the Supreme Court.

But if by that phrase the charge is made that I would appoint and the Senate would confirm Justices worthy to sit beside present members of the Court who understand those modern conditions, that I will appoint Justices who will not undertake to override the judgment of the Congress on legislative policy, that I will appoint Justices who will act as Justices and not as legislators—if the appointment of such Justices can be called "packing the Courts," then I say that I and with me the vast majority of the American people favor doing just that thing—now.

Is it a dangerous precedent for the Congress to change the number of the Justices? The Congress has always had, and will have, that power. The number of Justices has been changed several times before, in the Administrations of John Adams and Thomas Jefferson—both signers of the Declaration of Independence—Andrew Jackson, Abraham Lincoln and Ulysses S. Grant.

I suggest only the addition of Justices to the bench in accordance with a clearly defined principle relating to a clearly defined age limit. Fundamentally, if in the future, America cannot trust the Congress it elects to refrain from abuse of our Constitutional usages, democracy will have failed far beyond the importance to it of any kind of precedent concerning the Judiciary.

We think it so much in the public interest to maintain a vigorous judiciary that we encourage the retirement of elderly Judges by offering them a life pension at full salary. Why then should we leave the fulfillment of this public policy to chance or make it dependent upon the desire or prejudice of any individual Justice?

It is the clear intention of our public policy to provide for a constant flow of new and younger blood into the Judiciary. Normally every President appoints a large number of District and Circuit Judges and a few members of the Supreme Court. Until my first term practically every President of the United States had appointed at least one member of the Supreme Court. President Taft appointed five members and named a Chief Justice; President Wilson, three; President Harding, four, including a Chief Justice; President Coolidge, one; President Hoover, three, including a Chief Justice.

Such a succession of appointments should have provided a Court well-balanced as to age. But chance and the disinclination of individuals to leave the Supreme bench have now given us a Court in which five Justices will be over seventy-five years of age before next June and one over seventy. Thus a sound public policy has been defeated.

I now propose that we establish by law an assurance against any such ill-balanced Court in the future. I propose that hereafter, when a Judge reaches the age of seventy, a new and younger Judge shall be added to the Court automatically. In this way I propose to enforce a sound public policy by law instead of leaving the composition of our Federal Courts, including the highest, to be determined by chance or the personal decision of individuals.

If such a law as I propose is regarded as establishing a new precedent, is it not a most desirable precedent?

Like all lawyers, like all Americans, I regret the necessity of this controversy. But the welfare of the United States, and indeed of the Constitution itself, is what we all must think about first. Our difficulty with the Court today rises not from the Court as an institution but from human beings within it. But we cannot yield our constitutional destiny to the personal judgment of a few men who, being fearful of the future, would deny us the necessary means of dealing with the present.

This plan of mine is no attack on the Court; it seeks to restore the Court to its rightful and historic place in our system of Constitutional Government and to have it resume its high task of building anew on the Constitution "a system of living law." The Court itself can best undo what the Court has done. . . .

FRANKLIN D. ROOSEVELT

Speeches on Conservation and the Environment
1936–1937

Conservation was one of the causes closest to Roosevelt's heart. As early as 1912, he had declared that when it came to the use of natural resources, individual desire for profit should be subordinated to the welfare of the wider community, and he reiterated this theme throughout his presidency. Although FDR was interested in all aspects of conservation, he was especially concerned, as historian Edgar B. Nixon has noted, with "the devastation of our forests, the destruction of our soil, and the needless spoliation of our great scenic and wilderness areas." Roosevelt often used ceremonial occasions, such as the dedication of a national park or the opening of a dam to

Edgar B. Nixon, ed., *Franklin Delano Roosevelt and Conservation, 1911–1945* (Hyde Park, N.Y.: Franklin Delano Roosevelt Library, 1957), 1:537–39; 2:132–33.

provide inexpensive hydroelectric power, to talk about the responsibility owed to future generations, to "the children who will succeed to the land a few years hence."

Shenandoah National Park, Virginia, July 3, 1936

. . . I am very glad to come back to Virginia.

The creation of this Park is one part of our great program of husbandry—the joint husbandry of human resources and natural resources. In every part of the country, local and state and federal authorities are engaged in preserving and developing our heritage of natural resources; and in this work they are equally conserving our priceless heritage of human values by giving to hundreds of thousands of men the opportunity of making an honest living.

I have seen this work in progress, for I came here two years ago. I have seen it in progress in many other parts of the land, and so I can say, I think, from first hand evidence, that the product of the labor of the men of the Civilian Conservation Corps, who have opened up the Shenandoah National Park and other parks to the use and the enjoyment of our citizens, that product is as significant as though instead of working for the Government they had been working in a mill or in a factory. They have a right to be as proud of their labor here as if they had been engaged in private employment.

In by-gone years we have seen, even we of this generation have seen the terrible tragedy of our age—the tragedy of waste. Waste of our people, waste of our land. It was neither the will nor the destiny—I think that has been sufficiently proved—neither the will nor the destiny of our Nation that this waste of human and material resources should continue any longer. That was the compelling reason that led us to put our idle people to the task of ending the waste of our land.

Think of it—the thousands of young men, their involuntary idleness three years ago—that ended when they came here to the camps on the Blue Ridge; and since then they have not been idle. Today they have ended more than their own idleness, they have ended the idleness of the Shenandoah National Park. It is going to be a busy and a useful place in the years to come, just as the work of these young men will, I am very confident, lead them to busy and useful lives in the years to come.

Our country is going to need many other young men as they come to manhood, need them for work like this—for other Shenandoahs.

Is it a dream? Or perhaps will I be accused of an exaggerated passion for planning if I paint for you a picture? You who are here know of the great usefulness to humanity which this Skyline Drive achieves from now on and of the greater usefulness which its extension, south through Virginia and North Carolina and Tennessee to the Great Smoky Mountains National Park—we know what that will achieve.

And in almost every other part of the Union there is a similar need for recreational areas, for Parkways that will give men and women of moderate means the opportunity, the invigoration and the luxury of touring and camping amid scenes of great natural beauty like this.

All across the nation—and it's three thousand miles—at this time of the year, and in many parts of the nation at all times of the year, people are starting out on their vacations, vacations to be spent in part or in whole in National and State Parks. Those people will put up at roadside camps or pitch their tents under the stars, with an open fire to cook by, with the smell of the woods, and the wind in the trees. They will forget the rush and the strain of all the other long weeks of the year, and for a short time at least, the days will be good for their bodies and good for their souls. Once more they will lay hold of the perspective that comes to men and women who every morning and every night can lift up their eyes to Mother Nature.

There is merit for all of us in the ancient tale of mythology, the tale of the Giant Antaeus, who every time that he touched his Mother Earth arose with strength renewed a hundred fold.

This Park, therefore, together with its many sisters that are coming to completion in every part of our land, is in the largest sense a work of conservation. Through all of them, we are preserving the beauty and the wealth of the hills, the mountains, the plains, the trees and the streams. Through all of them we are maintaining useful work for our young men. Through all of them we are enriching the character and the happiness of our people.

We seek to pass on to our children a richer land and a stronger Nation.

And so my friends, I now take great pleasure in dedicating Shenandoah National Park, of dedicating it to this and to succeeding generations of Americans for the recreation, and for the re-creation which we find here.

Bonneville Dam, Oregon, September 28, 1937

Today I have a feeling of real satisfaction in witnessing the completion of another great national project, and of pleasure in the fact that in its inception, four years ago, I had some part. My interest in the whole of the valley of the great Columbia River goes back seventeen years to 1920 when I first studied its mighty possibilities. And again, in 1932, I visited Oregon and Washington and Idaho and on that visit I took occasion in Portland to express certain views which have since, through the action of the Congress, become a recorded part of American national policy.

Almost exactly three years ago, I inspected the early construction stages of this dam at Bonneville.

The more we study the water resources of the Nation, the more we accept the fact that their use is a matter of national concern, and that in our plans for their use our line of thinking must include great regions as well as narrower localities.

If, for example, we Americans had known as much and acted as effectively twenty or thirty or forty years ago as we do today in the development of the use of land in that great semiarid strip in the center of the country that runs from the Canadian border all the way down to Texas, we could have prevented in great part the abandonment of thousands and thousands of farms in portions of ten states and thus prevented the migration of thousands of destitute families from those areas into the States of Washington and Oregon and California. We would have done this by avoiding the plowing up of great areas that should have been kept in grazing range and by stricter regulations to prevent over-grazing. And at the same time we would have checked soil erosion, stopped the denudation of our forests and controlled disastrous fires.

Some of my friends who talk glibly about the right of any individual to do anything he wants with any of his property take the point of view that it is not the concern of Federal or state or local government to interfere with what they miscall "the liberty of the individual." With them I do not agree and never have agreed, because unlike them, I am thinking of the future of the United States. Yes, my conception of liberty does not permit an individual citizen or a group of citizens to commit acts of depredation against nature in such a way as to harm their neighbors, and especially to harm the future generations of Americans. . . .

2

The New Deal

The year 1935 witnessed a decisive turn toward fundamental social reform. The Social Security Act laid the foundation of the welfare state; the National Labor Relations Act enhanced the power of trade unions; and the Wealth Tax Act levied significantly higher rates on the well-to-do. But 1935 marked a "watershed," as historian Arthur M. Schlesinger, Jr., has termed it, for other reasons as well. The Roosevelt administration developed an ambitious plan to provide relief through public employment; it took steps to combat rural poverty and alleviate the plight of migrant workers; it set new limits on the power of public utility holding companies; it stepped up efforts to bring electricity to farms throughout the nation; and it imposed tougher federal controls on the nation's banking system. These initiatives, the journalist William Allen White remarked, represented a "belated attempt to bring the American people up to the modern standards of English-speaking countries."

ROBERT F. WAGNER

The National Labor Relations Act
February 21, 1935

Throughout a career spanning more than twenty years in the U.S. Senate (1927–1949), Robert F. Wagner of New York was the leading advocate of the rights of organized labor. In February 1935, he introduced what would become the National Labor Relations Act, popularly known as the Wagner Act, but he did not yet have FDR's backing. It was only in May, after the

Congressional Record, 74th Cong., 1st sess., Vol. 79, 2371–72.

*Senate passed the measure and the House was prepared to follow suit, that
the president announced his support. Wagner's speech shows that he viewed
the bill as a response to the inadequacy of Section 7(a) of the National Industrial Recovery Act of 1933, which in theory guaranteed workers the right
to organize but in practice more often than not led to the creation of company unions — employer-dominated "sham or dummy" unions, as Wagner
called them. The measure he sponsored outlawed such unions, proscribed
other unfair labor practices, and established the principle of majority rule:
The union that won a majority of votes would have to be recognized by the
employer as the bargaining agent for all workers. "There can be no freedom
in an atmosphere of bondage," Wagner said, and the act that bore his name
was designed to create the kind of freedom few workers had ever enjoyed.*

The recovery program has sought to bestow upon the business man and
the worker a new freedom to grapple with the great economic challenges of our times. We have released the business man from the undis-
criminating enforcement of the antitrust laws, which had been subjecting him to the attacks of the price cutters and wage reducers — the
pirates of industry. In order to deal out the equal treatment upon which
a just democratic society must rest, we at the same time guaranteed the
freedom of action of the worker. In fact, the now famous section 7(a), by
stating that employees should be allowed to cooperate among themselves if they desired to do so, merely restated principles that Congress
has avowed for half a century.

Congress is familiar with the events of the past 2 years. While industry's freedom of action has been encouraged until the trade association
movement has blanketed the entire country, employees attempting in
good faith to exercise their liberties under section 7(a) have met with repeated rebuffs. It was to check this evil that the President in his wisdom
created the National Labor Board in August 1933, out of which has
emerged the present National Labor Relations Board.

The Board has performed a marvelous service in composing disputes
and sending millions of workers back to their jobs upon terms beneficial
to every interest. But it was handicapped from the beginning, and it is
gradually but surely losing its effectiveness, because of the practical inability to enforce its decisions. At present it may refer its findings to the
National Recovery Administration and await some action by that agency,
such as the removal of the Blue Eagle. We all know that the entire enforcement procedure of the N.R.A. is closely interlinked with the voluntary spirit of the codes. Business in the large is allowed to police itself

through the code authorities. This voluntarism is without question admirable in respect to provisions for fair competition that have been written by industry and with which business is in complete accord. But it is wholly unadapted to the enforcement of a specific law of Congress which becomes a crucial issue only in those very cases where it is opposed by the guiding spirits of the code authorities. Secondly, the Board may refer a case to the Department of Justice. But since the Board has no power to subpoena records or witnesses, its hearings are largely ex parte and its records so infirm that the Department of Justice is usually unable to act. Finally, the existence of numerous industrial boards whose interpretations of section 7(a) are not subject to the coordinating influence of a supreme National Labor Relations Board, is creating a maze of confusion and contradictions. While there is a different code for each trade, there is only one section 7(a), and no definite law written by Congress can mean something different in each industry. These difficulties are reducing section 7(a) to a sham and a delusion.

The break-down of section 7(a) brings results equally disastrous to industry and to labor. Last summer it led to a procession of bloody and costly strikes, which in some cases swelled almost to the magnitude of national emergencies. It is not material at this time to inquire where the balance of right and wrong rested in respect to these various controversies. If it is true that employees find it difficult to remain acquiescent when they lose the main privilege promised them by the Recovery Act, it is equally true that employers are tremendously handicapped when it is impossible to determine exactly what their rights are. Everybody needs a law that is precise and certain.

There has been a second and even more serious consequence of the break-down of section 7(a). When employees are denied the freedom to act in concert even when they desire to do so, they cannot exercise a restraining influence upon the wayward members of their own groups, and they cannot participate in our national endeavor to coordinate production and purchasing power. The consequences are already visible in the widening gap between wages and profits. If these consequences are allowed to produce their full harvest, the whole country will suffer from a new economic decline.

The national labor relations bill which I now propose is novel neither in philosophy nor in content. It creates no new substantive rights. It merely provides that employees, if they desire to do so, shall be free to organize for their mutual protection or benefit. Quite aside from section 7(a), this principle has been embodied in the Norris-LaGuardia Act, in amendments to the Railway Labor Act passed last year, and in a long train of other enactments of Congress.

There is not a scintilla of truth in the wide-spread propaganda to the effect that this bill would tend to create a so-called "labor dictatorship." It does not encourage national unionism. It does not favor any particular union. It does not display any preference toward craft or industrial organizations. Most important of all, it does not force or even counsel any employee to join any union if he prefers to deal directly or individually with his employers. It seeks merely to make the worker a free man in the economic as well as the political field. Certainly the preservation of long-recognized fundamental rights is the only basis for frank and friendly relations in industry.

The erroneous impression that the bill expresses a bias for some particular form of union organization probably arises because it outlaws the company-dominated union. Let me emphasize that nothing in the measure discourages employees from uniting on an independent- or company-union basis, if by these terms we mean simply an organization confined to the limits of one plant or one employer. Nothing in the bill prevents employers from maintaining free and direct relations with their workers or from participating in group insurance, mutual welfare, pension systems, and other such activities. The only prohibition is against the sham or dummy union which is dominated by the employer, which is supported by the employer, which cannot change its rules or regulations without his consent, and which cannot live except by the grace of the employer's whims. To say that that kind of a union must be preserved in order to give employees freedom of selection is a contradiction in terms. There can be no freedom in an atmosphere of bondage. No organization can be free to represent the workers when it is the mere creature of the employer.

Equally erroneous is the belief that the bill creates a closed shop for all industry. It does not force any employer to make a closed-shop agreement. It does not even state that Congress favors the policy of the closed shop. It merely provides that employers and employees may voluntarily make closed-shop agreements in any State where they are now legal. Far from suggesting a change, it merely preserves the status quo.

A great deal of interest centers around the question of majority rule. The national labor relations bill provides that representatives selected by the majority of employees in an appropriate unit shall represent all the employees within that unit for the purposes of collective bargaining. This does not imply that an employee who is not a member of the majority group can be forced to enter the union which the majority favors. It means simply that the majority may decide who are to be the spokesmen for all in making agreements concerning wages, hours, and other conditions of employment. Once such agreements are made the bill provides that their terms must be applied without favor or discrimination to all employees. These provisions conform to the democratic procedure that is followed in every business and in our governmental life, and that was embodied by Congress in the Railway Labor Act last year. Without them the phrase "collective bargaining" is devoid of meaning, and the very few unfair employers are encouraged to divide their workers against themselves.

Finally, the National Labor Relations Board is established permanently, with jurisdiction over other boards dealing with cases under section 7(a) or under its equivalent as written into this bill. Nothing could be more unfounded than the charges that the Board would be invested with arbitrary or dictatorial or even unusual powers. Its powers are modeled upon those of the Federal Trade Commission and numerous other governmental agencies. Its orders would be enforceable not by the Board, but by recourse to the courts of the United States, with every affected party entitled to all the safeguards of appeal.

The enactment of this measure will clarify the industrial atmosphere and reduce the likelihood of another conflagration of strife such as we witnessed last summer. It will stabilize and improve business by laying the foundations for the amity and fair dealing upon which permanent progress must rest. It will give notice to all that the solemn pledge made by Congress when it enacted section 7(a) cannot be ignored with impunity, and that a cardinal principle of the new deal for all and not some of our people is going to be supported and preserved by the Government.

FRANCES PERKINS

The Social Security Act

September 2, 1935

In June 1934, FDR appointed a cabinet-level committee to draft a bill to guarantee the "economic security of individuals." He placed Secretary of Labor Frances Perkins in charge, telling her, "You care about this thing. You

Frances Perkins, "The Social Security Act," *Vital Speeches of the Day* (Pelham, N.Y.: City News Publishing Co., 1935), 1:792–94.

believe in it ... and you will drive it through." *The report of the Committee on Economic Security eventually led Congress to pass the Social Security Act, which FDR signed in August 1935. Despite its many limitations and the exclusion of many workers from its provisions, the act institutionalized government reponsibility for the disadvantaged. It created a federal old-age pension plan, a joint federal-state system of unemployment insurance, and programs to care for the blind, to train the physically handicapped, and to aid dependent children. When one social reformer complained to Perkins that the measure failed to cover many workers and set standards that were too low, she replied that it deserved support because it represented "a substantial, necessary beginning," a point she reiterated in her radio address explaining the act's provisions to the public.*

People who work for a living in the United States of America can join with all other good citizens on this forty-eighth anniversary of Labor Day in satisfaction that the Congress has passed the Social Security Act. This act establishes unemployment insurance as a substitute for haphazard methods of assistance in periods when men and women willing and able to work are without jobs. It provides for old-age pensions which mark great progress over the measures upon which we have hitherto depended in caring for those who have been unable to provide for the years when they no longer can work. It also provides security for dependent and crippled children, mothers, the indigent disabled and the blind.

Old people who are in need, unemployables, children, mothers and the sightless, will find systematic regular provisions for needs. The Act limits the Federal aid to not more than $15 per month for the individual, provided the State in which he resides appropriates a like amount. There is nothing to prevent a State from contributing more than $15 per month in special cases and there is no requirement to allow as much as $15 from either State or Federal funds when a particular case has some personal provision and needs less than the total allowed.

Following essentially the same procedure, the Act as passed provides for Federal assistance to the States in caring for the blind, a contribution by the State of up to $15 a month to be matched in turn by a like contribution by the Federal Government. The Act also contains provision for assistance to the States in providing payments to dependent children under sixteen years of age. There also is provision in the Act for cooperation with medical and health organizations charged with rehabilitation of physically handicapped children. The necessity for adequate service in the fields of public and maternal health and child welfare calls for the extension of these services to meet individual community needs.

Consider for a moment those portions of the Act which, while they will not be effective this present year, yet will exert a profound and far-reaching effect upon millions of citizens. I refer to the provision for a system of old-age benefits supported by the contributions of employer and employees, and to the section which sets up the initial machinery for unemployment insurance.

Old-age benefits in the form of monthly payments are to be paid to individuals who have worked and contributed to the insurance fund in direct proportion to the total wages earned by such individuals in the course of their employment subsequent to 1936. The minimum monthly payment is to be $10, the maximum $85. These payments will begin in the year 1942 and will be to those who have worked and contributed.

Because of difficulty of administration not all employments are covered in this plan at this time so that the law is not entirely complete in coverage, but it is sufficiently broad to cover all normally employed industrial workers.

As an example of the practical operation of the old-age benefit system, consider for a moment a typical young man of thirty-five years of age, and let us compute the benefits which will accrue to him. Assuming that his income will average $100 per month over the period of thirty years until he reaches the age of sixty-five, the benefit payments due him from the insurance fund will provide him with $42.50 per month for the remainder of his life. If he has been fortunate enough to have an income of $200 per month, his income will subsequently be $61.25 per month. In the event that death occurs prior to the age of sixty-five, 3½% of the total wages earned by him subsequent to 1936 will be returned to his dependents. If death occurs after the age of sixty-five, his dependents receive the same amount, less any benefits paid to him during his lifetime.

This vast system of old-age benefits requires contributions both by employer and employee, each to contribute 3% of the total wage paid to the employee. This tax, collected by the Bureau of Internal Revenue, will be graduated, ranging from 1% in 1937 to the maximum 3% in 1939 and thereafter. That is, on this man's average income of $100 a month he will pay to the usual fund $3 a month and his employer will also pay the same amount over his working years.

In conjunction with the system of old-age benefits, the Act recognizes that unemployment insurance is an integral part of any plan for the economic security of millions of gainfully employed workers. It provides for a plan of cooperative Federal-State action by which a State may enact an insurance system, compatible with Federal requirements and best suited to its individual needs.

The Federal Government attempts to promote and effectuate these State systems, by levying a uniform Federal pay-roll tax of 3% on employers employing eight or more workers, with the proviso that an employer who contributes to a State unemployment compensation system will receive a credit of 90% of this Federal tax. After 1937, additional credit is also allowable to any employer who, because of favorable employment experience or adequate reserves, is permitted by the State to reduce his payments.

In addition, the Act provides that after the current fiscal year the Federal Government allocate annually to the States $49,000,000 solely for the administration of their respective insurance systems, thus assuring that all money paid for State unemployment compensation will be reserved for the purpose of compensation to the worker. It has been necessary, at the present time, to eliminate essentially the same groups from participation under the unemployment insurance plan as in the old-age benefit plan, though it is possible that at some future time a more complete coverage will be formulated. . . .

With the States rests now the responsibility of devising and enacting measures which will result in the maximum benefits to the American workman in the field of unemployment compensation. I am confident that impending State action will not fail to take cognizance of this responsibility. The people of the different States favor the program designed to bring them greater security in the future and their legislatures will speedily pass appropriate laws so that all may help to promote the general welfare.

Federal legislation was framed in the thought that the attack upon the problems of insecurity should be a cooperative venture participated in by both the Federal and State Governments, preserving the benefits of local administration and national leadership. It was thought unwise to have the Federal Government decide all questions of policy and dictate completely what the States should do. Only very necessary minimum standards are included in the Federal measure leaving wide latitude to the States.

While the different State laws on unemployment insurance must make all contributions compulsory, the States, in addition to deciding how these contributions shall be levied, have freedom in determining their own waiting periods, benefit rates, maximum benefit periods and the like. Care should be taken that these laws do not contain benefit provisions in excess of collections. While unemployment varies greatly in different States, there is no certainty that States which have had less normal unemployment heretofore will in the future have a more favorable experience than the average for the country. It is obvious that in the best interests of the worker, industry and society, there must be a certain uniformity of standards. It is obvious, too, that we must prevent the penalizing of competitive industry in any State which plans the early adoption of a sound system of unemployment insurance, and provide effective guarantees against the possibility of industry in one State having an advantage over that of another. This the uniform Federal tax does, as it costs the employer the same whether he pays the levy to the Federal Government or makes a contribution to a State unemployment insurance fund. The amount of the tax itself is a relative assurance that benefits will be standardized in all States, since under the law the entire collection must be spent on benefits to unemployed.

The social security measure looks primarily to the future and is only a part of the administration's plan to promote sound and stable economic life. We cannot think of it as disassociated from the Government's program to save the homes, the farms, the businesses and banks of the Nation, and especially must we consider it a companion measure to the Works Relief Act which does undertake to provide immediate increase in employment and corresponding stimulation to private industry by purchase of supplies.

While it is not anticipated as a complete remedy for the abnormal conditions confronting us at the present time, it is designed to afford protection for the individual against future major economic vicissitudes. It is a sound and reasonable plan and framed with due regard for the present state of economic recovery. It does not represent a complete solution of the problems of economic security, but it does represent a substantial, necessary beginning. It has been developed after careful and intelligent consideration of all the facts and all of the programs that have been suggested or applied anywhere.

Few legislative proposals have had as careful study, as thorough and conscientious deliberation, as that which went into the preparation of the social security programs. It is embodied in perhaps the most useful and fundamental single piece of Federal legislation in the interest of wage earners in the United States. As President Roosevelt said when he signed the measure: "If the Senate and House of Representatives in their long and arduous session had done nothing more than pass this bill, the session would be regarded as historic for all time."

This is truly legislation in the interest of the national welfare. We must recognize that if we are to maintain a healthy economy and thriving production, we need to maintain the standard of living of the lower income groups of our population who constitute ninety per cent of our purchasing power. The President's Committee on Economic Security, of which I had the honor to be chairman, in drawing up the plan, was convinced that its enactment into law would not only carry us a long way toward the goal of economic security for the individual, but also a long way toward the promotion and stabilization of mass purchasing power without which the present economic system cannot endure. . . .

The passage of this act with so few dissenting votes and with so much intelligent public support is deeply significant of the progress which the American people have made in thought in the social field and awareness of methods of using cooperation through government to overcome social hazards against which the individual alone is inadequate.

During the fifteen years I have been advocating such legislation as this I have learned that the American people want such security as the law provides. It will make this great Republic a better and a happier place in which to live — for us, our children and our children's children. It is a profound and sacred satisfaction to have had some part in securing this great boon to the people of our country. . . .

JOHN STEINBECK
The Crisis in Agriculture
September 12, 1936

Among the groups not covered by the Social Security Act were farm laborers, the most destitute of whom were migrant workers. The individual who most effectively publicized their plight was the writer John Steinbeck. He first began to investigate the issue in August 1936, when the San Francisco News *invited him to contribute a series of articles on migratory workers in California. In September, traveling through the San Joaquin Valley, Steinbeck gained firsthand knowledge of the workers' squalid working and living conditions. He also wrote a feature article for* The Nation, *a leading liberal journal, based on background information he had earlier obtained from the Resettlement Administration and other federal agencies. His article*

John Steinbeck, "Dubious Battle in California," *The Nation,* September 12, 1936, 302–4.

advanced some of the themes that he would later use in his famous novel The Grapes of Wrath *(1939), such as the contrast between the government-run camps and the squatter camps. In March 1938, as he began work on the novel, he said, "I'm trying to write history while it is happening and I don't want it to be wrong."*

In sixty years a complete revolution has taken place in California agriculture. Once its principal products were hay and cattle. Today fruits and vegetables are its most profitable crops. With the change in the nature of farming there has come a parallel change in the nature and amount of the labor necessary to carry it on. Truck gardens, while they give a heavy yield per acre, require much more labor and equipment than the raising of hay and livestock. At the same time these crops are seasonal, which means that they are largely handled by migratory workers. Along with the intensification of farming made necessary by truck gardening has come another important development. The number of large-scale farms, involving the investment of thousands of dollars, has increased; so has the number of very small farms of from five to ten acres. But the middle farm, of from 100 to 300 acres is in process of elimination.

There are in California, therefore, two distinct classes of farmers widely separated in standard of living, desires, needs, and sympathies: the very small farmer who more often than not takes the side of the workers in disputes, and the speculative farmer, like A. J. Chandler, publisher of the *Los Angeles Times,* or like Herbert Hoover and William Randolph Hearst, absentee owners who possess huge sections of land. Allied with these large individual growers have been the big incorporated farms, owned by their stockholders and farmed by instructed managers, and a large number of bank farms, acquired by foreclosure and operated by superintendents whose labor policy is dictated by the bank. For example, the Bank of America is very nearly the largest farm owner and operator in the state of California.

These two classes have little or no common ground; while the small farmer is likely to belong to the grange, the speculative farmer belongs to some such organization as the Associated Farmers of California, which is closely tied to the state Chamber of Commerce. This group has as its major activity resistance to any attempt of farm labor to organize. Its avowed purpose has been the distribution of news reports and leaflets tending to show that every attempt to organize agricultural workers was the work of red agitators and that every organization was Communist inspired.

The completion of the transcontinental railroads left in the country many thousands of Chinese and some Hindus who had been imported for the work. At about the same time the increase of fruit crops, with their heavy seasonal need for pickers, created a demand for this mass of cheap labor. These people, however, did not long remain on the land. They migrated to the cities, rented small plots of land there, and, worst of all, organized in the so-called "tongs," which were able to direct their efforts as a group. Soon the whites were inflamed to race hatred, riots broke out against the Chinese, and repressive activities were undertaken all over the state, until these people, who had been a tractable and cheap source of labor, were driven from the fields.

To take the place of the Chinese, the Japanese were encouraged to come into California; and they, even more than the Chinese, showed an ability not only to obtain land for their subsistence but to organize. The "Yellow Peril" agitation was the result. Then, soon after the turn of the century Mexicans were imported in great numbers. For a while they were industrious workers, until the process of importing twice as many as were needed in order to depress wages made their earnings drop below any conceivable living standard. In such conditions they did what the others had done; they began to organize. The large growers immediately opened fire on them. The newspapers were full of the radicalism of the Mexican unions. Riots became common in the Imperial Valley and in the grape country in and adjacent to Kern County. Another wave of importations was arranged, from the Philippine Islands, and the cycle was repeated — wage depression due to abundant labor, organization, and the inevitable race hatred and riots.

This brings us almost to the present. The drought in the Middle West has very recently made available an enormous amount of cheap labor. Workers have been coming to California in nondescript cars from Oklahoma, Nebraska, Texas, and other states, parts of which have been rendered uninhabitable by drought. Poverty-stricken after the destruction of their farms, their last reserves used up in making the trip, they have arrived so beaten and destitute that they have been willing at first to work under any conditions and for any wages offered. This migration started on a considerable scale about two years ago and is increasing all the time.

For a time it looked as though the present cycle would be identical with the earlier ones, but there are several factors in this influx which differentiate it from the others. In the first place, the migrants are undeniably American and not deportable. In the second place, they were not lured to California by a promise of good wages, but are refugees as surely as though they had fled from destruction by an invader. In the third place, they are not drawn from a peon class, but have either owned small farms or been farm hands in the early American sense, in which the "hand" is a member of the employing family. They have one fixed idea, and that is to acquire land and settle on it. Probably the most important difference is that they are not easily intimidated. They are courageous, intelligent, and resourceful. Having gone through the horrors of the drought and with immense effort having escaped from it, they cannot be herded, attacked, starved, or frightened as all the others were.

Let us see what the emigrants from the dust bowl find when they arrive in California. The ranks of permanent and settled labor are filled. In most cases all resources have been spent in making the trip from the dust bowl. Unlike the Chinese and the Filipinos, the men rarely come alone. They bring wives and children, now and then a few chickens and their pitiful household goods, though in most cases these have been sold to buy gasoline for the trip. It is quite usual for a man, his wife, and from three to eight children to arrive in California with no possessions but the rattletrap car they travel in and the ragged clothes on their bodies. They often lack bedding and cooking utensils.

During the spring, summer, and part of the fall the man may find some kind of agricultural work. The top pay for a successful year will not be over $400, and if he has any trouble or is not agile, strong, and quick it may well be only $150. It will be seen that rent is out of the question. Clothes cannot be bought. Every available cent must go for food and a reserve to move the car from harvest to harvest. The migrant will stop in one of two federal camps, in a state camp, in houses put up by the large or small farmers, or in the notorious squatters' camps. In the state and federal camps he will find sanitary arrangements and a place to pitch his tent. The camps maintained by the large farmers are of two classes — houses which are rented to the workers at what are called nominal prices, $4 to $8 a month, and camp grounds which are little if any better than the squatters' camps. Since rent is such a problem, let us see how the houses are fitted. Ordinarily there is one room, no running water; one toilet and one bathroom are provided for two or three hundred persons. Indeed, one large farmer was accused in a Growers' Association meeting of being "kind of communistic" because he advocated separate toilets for men and women. Some of the large ranches maintain what are called model workers' houses. One such ranch, run by a very prominent man, has neat single-room houses built of whitewashed adobe. They are said to have cost $500 apiece. They are rented for $5 a month. This ranch pays twenty cents an hour as opposed to the thirty cents paid at other ranches and indorsed by the grange in the community. Since this rugged individual is saving 33⅓ per cent of his labor cost and still charging $5 a month rent for his houses, it will be readily seen that he is getting a very fair return on his money besides being generally praised as a philanthropist. The reputation of this ranch, however, is that the migrants stay only long enough to get money to buy gasoline with, and then move on.

The small farmers are not able to maintain camps of any comfort or with any sanitary facilities except one or two holes dug for toilets. The final resource is the squatters' camp, usually located on the bank of some watercourse. The people pack into them. They use the watercourse for drinking, bathing, washing their clothes, and to receive their refuse, with the result that epidemics start easily and are difficult to check. Stanislaus County, for example, has a nice culture of hookworm in the mud by its squatters' camp. The people in these camps, because of long-continued privation, are in no shape to fight illness. It is often said that no one starves in the United States, yet in Santa Clara County last year five babies were certified by the local coroner to have died of "malnutrition," the modern word for starvation, and the less shocking word, although in its connotation it is perhaps more horrible since it indicates that the suffering has been long drawn out.

In these squatters' camps the migrant will find squalor beyond anything he has yet had to experience and intimidation almost unchecked. At one camp it is the custom of deputy sheriffs, who are also employees of a great ranch nearby, to drive by the camp for hours at a time, staring into the tents as though trying to memorize faces. The communities in which these camps exist want migratory workers to come for the month required to pick the harvest, and to move on when it is over. If they do not move on, they are urged to with guns.

These are some of the conditions California offers the refugees from the dust bowl. But the refugees are even less content with the starvation wages and the rural slums than were the Chinese, the Filipinos, and the Mexicans. Having their families with them, they are not so mobile as the earlier immigrants were. If starvation sets in, the whole family starves, instead of just one man. Therefore they have been quick to see that they must organize for their own safety.

Attempts to organize have been met with a savagery from the large growers beyond anything yet attempted. In Kern County a short time ago a group met to organize under the A. F. of L. They made out their form and petition for a charter and put it in the mail for Washington. That night a representative of Associated Farmers wired Washington for information concerning a charter granted to these workers. The Wash-

ington office naturally replied that it had no knowledge of such a charter. In the Bakersfield papers the next day appeared a story that the A. F.
of L. denied the affiliation; consequently the proposed union must be of
Communist origin.

But the use of the term communism as a bugbear has nearly lost its
sting. An official of a speculative-farmer group, when asked what he
meant by a Communist, replied: "Why, he's the guy that wants twenty-
five cents an hour when we're paying twenty." This realistic and cynical
definition has finally been understood by the workers, so that the term
is no longer the frightening thing it was. And when a county judge said,
"California agriculture demands that we create and maintain a peonage,"
the future of unorganized agricultural labor was made clear to every man
in the field.

The usual repressive measures have been used against these migrants: shooting by deputy sheriffs in "self-defense," jailing without
charge, refusal of trial by jury, torture and beating by night riders. But
even in the short time that these American migrants have been out here
there has been a change. It is understood that they are being attacked
not because they want higher wages, not because they are Communists,
but simply because they want to organize. And to the men, since this
defines the thing not to be allowed, it also defines the thing that is completely necessary to the safety of the workers.

This season has seen the beginning of a new form of intimidation not
used before. It is the whispering campaign which proved so successful
among business rivals. As in business, it is particularly deadly here because its source cannot be traced and because it is easily spread. One of
the items of this campaign is the rumor that in the event of labor troubles
the deputy sheriffs inducted to break up picket lines will be armed not
with tear gas but with poison gas. The second is aimed at the women and
marks a new low in tactics. It is to the effect that in the event of labor
troubles the water supply used by strikers will be infected with typhoid
germs. The fact that these bits of information are current over a good
part of the state indicates that they have been widely planted.

The effect has been far from that desired. There is now in California
anger instead of fear. The stupidity of the large grower has changed terror into defensive fury. The granges, working close to the soil and to the
men, and knowing the temper of the men of this new race, have tried to
put through wages that will allow a living, however small. But the large
growers, who have been shown to be the only group making a considerable profit from agriculture, are devoting their money to tear gas and
rifle ammunition. The men will organize and the large growers will meet
organization with force. It is easy to prophesy this. In Kern County the

grange has voted $1 a hundred pounds for cotton pickers for the first picking. The Associated Farmers have not yielded from seventy-five cents. There is tension in the valley, and fear for the future.

It is fervently to be hoped that the great group of migrant workers so necessary to the harvesting of California's crops may be given the right to live decently, that they may not be so badgered, tormented, and hurt that in the end they become avengers of the hundreds of thousands who have been tortured and starved before them.

HARRY HOPKINS

Federal Relief

September 19, 1936

Just a week after the publication of Steinbeck's article, Harry Hopkins, director of the Works Progress Administration (WPA), appeared at the Ambassador Hotel in Los Angeles to defend New Deal relief policies. Hopkins had directed relief efforts in New York State when FDR was governor, and he had then moved to Washington in 1933 to head the new federal programs: the Federal Emergency Relief Administration, the Civil Works Administration, and finally the WPA, created in 1935. "The end of Government," Hopkins once declared, "is that people, individuals shall be allowed to live a more abundant life, and Government has no other purpose than to take care of the people that live within our borders." His speech in Los Angeles not only illustrates his no-nonsense, tell-it-like-it-is style, but it also explains his underlying philosophy: People who are out of work are not morally at fault but "are just like the rest of us"; those on relief must be permitted to maintain their dignity and self-respect; mistakes are inevitable in the administering of a vast program but must always be made in the interest of helping people. Hopkins tersely summarized his outlook by saying "hunger is not debatable."

. . . I gained six pounds this summer and am looking pretty well after all the things people have called me, and the reason is I don't worry any more. A fellow told me the story about the eighteen year old girl that had

Harry Hopkins, "Address at WPA Luncheon," Harry L. Hopkins Papers, Franklin D. Roosevelt Library.

her first date. Her father sent for her and told her there were certain things she should know. "This young fellow is very apt to hold your hand, and daughter, that is all right. Then he will want to put his arm around you, and that is all right. Then he will want you to put your head on his shoulder — you must not do that because your mother will worry." So the young girl went out and the next morning her father asked her how the evening had gone. She replied, "Well, Dad, everything happened just as you said it would, he held my hand, then he put his arm around me, then he wanted me to put my head on his shoulder, but I said, 'Hell no! — you put your head on my shoulder and let your mother worry.'" . . .

I am going to discuss with you very briefly some of the things that have happened to me in the last three or four years, and some of the things that would have happened to you if you had had this job. You didn't have it — you could sit around your dinner table and discuss these things — about what you would and would not do. "What a terrible fellow this bird Hopkins is." But if you had had my job you would have had to sign on a dotted line — you would have had to put it in writing. You would have had to say "yes" or "no" and you would have had to make a lot of decisions, and furthermore you would have had to make these decisions fast. You couldn't have called a meeting of the board of directors or written an article to see how the public would react, or sent out trial balloons to find out what the people might think. People were hungry. Twenty-two million of them in the United States.

Now, a lot of people don't realize there were more people on the relief rolls late in 1932 and early in 1933 than have ever been in America since, and there are fewer in America today than there have ever been. You would have bumped right into that, because we found these millions of people in the United States. Families — many of them getting two dollars a month relief, and you would have had to decide right off the bat whether you were going to go on giving them $2 or $4 or $8 a month. You would have had to decide who should and who should not get relief. Would you give relief to everybody that knocked on the door and asked for it, and would you make an investigation of their need, and what kind of an investigation? If a man had an insurance policy for $200 would you make him cash it in? You couldn't be vague on that point. You couldn't tell these State Administrators, "Do anything you please, make up your own minds." You would have had to write a letter out here very specifically saying what you would do about it. If he had $100 in a savings bank — every dime he had — would he have to take it out and spend it before you gave him relief? You couldn't have sat around the table at

Washington and talked about it — you would have had to write a letter and decide it, the whole business about this investigation. What kind of people should make these investigations — how many there should be. Every time you had to spend any money for investigations it was charged up against administration — the people would yell — and if you didn't make an investigation, an adequate one, then they would jump on you because you weren't making an adequate investigation. And you would have had to decide this business with the millions of people involved. Investigators that these people had never seen in their lives would go in and ask whether they had a bank account or an insurance policy — how far behind they were in their rent, did they have any relatives. You would have had to decide this whole business about investigating needs and you would have had headaches about whether these people on relief were in need. I might as well say here and now, we have never yet worked out the technique of investigating people who asked for relief. Some way, somehow in America, we have got to find a technique that is dignified, that is an American way of determining who should and who should not get a benefit.

Now let me tell you this about these investigations, because this gets into one of the major criticisms of this show. The public says these people on relief don't need it. They say they are chiselers and cheats. All right, there isn't a single person in this room, that if a hundred people walked up to the desk and you were going to put 50 on relief — nobody in this room would pick the same fifty — and any fifty picked out, I could go out three months later and find five percent of them that didn't need relief and shouldn't have it — just as you could find five percent that I had picked that didn't need relief. Don't fool yourself, there is no magic about this business of determining who does and who does not need relief — it is always a matter of opinion. I had to exercise my opinion — you didn't. We have made many hundreds of investigations as to whether these people were in need; we have made them by the Chambers of Commerce, by Rotary Clubs, by all kinds of people, and the result is always the same. They come back and they say 95% of these people need relief and the other 5% should be off. If I were any of you, I would be awfully careful if someone wants to appoint you on a committee to go out and visit some of these people in their homes. I would be awfully careful if I had to talk to the wives.

A lot of people say that the people are getting too much, that the wages are too high. The average relief to the whole crowd has only been $27.00 per month. Today in the WPA $50.00 per month is the average wage. Try and live on $50.00 per month. See how far it goes.

I have never seen a person in my life since I have been in this game, I don't care who they were, who didn't know some particular person, some intimate friend of theirs, perhaps a relative, who would come to me and say, "Hopkins, I know this fellow is in need" — and they know five or six more. The answer is, you can sympathize with five or six, but you can't sympathize with five or six million, and so you begin to generalize about things you hear often in clubs, about whether or not they are in need. I am getting sick and tired of these people on the WPA and local relief rolls being called chiselers and cheats. It doesn't do any good to call these people names, because they are just like the rest of us. They don't drink any more than the rest of us, they don't lie any more, they're no lazier than the rest of us — they're pretty much a cross section of the American people who can't get a job. . . .

We had a law known as the Elizabethan Poor Law, an alien institution. The idea was to make these people as uncomfortable as possible. If you give them relief, hand them out a niggardly amount to keep body and soul together. That is what went on in this country, except in a few cities. Of all the outrageous things that were done to American people, treating these people like outcasts. Behind that is a moral philosophy, if anyone is poor it's because something is wrong with them. Give them just as little relief as possible so you won't encourage them. They want these unemployed to walk up timidly and knock on the door, and why should they? They are American citizens like the rest of us. It is no fault of their own that they are out of work, and it is the business of society to take care of them. It shouldn't be done as an act of degradation. I made up my mind early in this game that relief was a matter of right and not a matter of charity.

Then you would have had to decide, once you had made up your mind to put them on relief, what kind of relief you were going to give them. When I got to Washington we had the soup kitchen, bread lines. Should you feed the unemployed in a bread line or a soup kitchen and let them stand in line? Should you feed them in great commissaries? Should we buy our food wholesale and give these fellows a basket and let them walk out? These things were going on all over America. A lot of people believed in soup kitchens. A lot of people thought it was all right to let a fellow stand in line for hours. Well, that seemed terrible to me. It was cheaper — there's no question about it. We did not have to do business with any wholesaler or middleman in the country. We could have bought things just as cheaply as Sears Roebuck. While we had an average of 15% of the population on relief, we had 80% of the people in some cities. . . .

A lot of conservative business men were the people that were urging me to set up commissaries, the cheapest way you possibly can, no matter what it does to the unemployed. You would have had to decide this business about grocery orders. When we threw the commissary over we printed millions of grocery orders. They would take these orders to the grocer for $3. They would walk in — usually they would have to wait because these pink and blue slips of ours became very familiar and the grocers would make them wait until the cash customers were taken care of. Often in buying groceries, a grocer would fill the order for $2.75 and give them 25¢ in cash. The reason they did this was that we never had a hair cut on these orders. They couldn't buy safety razor blades and they couldn't go to the movies. In America there are hundreds of thousands of families that went month on end and never saw a dime. . . .

Work is a moral habit in America. I was taught very early in the game that you had to work to have any status in society. Did you ever see a rich man putting on a front about working, who didn't say on Friday or Saturday that he had to go to the office to take care of something? And I don't blame him a bit. And don't you suppose the unemployed are in the same fix as the rest of us? These men, millions of them, going home every night, and they're out of work. They lose their self respect in no time. I think the most outrageous suggestion that is running around in America today is the idea that we should take these unemployed people and let them sit at home and hand them a basket of groceries once a week. And you would have had to decide what kind of work you were going to give them, what kind of projects, and you finally would have jumped right into boondoggling. . . .

You would have had to decide about 560,000 white collar men. Would you make them suffer? Would you put them out in a ditch with a pick axe and make them like it, musicians, actors? We decided to take the skills of these people wherever we found them and put them to work to save their skills when the public wanted them. Sure we put musicians into orchestras. Sure we let artists paint. It was all right for the great foundations to give fellowships to artists, but when the United States Government did it because these fellows were busted and broke, then it becomes boondoggling, a waste of money. A great many rich men in America maintain their whole standing in the community by doing boondoggling, and some of the finest things in America are of that character. There must have been some men or women in this town who have put up money for a great orchestra. Now we have been doing the same thing when the arts no longer have a patron. We have artists, writers, doctors,

lawyers and nurses. Why we even have sunk so low as to put blind people
to work on projects for the blind. I think these projects are good. I think
they are getting better all the time. I think the unit of production is better. They are better supervised than they were. Any contractor knows
that it depends on the man who is actually in charge of a crew of men.
And one foreman will get more performance than another. One of the
difficulties we get into is because of this question of skills. Sometimes a
project comes to us that is an excellent project, but they haven't got the
kind of skilled workmen in that community that it takes to develop that
project. We have some skilled workers here but not many. We have to develop a project around the skills of the people. Otherwise we are going
to be competing with private business for our workers. . . .

I want to finish by saying two things. I have never liked poverty. I have
never believed that with our capitalistic system people have to be poor. I
think it is an outrage that we should permit hundreds and hundreds of
thousands of people to be ill clad, to live in miserable homes, not to have
enough to eat; not to be able to send their children to school for the only
reason that they are poor. I don't believe ever again in America are we going to permit the things to happen that have happened in the past to
people. We are never going back again, in my opinion, to the days of
putting the old people in the alms houses, when a decent dignified pension at home will keep them there. We are coming to the day when we
are going to have decent houses for the poor, when there is genuine and
real security for everybody. I have gone all over the moral hurdles that
people are poor because they are bad. I don't believe it. A system of government on that basis is fallacious. I think further than that, that this economic system of ours is an ideal instrument to increase this national income of ours, not back to 80 billion where it was, but up to 100 billion or
120 billion. The capitalistic system lends itself to providing a national income that will give real security for all.

Now I want to say this, I have been at this thing for three and a half
years. I have never been a public official before. I was brought up in that
school of thought that believed that no one went on the public payroll except for political purposes or because he was incompetent or unless he
had a job that he didn't work at. One of the most insidious things is the
propaganda that something is wrong about one that works for the
people. I have learned something in these three and a half years. I have
taken a look at a lot of these public servants. . . .

I have come to resent an attitude on the part of some people in America that you should never be part of this business of public service. I am
proud of having worked for the Government. It has been a great experi-

ence for me. I have signed my name to about $6,000,000,000 in the last three and a half years. None of it has stuck to the fingers of our administrators. You might think some of it has been wasted. If it has been wasted it was in the interest of the unemployed. You might say we have made mistakes. I haven't a thing to apologize for about our so-called mistakes. If we have made mistakes we have made them in the interests of the people that were broke.

When this thing is all over and I am out of the Government the things I am going to regret are the things I have failed to do for the unemployed. I don't know whether you would have liked the job. Every night when you went home and after you got home and remembered there was a telegram you didn't answer, the fact that you failed to answer the telegram and the telephone call may have resulted in somebody not eating. That is the kind of a job I have had for the last three and a half years, and still have. When it is all over, the thing I am going to be proudest of are the people all over America, public officials, volunteers, paid workers, thousands of people of all political and religious faiths who joined in this enterprise of taking care of people in need. It has been a great thing. I am not ashamed of one of them and I hope when I am through they are not going to be ashamed of me, and as I go around this country and see the unemployment and see the people who are running this show of ours, I am tremendously proud of this country of ours and I am tremendously proud that I am a citizen of it. Thank you very much.

HALLIE FLANAGAN

The Federal Theatre Project
May 11, 1938

To head the WPA's Federal Theatre Project, Hopkins selected Hallie Flanagan, whom he had known since their undergraduate days at Grinnell College. Flanagan had gone on to become director of experimental theater at Vassar College. In 1935, when she met with the heads of the Writers' Project (Henry Alsberg), the Music Project (Nikolai Sokoloff), and the Arts

Hallie Flanagan, introduction to *Federal Theatre Plays* (New York: Random House, 1938), vii–xiii.

Project (Holger Cahill), she said that all their efforts could be "part of a tremendous re-thinking, re-building, and re-dreaming of America," a point she reiterates here in her introduction to the published version of three Federal Theatre Project plays. One of the best known of those productions, Power by Arthur Arent, frankly advocated greater consumer control over public utilities and sang the praises of the Tennessee Valley Authority. "This is a great show," Harry Hopkins told the company backstage. "It's fast and funny, it makes you laugh and it makes you cry and it makes you think — I don't know what more anyone can ask of a show."

Government support of the theatre brings the United States into the best historic theatre tradition and into the best contemporary theatre practice. Four centuries before Christ, Athens believed that plays were worth paying for out of public money; today France, Germany, Norway, Sweden, Denmark, Russia, Italy and practically all other civilized countries appropriate money for the theatre.

However, it was not because of historic theatre tradition nor because of contemporary theatre practice that the Federal Theatre came into being. It came into being because in the summer of 1935 the relief rolls of American cities showed that thousands of unemployed theatre professionals, affected not only by economic depression but by the rapid development of the cinema and the radio, were destitute. The Federal Theatre came into being because the Government of the United States took the position that the talents of these professional theatre workers, together with the skills of painters, musicians and writers, made up a part of the national wealth which America could not afford to lose.

Therefore, on August 29, 1935, the Federal Theatre Project, a branch of the Works Progress Administration, under Harry Hopkins, was set up.

The story of how these theatre workers — actors, directors, designers, writers, dancers, musicians, technicians receiving only the small security wage set by Congress, with no stellar billings, and in the face of polite or impolite public amusement — leapt to meet their chance, is a drama more exciting than any which has yet reached our stage. . . .

It is a story of vaudeville companies playing before amazing audiences in schools, playgrounds, camps, prisons, reformatories, asylums, hospitals. It is the story of play bureaus sending out scripts and theatre research to 20,000 schools, farm granges and 4H clubs in rural areas. It is the story of ambitious youth experimenting in the fields of light, direction, design, writing and radio.

Fifteen hundred people returned to good jobs in private industry are a part of the story, as are eight thousand who remain, working with increasing imagination in forty theatres in twenty States, lacing the intervening countryside with local, regional tours. The story of Federal Theatre is the story also of its audience, a vast, exciting new audience of rich and poor, old and young; students in colleges, housewives in small towns, lumberjacks in Oregon, sharecroppers in the South. Federal Theatre is the story of a hundred thousand children who never saw a play before. . . .

Our Federal Theatre is a pioneer theatre. Our companies go through pioneer hardships; they play the turpentine circuit in Florida; they play the CCC camps in the dead of winter in the remote Northern woods. They played the devastated areas in the wake of the flood, acting on improvised stages before thousands of homeless flood victims. We underestimate the quality called patriotism if we think it does not bring to any Federal Theatre troupe a thrill of pride to portray the early days of a country which has recently, through Congressional action, given a new lease of life to the theatre.

Just as William Du Bois' *Haiti* represents our Negro theatre and *Prologue to Glory* our American historical series, *One-Third of a Nation* represents a type of drama developed on the project, an attempt to dramatize the struggle of the average American today for knowledge about his country and his world. The history of the Living Newspaper . . . is a form particularly adapted to a theatre which counts its greatest wealth in man power. . . .

The history of the Living Newspaper illustrates the fact that in a larger sense, also, the Federal Theatre is a pioneer theatre, because it is part of a tremendous rethinking, redreaming, and rebuilding of America. Being a part of a great nationwide work project, our actors are one, not only with the musicians playing symphonies in Federal orchestras; with writers re-creating the American scene; with artists compiling from the rich and almost forgotten past the *Index of American Design;* but they are also one with thousands of men building roads and bridges and sewers; one with doctors and nurses giving clinical aid to a million destitute men, women and children; one with workers carrying traveling libraries into desolate areas; one with scientists studying mosquito control and reforestation and swamp drainage and soil erosion.

What has all this to do with the theatre?

It has everything to do with the Federal Theatre. For these activities represent a new frontier in America, a frontier against disease, dirt, poverty, illiteracy, unemployment, despair, and at the same time against selfishness, special privilege and social apathy. The struggles along this frontier are not political in any narrow sense. They would exist under any administration. Taken collectively they illustrate what William James meant when he talked about a moral equivalent for war.

In this struggle our actors know what they are talking about. In this larger drama they are themselves protagonists.

3

Eleanor Roosevelt and American Women

During her years in the White House, Eleanor Roosevelt reshaped the role of first lady. Her success can be attributed not only to her humane sensibilities, intelligence, and fierce sense of independence but also to the nature of her relationship with her husband. By the time FDR was elected president, their relationship, as biographer Allida M. Black has observed, "had begun to move away from a traditional marriage and more toward a professional collaboration between peers." In books, articles, speeches, press conferences, and her daily newspaper column, "My Day," Eleanor Roosevelt supported her husband's broad objectives while managing to champion the causes in which she believed most deeply: equality for women, racial justice, federal support for the arts, the expansion of educational opportunities and vocational training programs for young people, and support for subsistence homestead communities. She favored programs designed to ensure, in her own words, "that a family shall have sufficient means of livelihood and the assurance of an ability to pay their expenses."

ELEANOR ROOSEVELT

Women in the Labor Force
June 16, 1938

Two days after FDR's first inauguration, Eleanor Roosevelt did something no president's wife had ever done before: She held her own press conference. She ultimately held 348 of them. To ensure that women reporters would

Maurine Beasley, ed., *The White House Press Conferences of Eleanor Roosevelt* (New York: Garland Publishing, 1983), 50–56.

have access to a source exclusively their own — and thereby put pressure on news organizations to hire women — she usually allowed only women to attend. Although official transcripts were not made, shorthand notes were kept by several reporters, among them Martha Strayer of the Washington Daily News, *who took down the press conference of June 16, 1938. The issue under discussion — whether married women ought to work outside the home — was highly controversial in an era of widespread unemployment among men. In 1936, when a Gallup poll asked people if they thought wives should work if their husbands had jobs, 82 percent of those who responded (and 75 percent of the women) answered in the negative. Whatever attitudes the poll revealed, the proportion of women wage earners who were married increased from 29 percent in 1930 to 35 percent in 1940.*

Topic: [Married women in the labor force.]

Miss [Mary] Anderson [head of the Women's Bureau, Department of Labor]: The question is the married woman in employment.

There has been a great deal said of taking married women out of employment and that would cure the unemployment situation. When we realize that we have a little more than three million in employment that are married, it seems rather a large number. But when we find out just how throwing people out of employment would employ all of the men, as they always say, and when we realize that the men [family breadwinners] that are out of employment — probably nearly half of those are women, and married women at that — it's a question of how much we would dislocate our whole fabric and how many we would throw on relief if we do anything like taking married women out of employment.

This little bit might be interesting: In 1921, during the unemployment period of that time, we had in the Women's Bureau thousands of letters telling us that if all the women were taken out of employment, that would cure the unemployment situation at that time. Since 1930, up to now, we have not had one single letter saying that very thing. All of the effort that is being put forth by individuals are about gains of married women. So that we have really established in this time the right of women to be employed.

They used to say they work for [pin] money, but they don't use that anymore. Married women are working for the same reason others are working: That is, to live, and for dependents to live. I'm sorry we haven't enough information so that one would understand that married women have dependents. But I think from this scattered information we have been able to get into the Women's Bureau, we have found that they have dependents, the same as anyone else; and the married woman works because the husband isn't getting enough money to keep the family, or because they have had sickness and they are paying the back debts, or they are paying for a house, or they are becoming a family, with all the things that belong to a family.

The married woman, of course, has assumed the burden of that. We talk about that and say taking married women out of employment would dislocate and hurt a great many families throughout the country.

Some people have been saying that, after all, if women had not been working, probably we would have better wages, probably there would have been a different kind of civilization. Perhaps so. I don't know. Yet, the fact is that the individual family has to be taken care of; and if the woman can do that, she could help, regardless of what we think of civilization or anything else.

Mrs. Roosevelt: Couldn't that same thing be said about certain groups that have been low-wage groups?

Miss Anderson: Yes. We might say, too, that the married women, as women do, have helped in the family. We haven't established a family wage. We haven't established enough wages for the husband to take care of his family. Till we can, we haven't any right or we can't really say whether a married woman should work or not. I think that's her individual right. It depends upon her wish, after all.

Where the married women are working and there is a low wage, which the majority of them are working under, there, too, she has to see to it that that little wage supplements the family income; because with that low wage, she doesn't escape her family responsibilities of working in a home. She has to look after the children. She has to cook the food. She has to see that the house is clean. She has to do the wash. She has really taken on two jobs — two full-time jobs. She isn't going to do that unless there is a real necessity for it. So it seems to me that when we speak about married women working and that they take three million men out, you can't do it. It's impossible.

I might say that the statistics say that 36 percent of the married women working are in domestic and personal service. Now, no one would ever say that men have ever done that, that it's a man's job. That's the largest proportion of married women. Clerical, 12 percent. Trade area, 11 percent. Professional, 10 percent. Agriculture, 9 percent.

I question the information, because I think we have to have and want much more and much better information on the question of the family and the reason for the married women working. We're hoping that some day, somebody will make that investigation, so that we can have real facts and focus on the question.

Mrs. Weed [apparently Helena Hill Weed, a member of the National Woman's party]: Have you ever heard any factory make their provision that the places vacated by women shall be filled by unemployed men?

Miss Anderson: Less so in professional and business.

Mrs. Weed: I think it has been used a great deal to get rid of people they want to get rid of.

A woman has a right to work because she wants to. She has the right, if she can get a job, to work if she wants to. There are factions that challenge that right, saying it's also a cause of unemployment and a great deal of dismissals.

Railroads have from time to time been trying to make that provision. I shouldn't say they are down in the general trend towards the dismissal of women.

Mrs. Roosevelt: I should say that it was more that people look for assistance and, to correct the unemployment situation, pick on that particular thing as one of the easiest methods to theorize about. . . .

For some people, work is almost a necessity to development. It may be that it's not always the keeping of a home which is the type of work that they are supposed to do and that you can't deny permanently to any human being the right. You might say temporarily, because in this situation perhaps you couldn't take a salary for a length of time if there is a stress of some kind, but you certainly can't deny that human being the right of development permanently.

I have always cited the fact that work was necessary to the development of the country and dignified the individual and was of value to the community, and that any young man who could live on his income without working and who did not work has always had the feeling that he was a slacker.

Why we should feel that in an age when someone's work is not needed in the home, she should, out of necessity, be made a slacker, is something I have never been able to understand in the value of citizens to every community.

I think the theory on which we have built does not go with the theory we are trying to push on women today. It was all right when your home required every bit of work that you could get out of every woman in the house; because then the full capacity was being used and there were all kinds of ways of using it, and today it doesn't require that anymore. Therefore, we are really forcing upon women a position which we have held from the beginning in this country was not good for the country.

May [apparently May Craig, a correspondent for Maine newspapers]: When the President went to Arthurdale [May 27, 1938], there was a press release telling about the project; and it said, in regard to the factory, that any woman who could properly be spared from her home duties could get a job in the factory.

Mrs. Roosevelt: I think she, herself, decides that. Actually, the families there are very large. A mother could hardly leave home a minute. Being large families, there are a good many girls who have wanted to work, but it's left entirely to them. I mean, nobody decides for them. They decide for themselves.

It happens that in the factory, girls and women are employed, not men. I think there may be one or two men, but it's almost entirely women and girls. That was understandable, because there were quite a number of young women and girls who really needed work, because they would have just been an added burden on their families if there had not been some outlet for their work. But, of course, they married very young and have very large families. So how long any one of them will continue is up to them.

If you had looked into family after family, you would have found that a number of the girls marry the minute they leave high school. They may work a short time, but a family begins to arrive very quickly, and for a short time they can't work.

There are one or two women who have been able to work because their children were old enough not to need them so much at home or helped at home or something of that sort. That's not a question that's decided by the individual. It's decided by the families.

A short time ago, I got a number of letters [questioning employment of women], and it wasn't merely drawing my attention, because one of the heads of a department here got a letter which he sent to me — I think because he had a sense of bewilderment as to what it was all about — and I got the answer for him and decided that perhaps the answer would be valuable in the country as a whole, because I had had several letters.

I am always getting letters from people who have theories of the way you can do away with unemployment. That had been one of the ways.

Mrs. Weed: I expected you to say that there might be, in times of stress, a reason for women to work without salary.

Mrs. Roosevelt: Not for women to give up their work. I think you have to realize that there are always individual situations.

For instance, I know of a family where the woman was working, and working to give a very much better education to her children. There was no real reason why she couldn't do it, because the children were grown and almost of college age. But there developed in their community a very serious employment situation. It was a temporary situation, but it was almost a necessity to cut down in the kind of work in which her husband was employed.

They did cut a number of employees, and she voluntarily took the cut, and the children did manage to pull themselves through. She did go back, but it was an exceptional situation that had to be met over a temporary period. It happened to be a situation which the employees understood as well as the employer.

I can't think that you could lay down hard and fast rules, that individual situations do arise, and people should be allowed to use their own intelligence about that. You can't ever, I don't think, say that any one thing will ever fit every situation. It doesn't. It's like saying such and such a thing is always right. You and I know such and such a thing is never always right. It may be right for one person and wrong for another person in almost the same situation. So that laying down hard and fast rules is very difficult, and I think you should leave a certain flexibility to allow for judgment.

Mrs. Weed: Do you think there is a greater moral obligation on women to give up their work, when they have other means of support, than there is on men in the same circumstances, married or single?

Mrs. Roosevelt: I think if the single woman has to support herself, the question does not arise if she is under more moral obligation than a man.

So I think it boils down to a married woman, and then comes the question whether the man or woman should be the main support in a family. My own instinct is a feeling that most women, if it comes to a decision, have more ability to find employment for themselves than most men have. But that doesn't always hold true.

I happen to know of a couple where the woman earns money and the man runs a farm. It's the kind of work which doesn't bring in a large amount of income but which makes living a very pleasant, happy thing, and he is happy and does the kind of thing he enjoys. It's a happy family. My instinct is to say that, as a rule, a woman is more adjustable.

May [Craig?]: What is a woman's duty? Her first duty is to stay home and take care of her family, and the other is to take a job in the economic situation when jobs are scarce.

Mrs. Roosevelt: Who is going to be the person to decide whether it is a woman's duty to stay at home and take care of her family?

Second, who should say that where the skills of the woman were such that she could do that particular job better than anybody else, better than she could do any other, probably it would be economically sound as well as spiritually a good thing? On the other hand, there may be a great many people for whom it would neither be spiritually or economically the best thing for their children or for that individual.

MOLLY DEWSON

Women and the New Deal
April 8, 1936

One of Eleanor Roosevelt's most devoted admirers was Mary F. ("Molly") Dewson, who headed the Women's Division of the Democratic National Committee. Described by her biographer, Susan Ware, as "a political boss with a feminist twist," Dewson worked unceasingly to increase the role of women in public life, to give women a larger voice in Democratic party councils, and to further what she termed "the human aspects of the New Deal." Eventually, she noted proudly, more than one hundred women held prominent positions in New Deal bureaus and agencies. In April 1936, following a two-month tour of the western states that convinced her that women's votes were crucial in FDR's upcoming campaign, she submitted this report on the emerging role of women in the Democratic party. She sent a copy to Eleanor Roosevelt, who told her, "I think your report is excellent. I read it with a great deal of interest."

The attitude of Democratic women toward politics and the attitude of Democratic politicians toward women in the party organization is very

Eleanor Roosevelt Papers, Franklin D. Roosevelt Library.

different from four years ago. This period has been epochal. The first great change since women won the ballot in 1920.

From 1920 to 1932 woman's status in politics was nebulous. A woman here and there made a career for herself like Congressman Mary T. Norton, but few functioned independently of the man who gave them prominence as a gesture toward woman suffrage. Those who accepted the drudgery of political chores worked with woman's habitual fidelity but without the illumination of ideas as to the significance of government or of ideals wrought from their experience.

Then came President Roosevelt. He appreciated the ability of women. He believed they could stand heavy responsibility and the gaff [ordeal] of public office. He put them in key positions throughout the Administration and in numbers proportionate to women's position in business, in the professions and in public affairs. These women have justified his belief. Their appointment and their success has encouraged women in their struggle to break down age old prejudice against their taking their place outside the home from which long since many former duties have departed in the wake of our mechanized civilization.

But his gift to women has been far greater than this recognition of individuals. There he accelerated a growing movement. Roosevelt has made women conscious of government and what it can do for them and their families and communities and what, alas!, it can do to them. No longer does government seem an alien thing either distant and incomprehensible or harsh and requiring. Experience had taught women the welfare of their families is bound up in the general welfare but it took Roosevelt to show them that government exists to help make life for the whole people "finer, better, happier." Woman's genius to conserve and protect the lives and happiness of others is aroused.

The party organization has been revivified by women who now see it as an instrument to attain their hopes and dreams of a measure of economic stability and security for every-day persons. Fifteen thousand of them the last two years, have been studying some part of Roosevelt's program to lighten unfair burdens, to strike a balance between diverse interests and to curb intolerable license to exploit. Many thousands more have been listening to the efforts and achievements of the administration as told by these students, often in far away places cut off by a controlled press from government releases on its progress in setting its house in order.

Democratic women everywhere are asking for information and facts. *The Democratic Digest* is the answer of the Women's Division of the Democratic National Committee. The circulation of this thirty-six page magazine, without a single deadhead, quadrupled last year, and now state after state is undertaking a special edition carrying supplementary news on its local government.

The campaign literature is designed in 1936 as in 1932 to put the main facts in the hands of every woman so that she will have a clear cut picture of the situation. The practical mind of woman, now that it has begun to function on governmental questions wishes to know and understand the issues. Vilifying, bombast and unsupported generalizations are distasteful to women.

In 1932 Roosevelt made no special appeal to women to support him. He saw no interests that were not their interests and by this simple act he testified to his belief that whatever has to do with the general welfare be it the problems of children, or of economics are the common concern of both men and women.

Long ago a poet said I would rather write the songs of a nation than its laws. No one can prophesy the duration of any law. It may serve its day or its purpose and pass. It may be superseded by some more practical, or constitutional device to secure the end sought. It is the goal that moulds the spirit of its time. Roosevelt's attitude toward women has meant a great lift upward; his attitude toward the aims of government has awakened in them a new hope that mankind will not founder from lack of vision.

Women's belief in their power to help and their determination to do so has been shown in many ways. They testified from their experience at code hearings of the National Recovery Administration in order that pitfalls might be avoided. They put over the great drive to get nationwide support for this attempt in cooperation by manufacturers, employees and consumers. It called for a familiar technique. They served on Consumers' Councils, more difficult because it was a fumbling toward the light in unknown territory. They initiated relief projects in their localities, seizing this unparalleled opportunity to kill two birds with one stone — give work to the unemployed and arrange that undernourished school children be fed; that home assistants be furnished in families over burdened by sickness and poverty, that our citizens of foreign birth be taught American ways, and for those innumerable activities which build a healthy society. They initiated these projects, explained their value to a critical but uninformed public and by their continuing interest kept them effective. They sold the Repair program of the Federal Housing Administration. They aided in the drafting of the Social Security Act and in the passage of supplementary legislation in the states.

Last and most significant of the new awakening the Democratic Party has made fresh recruits from among those women who had previously thought there was no place for them in politics, or who had not realized that since it is the parties that pass or do not pass desired legislation the effective place to work is from the inside. They volunteered because they believed they could be of service in explaining Roosevelt's program. They joined in the great educational effort of the Women's Division carried on through regional and state conferences, and county and town meetings. . . .

In stating the changes taking shape during the last four years, one great influence may not be omitted. Mrs. Roosevelt's presence in the White House has focused the interest of innumerable women on the affairs of common concern to every citizen — women whose attention had previously been limited to personal affairs by a habit of thought created in simpler days and later fostered by the great expansion of wealth and subsequent cheaper human standards. As reporter to the President Mrs. Roosevelt has observed the lives of the people from one end of the country to the other. She has talked about what she has seen and the women have listened. She has made all parts of the country seem nearer but the greatest distance spanned has been in the minds of those who have heard her stories of how others live. With her as its mistress the White House has ceased to be just an historic shrine and has become a symbol of friendliness, affection and cheer for all the people.

What is alive grows and its future form depends on its present inclination. I have reported the marked trends developing in the attitude of Democratic women toward politics and of Democratic men toward women in the party organization. These changes are tentative beginnings. They have not stiffened into custom. No one can deny they are good and sound and to rejoice that under a continuance of the present administration they will persist.

ELEANOR ROOSEVELT

Women in Politics

March–April 1940

Like Molly Dewson, Eleanor Roosevelt believed that women, generally speaking, were more concerned with welfare, justice, reform, and peace than were men. In 1940 she published this essay on women's role in politics in Good Housekeeping, *a magazine that had no particular political slant and whose readership consisted primarily of homemakers. She conceded that women behaved politically as individuals rather than as members of a group, dividing, as did male voters, along liberal and conservative lines. But she nevertheless insisted that the granting of suffrage to women coincided with government "taking increasing cognizance of humanitarian questions." She also explored an apparent — and enduring — paradox: The betterment of women's position seemed to require both that they become more conscious of their identity as women and that they demand being treated as individuals rather than as members of a group.*

Now that we have considered what has happened to women in the political arena since they were granted the right of suffrage, I think it is only fair to deal with that perennial question: "What have women accomplished for human betterment with the vote?"

Of course, I never felt that there was any particular reason why we should expect miracles to occur as a result of giving women the right to vote. It was denied them for so long that men acquired great interest in public questions and women felt these questions were not their responsibility. Therefore, women for many years have been accustomed to centering their interests in the home or in allied activities. They have left the administration of government almost exclusively in the hands of men.

Changing the habits of thought of any group of people, men or women, is not a rapid process, so I am not in the least surprised, at the end of twenty-one years of suffrage, that the answer to: "What have women accomplished by their vote?" is frequently a shrug of the shoulders.

Eleanor Roosevelt, "Women in Politics," *Good Housekeeping,* March 1940, 45, 68; April 1940, 201–3.

Women have used this suffrage, as far as I can tell, approximately as much as men have. There is a great percentage of people, eligible to vote, who do not vote on election day, and there is no proof that they are predominately either men or women. And, strange though it may seem, women apparently make up their minds on public questions in much the say way that men do.

I think it is fairly obvious that women have voted on most questions as individuals and not as a group, in much the same way that men do, and that they are influenced by their environment and their experience and background, just as men are.

There are women, however, who, either because they have no confidence in themselves, or because of the age-old tradition that men are superior for some reason or other, will say: "Oh, Mrs. Roosevelt, it is all right for you to urge women to think independently and clearly on all these social questions, but I still like to take my guidance from the men and do as they tell me." Well, perhaps there are some men who, for the sake of peace in the family, accept a woman's point of view even on political questions.

You will find, I think, women divided in the same groupings that have divided men, and they approach any question before the electorate in much the same way. There are liberals and conservatives among the women as well as among the men. As far as I can judge, only one thing stands out — namely, that on the whole, during the last twenty years, government has been taking increasing cognizance of humanitarian questions, things that deal with the happiness of human beings, such as health, education, security. There is nothing, of course, to prove that this is entirely because of the women's interest, and yet I think it is significant that this change has come about during the period when women have been exercising their franchise. It makes me surmise that women who do take an interest in public questions have thrust these interests to the fore, and obliged their fellow citizens to consider them. Whereas in the past these human problems have remained more or less in the background, today they are discussed by every governing body.

No revolution has come about because women have been given the vote, and it is perfectly true that many women are not thrilled by their opportunity to take part in political-party work. They probably do not like it so well as the men do, for we do not find them competing for places on party committees or for actual recognition in the political positions.

The women, however, are gradually increasing their activities. There are more women in civil-service positions and there are more women in rather inconspicuous, but important positions in city, state, and federal governments where technical knowledge is required.

When I went to Washington, I was so much impressed by the work they were doing that I started to have parties for women executives in various departments, and I discovered an astonishing number of women doing very important work, but getting comparatively little recognition because government is still a man's world.

As a result of all this, however, I find the influence of women emerging into a more important sphere. There was a time when no one asked: "What will the women think about this?" Now that question comes up often. It is true that we had more women in elective positions a few years ago; but I think the change is so slight that it is just a temporary fluctuation, and due to the fact that women haven't yet gained real confidence in themselves in that type of competition. Women are quite willing to compete in an examination that tests their knowledge even though there is still a prejudice against appointing them to certain positions because of their sex. To come out and fight a political campaign, however, is still difficult for most women. That is one reason why a woman who does hold an office, either elective or appointive, so often obtains it at her husband's death or as a result of his interests. She is continuing work she might never have taken up on her own initiative.

We have had, of course, a few failures among women who have taken office either because men have urged them to do so, or because they have followed in their husbands' footsteps. When a woman fails, it is much more serious than when a man fails, because the average woman attributes the failure not to the individual, but to the fact that she is a woman. . . .

Looking for concrete achievements, I feel we can really credit to the women only one over this period of years, and that is the one already mentioned — the government's attitude of concern for the welfare of human beings. On the whole, more interest is now taken in social questions. The government is concerned about housing, about the care of citizens who temporarily are unable to take care of themselves, about the care of handicapped children, whether handicapped by poor homes or by straitened circumstances. This is a general change, which I attribute to the fact that men had to appeal for the vote of the women and have therefore taken a greater interest in subjects they feel may draw women to their support. . . .

Where are we going as women? Do we know where we are going? Do we know where we want to go?

I have a suggestion to make that will probably seem to you entirely paradoxical. Yet at the present juncture of civilization, it seems to me the only way for women to grow.

Women must become more conscious of themselves as women and of their ability to function as a group. At the same time they must try to wipe from men's consciousness the need to consider them as a group or as women in their everyday activities, especially as workers in industry or the professions.

Let us consider first what women can do united in a cause.

It is perfectly obvious that women are not all alike. They do not think alike, nor do they feel alike on many subjects. Therefore, you can no more unite all women on a great variety of subjects than you can unite all men.

If I am right that, as I stated above, women have caused a basic change in the attitude of government toward human beings, then there are certain fundamental things that mean more to the great majority of women than to the great majority of men. These things are undoubtedly tied up with women's biological functions. The women bear the children, and love them even before they come into the world. Some of you will say that the maternal instinct is not universal in women, and that now and then you will find a man whose paternal instinct is very strong — even stronger than his wife's maternal instinct. These are the exceptions which prove the rule, however. The pride most men feel in the little new bundle of humanity must grow gradually into love and devotion. I will not deny that this love develops fast with everything a man does for the new small and helpless human being which belongs to him; but a man can nearly always be more objective about his children than a woman can be.

This ability to be objective about children is one thing women have to fight to acquire; never, no matter what a child may do or how old he may be, is a woman quite divorced from the baby who once lay so helpless in her arms. This is the first fundamental truth for us to recognize, and we find it in greater or less degree in women who have never had a child. From it springs that concern about the home, the shelter for the children. And here is the great point of unity for the majority of women. . . .

Now let us consider women in the other phases of activity where they wish to be persons and wipe out the sex consideration.

Opposition to women who work is usually based on the theory that men have to support families. This, of course, is only saying something that sounds well, for we know that almost all working women are supporting someone besides themselves. And women themselves are partly to blame for the fact that equal pay for equal work has not become an actuality. They have accepted lower pay very often and taken advantage of it occasionally, too, as an excuse for not doing their share of their particular job.

If women want equal consideration, they must prepare themselves to adjust to other people and make no appeals on the ground of sex. Whether women take part in the business or in the political world, this is equally true.

A woman who cannot engage in an occupation and hold it because of her own ability had much better get out of that particular occupation, and do something else, where her ability will count. Otherwise, she is hanging on by her eyebrows, trying to exploit one person after another, and in the end she is going to be unsuccessful and drag down with her other women who are trying to do honest work. . . .

There is one place, however, where sex must be a cleavage in daily activity. Women run their homes as women. They live their social lives as women, and they have a right to call upon man's chivalry and to use their wiles to make men do the things that make life's contacts pleasanter in these two spheres. Sex is a weapon and one that women have a right to use, because this is a part of life in which men and women live as men and women and complement, but do not compete with each other. They are both needed in the world of business and politics to bring their different points of view and different methods of doing things to the service of civilization as individuals, with no consideration of sex involved; but in the home and in social life they must emphasize the difference between the sexes because it adds to the flavor of life together. . . .

It will always take all kinds of women to make up a world, and only now and then will they unite their interests. When they do, I think it is safe to say that something historically important will happen.

4

Documenting the Depression: The Photographs of Dorothea Lange

In 1935 Rexford Guy Tugwell, the head of the newly created Resettlement Administration, appointed Roy Stryker to its Information Division. Since Stryker's job involved publicizing the agency's programs, he hired a number of documentary photographers, among them Ben Shahn, Carl Mydams, Arthur Rothstein, Walker Evans, and Dorothea Lange. Already well known for her photographs depicting the human costs of the Depression, Lange also had collaborated with the economist Paul S. Taylor (whom she later married) on articles describing the plight of migrant workers. Over the next eight years, she would work for federal agencies: first for the Resettlement Administration and its successor, the Farm Security Administration, then after the United States entered World War II for the War Relocation Authority and the Office of War Information. "Documentary photography records the social scene of our time. It mirrors the present and documents for the future," she wrote. "It is preeminently suited to build a record of change."

Her photograph of the plantation overseer and his field hands depicts a social order that, on the surface, appears highly resistant to change. It was taken near Clarksdale, Mississippi, in July 1936. The white overseer's superior status is implicit in his placement in the foreground, his girth, his stance, and the way his foot is planted firmly on the bumper of his shiny automobile. The black field hands' subordination is suggested by their demeanor and positioning. Ironically, when the photograph was published two years later in *Land of the Free*, with text by the poet Archibald MacLeish, it was cropped so as to omit the black men. The white overseer was presented as a proud yeoman farmer. The photograph is essentially ambiguous, the historian Lawrence Levine contends: "It captured the image of a man who exemplified the exploitative, racist, undemocratic features of southern plantation life even while he also doubtless represented many of the qualities that built the type of in-

Plantation Overseer and His Field Hands, Mississippi Delta, 1936
(Library of Congress)

dividualistic freedom that has characterized America throughout so much of its history."

There was nothing ambiguous about Lange's most famous photograph, *Migrant Mother.* She took it in March 1936, in Nipomo, California, where cold weather had destroyed the pea crop and left the workers with nothing to do. "I saw and approached the hungry and desperate mother, as if drawn by a magnet," Lange recalled many years later. The woman (her name was Florence Thompson, although Lange did not identify her) was thirty-two years old. She told Lange that she and her children "had been living on frozen vegetables from the surrounding fields, and birds that the children killed. She had just sold the tires from her car to buy food." Lange's biographer, Milton Meltzer, explains that although she did not intend to produce a Madonna, "the image has achieved an independent existence, finding its place in the almost timeless tradition of art whose theme is Mother and Child."

Migrant Mother, Nipomo, California, 1936
(Library of Congress)

Mexican Migratory Field Worker's Home on the Edge of a Frozen Pea Field, Imperial Valley, California, 1937
(Library of Congress)

Small Independent Gas Station during Cotton Strike, Kern City, California,
November 1938
(Library of Congress)

Early in the spring of 1937, Lange traveled through California's Imperial Valley, where, once again, freezing conditions had destroyed much of the pea crop. "The region is swamped with homeless moving families," Lange wrote to Stryker. She found, she added, "a major migration of people, and a rotten mess." Her photographs were designed to support a Department of Labor report to the U.S. Senate on the conditions of migrant laborers. (In 1939 Lange and Paul Taylor collaborated on *An American Exodus: A Record of Human Erosion,* a volume documenting these problems.) Lange, who believed that her photographs "are loaded with ammunition," was frequently drawn to the theme of parental nurturance — here shown by a Mexican migratory field worker cradling his infant — even in the midst of the most awful squalor.

By October 1937, Lange was working for the Farm Security Administration. Camera in hand, she visited the San Joaquin Valley to show what the agency had done to assist tenant farmers, but she arrived in the midst of a strike by migrant cotton workers, whom the Congress of Industrial Organizations was attempting to organize. At the time, workers earned seventy-five cents for picking one hundred pounds of cotton; a strong person could pick about two hundred pounds a day. The workers wanted an increase to one dollar for one hundred pounds but failed to win the increase. In a letter to Stryker, Lange described this as "a long heartbreaking strike, unsuccessful." Her photograph of the "small independent gas station" was meant to convey the sense of solidarity between the small businessman who owned the gas station and the striking cotton workers.

5

Right . . . and Left . . . Face

The early years of the New Deal witnessed an outburst of political energy the likes of which had seldom been seen in the United States. Many of Franklin D. Roosevelt's policies threatened deeply held values and altered traditional patterns of power, and so they elicited heated responses from both the right and the left. Conservatives complained that the New Deal was going too far, that it was stirring up class hatred and destroying business confidence. By contrast, radicals believed that the New Deal was not going far enough in aiding the poor and the disadvantaged. The resulting political turmoil posed a severe challenge to the established two-party system at the state and even the national level.

HERBERT HOOVER

The Challenge to Liberty

1934

Herbert Hoover had suffered too humiliating a defeat in the 1932 election and was too closely identified with the conservative wing of the Republican party to be a viable candidate for renomination in 1936, but he remained one of Roosevelt's harshest critics. In numerous speeches, articles, and books, such as The Challenge to Liberty, *he maintained that the New Dealers had abandoned "the heritage of liberty" in leading the country on a futile quest for "security." Condemning the growth of regimentation, bureaucracy, and centralization, he spoke of "this New Deal attack upon free*

Herbert Hoover, *The Challenge to Liberty* (New York: Charles Scribner's Sons, 1934), 197–204.

institutions." To this argument, New Dealers would surely have replied, as the liberal Texas congressman Maury Maverick once did, that Americans wanted "freedom plus groceries." Yet Hoover raised an important issue when he claimed that big government would attempt to protect itself from criticism by blocking the free flow of information and therefore represented an insidious threat to freedom of speech and the press.

There are those who assert that revolution has swept the United States. That is not true. But there are some who are trying to bring it about. At least they are following the vocal technique which has led elsewhere to the tragedy of Liberty. Their slogans; their promise of Utopia; their denunciation of individual wickednesses as if these were the wards of Liberty; their misrepresentation of deep-seated causes; their will to destruction of confidence and consequent disorganization in order to justify action; their stirring of class feeling and hatred; their will to clip and atrophy the legislative arm; their resentment of criticism; their chatter of boycott, of threat and of force — all are typical enough of the methods of more violent action.

In our blind groping we have stumbled into philosophies which lead to the surrender of freedom. The proposals before our country do not necessarily lead to the European forms of Fascism, of Socialism, or of Communism, but they certainly lead definitely from the path of liberty. The danger lies in the tested human experience, that a step away from liberty itself impels a second step, a second compels a third. The appetite for power grows with every opportunity to assume it, and power over the rights of men leads not to humility but to arrogance, and arrogance incessantly demands more power. A few steps so dislocate social forces that some form of despotism becomes inevitable and Liberty dies.

No country or no society can be conducted by partly acknowledging the securities of Liberty and partly denying them, nor by recognizing some of them and denying others. That is part democracy and part tyranny. At once there are conflicts and interferences which not only damage the whole economic mechanism but drive unceasingly for more and more dictation.

Even partial regimentation cannot be made to work and still maintain live democratic institutions. Representative government will sooner or later be at conflict with it along the whole front, both in the incidentals of daily working and in the whole field of free choice by the people. If it be continued the Congress must further surrender its checks and balances on administration and its free criticism since these, with intensified duties to its constituents, create interferences that will make efficient administration of this regimented machine impossible.

For any plan of Regimentation to succeed it must have not only powers of rigid discipline but adamant continuity. Does anyone believe that with the interferences of the Congress and the storms of a free press any government can impose discipline and follow a consistent and undeviating course in directing the activities of 125,000,000 highly diversified people? Because such a course is impossible Fascism and Sovietism have suppressed both free speech and representative government. . . .

The American System has steadily evolved the protections of Liberty. In the early days of road traffic we secured a respect for liberties of others by standards of decency and courtesy in conduct between neighbors. But with the crowding of highways and streets we have invented Stop and Go signals which apply to everybody alike, in order to maintain the same ordered Liberty. But traffic signals are not a sacrifice of Liberty, they are the preservation of it. Under them each citizen moves more swiftly to his own individual purpose and attainment. That is a far different thing from the corner policeman being given the right to determine whether the citizen's mission warrants his passing and whether he is competent to execute it, and then telling him which way he should go, whether he likes it or not. That is the whole distance between ordered Liberty and Regimentation.

The achievements of our own economic system have brought us new problems in stability in business, in agriculture, and in employment, and greater security of living. But the first constructive step in solution is the preservation of Liberty, for in that sphere alone are the dynamic forces with which to solve our problems successfully.

The whole history of humanity has been a struggle against famine and want. Within less than half a century the American System has achieved a triumph in this age-long struggle by producing a plenty.

The other systems now urged for permanent adoption propose to solve the remaining problem of distribution of a hard-won plenty by restrictions which will abolish the plenty. To adopt this course would be an abject surrender. Worse, it would be a surrender to the complexities of distribution after the major battle, which is production, has been won. It may be repeated that if we undermine the stimulants to individual effort which come alone from the spirit of Liberty, we may well cease to discuss the greater "diffusion of income," "of wealth," "minimum standards," and "economic security," the "abolition of poverty," and its fears. Those are possibilities only in an economy of plenty. . . .

We cannot extend the mastery of government over the daily life of a people without somewhere making it master of people's souls and thoughts. That is going on today. It is part of all regimentation.

Even if the government conduct of business could give us the maximum of efficiency instead of least efficiency, it would be purchased at the cost of freedom. It would increase rather than decrease abuse and corruption, stifle initiative and invention, undermine the development of leadership, cripple the mental and spiritual energies of our people, extinguish equality of opportunity, and dry up the spirit of liberty and the forces which make progress.

It is a false Liberalism that interprets itself into government dictation, or operation of commerce, industry and agriculture. Every move in that direction poisons the very springs of true Liberalism. It poisons political equality, free thought, free press, and equality of opportunity. It is the road not to liberty but to less liberty. True Liberalism is found not in striving to spread bureaucracy, but in striving to set bounds to it. Liberalism is a force proceeding from the deep realization that economic freedom cannot be sacrificed if political freedom is to be preserved. True Liberalism seeks all legitimate freedom first in the confident belief that without such freedom the pursuit of other blessings is in vain.

The nation seeks for solution of its many difficulties. These solutions can come alone through the constructive forces from the system built upon Liberty. They cannot be achieved by the destructive forces of Regimentation. The purification of Liberty from abuses, the restoration of confidence in the rights of men, the release of the dynamic forces of initiative and enterprise are alone the methods by which these solutions can be found and the purpose of American life assured. . . .

AMERICAN LIBERTY LEAGUE

The New Deal vs. Democracy

July 15, 1936

Notwithstanding his indictment of the New Deal in the previous selection, Hoover did not think much of a newly formed conservative organization, the American Liberty League, which, he said, favored "the Wall Street

"The New Deal vs. Democracy," *American Liberty League Bulletin,* July 15, 1936, 2–3.

model" of liberty. The league was created in August 1934 by people who had originally supported FDR but now believed he had become too antibusiness and had surrounded himself with radical advisers. Financed largely by Pierre S. and Irenee Du Pont, the organization was led by such conservative Democratic politicians as John J. Raskob and Jouett Shouse. Shouse, who at first favored the name National Property League, said the league's goal was "to foster the right to work, earn, save, and acquire property and to preserve the ownership and lawful use of property when acquired." In the space of two years, the league enrolled 125,000 members, spent $1 million, and distributed 5 million pieces of literature, including a weekly bulletin, included here, in an effort to mobilize public sentiment against the New Deal. Shortly after Shouse informed FDR of the league's formation, Roosevelt was asked about it at a press conference. He replied, off the record:

> *It has been said there are two great Commandments — one is to love God, and the other to love your neighbor. A gentleman with a rather ribald sense of humor suggested that the two particular tenets of this new organization say you shall love God and then forget your neighbor, and he also raised the question as to whether the other name for their God was not "property."*

Jouett Shouse, President of the American Liberty League, in a radio address over a nation-wide hookup on the eve of the New Deal Convention in Philadelphia, discussed the basic conflict between the New Deal and the Democratic Party. Mr. Shouse spoke not only as President of the League, but also as former Chairman of the Democratic National Executive Committee. He summarized some of the New Deal performances as follows:

The New Deal has built up a huge bureaucracy which has shown no regard for the Constitutional rights and liberties of our citizens.

The New Deal has converted the Federal Civil Service into a barefaced spoils system.

The New Deal has used the money of taxpayers of all political parties to build up a propaganda machine to aid its efforts to continue in power.

The New Deal has prostituted the administration of the relief of the unfortunate to the ends of partisan politics.

The New Deal has spent huge sums upon public works, despite grave doubts as to the desirability or usefulness of the projects.

The New Deal has instituted a series of boondoggling enterprises which are as ridiculous as they are unwise.

The New Deal has all but destroyed the export market for American agricultural products.

The New Deal has opened American markets to import of foodstuffs which properly should be supplied by the American farmer.

The New Deal has harassed American business and has entered into competition in almost every possible way with private industry.

The New Deal has misused the Federal taxing power in an effort to promote visionary schemes for the redistribution of wealth.

The New Deal has imposed taxes heavier than were ever before placed upon the nation in time of peace and by reckless borrowing has saddled huge obligations upon generations yet unborn.

The New Deal has led the nation far along the road toward national bankruptcy and has increased the national debt to unprecedented size.

The New Deal has manifested its contempt for constitutional government.

The New Deal has sought to make the Legislative Branch of the government subservient to the will of the Executive.

The New Deal, through its official spokesman, has criticized decisions of the Supreme Court because in the interpretation of the basic law of the land that tribunal held pet New Deal acts unconstitutional.

The New Deal, in the words of Mr. Roosevelt himself, has set up "new instruments of public power," admittedly dangerous in the hands of men who might misuse that power.

In a word, the New Deal has sought to destroy the American system of government composed of three coordinate branches and to upset the dual sovereignty as between state and nation which the Constitution provides.

The New Deal represents the attempt in America to set up a totalitarian government, one which recognizes no sphere of individual or business life as immune from governmental authority and which submerges the welfare of the individual to that of the government.

Passing on to a discussion of what the future may bring forth, Mr. Shouse added:

Sooner or later, the present madness will pass. Sooner or later, a political promise will again be regarded as a sacred obligation. Sooner or later, we shall once more recognize that two and two make four. And when that time comes the Democrats who are Democrats from conviction and not from mere expediency will regain control of the Democratic Party and will make it once more the Party of Jefferson and Jackson and Cleveland and Wilson. . . . The processes of recovery have begun despite the tinkering of the New Deal but they must be carried forward with care, with courage, with perseverance. Democrats, therefore, who are left without a Party in present circumstances must decide the course they will pursue. They owe no duty of loyalty to the New Deal.

UPTON SINCLAIR

The EPIC Plan

1934

In August 1934, the same month the American Liberty League was founded, conservatives everywhere were thrown into a panic when Upton Sinclair captured the Democratic gubernatorial nomination in California. Widely known as a socialist and as the author of some forty books, many of them attacking the evils of capitalist society, Sinclair had registered as a Democrat so that he could run as a major-party candidate. Now he proposed to "End Poverty in California" by means of the EPIC Plan, reprinted here. He called for an economy based on use rather than on profit, claiming this proposal was American to the core, for it embodied "all our true pioneer virtues — self-reliance, initiative, frugality, equality, neighborliness." But in the fall election campaign, media professionals hired by the Republicans organized a highly successful smear campaign, branding "Sincliar," as they called him, an atheist and a communist, and ridiculing his plan by referring to it as "Easy Pickings in California." Sinclair received 880,000 votes but lost to his Republican rival, Frank Merriam, who received 1,139,000. The number of votes Sinclair received, especially in view of the campaign of misrepresentation, indicates, as historian James N. Gregory notes, "the extraordinary fluidity of American politics" at the time.

1. A legislative enactment for the establishment of State land colonies, whereby the unemployed may become self-sustaining and cease to be a burden upon the taxpayers. A public body, the California Authority for Land (the CAL) will take the idle land, and land sold for taxes and at foreclosure sales, and erect dormitories, kitchens, cafeterias, and social rooms, and cultivate the land using modern machinery under the guidance of experts.
2. A public body entitled the California Authority for Production (the CAP) will be authorized to acquire factories and production plants whereby the unemployed may produce the basic necessities required for themselves and for the land colonies,

Upton Sinclair, *Immediate Epic: The Final Statement of the Plan* (Los Angeles: End Poverty League, 1934).

and to operate these factories and house and feed and care for the workers. CAL and CAP will maintain a distribution system for the exchange of each other's products. The industries will include laundries, bakeries, canneries, clothing and shoe factories, cement-plants, brick-yards, lumber yards, thus constituting a complete industrial system and a new and self-sustaining world for those our present system cannot employ.

3. A public body entitled the California Authority for Money (the CAM) will handle the financing of CAL and CAP. This body will issue scrip to be paid to the workers and used in the exchanging of products within the system. It will also issue bonds to cover the purchase of land and factories, the erection of buildings and the purchase of machinery.

4. An act of the legislature repealing the present sales tax, and substituting a tax on stock transfers at the rate of 4 cents per share.

5. An act of the legislature providing for a State income tax, beginning with incomes of $5000 and steeply graduated until incomes of $50,000 would pay 30% tax.

6. An increase in the State inheritance tax, steeply graduated and applying to all property in the State regardless of where the owner may reside. The law would take 50% of sums above $50,000 bequeathed *to* any individual and 50% of sums above $250,000 bequeathed *by* any individual.

7. A law increasing the taxes on privately owned public utility corporations and banks.

8. A constitutional amendment revising the tax code of the State, providing that cities and counties shall exempt from taxation all homes occupied by the owners and ranches cultivated by the owners, wherever the assessed value of such homes and ranches is less than $3000. Upon properties assessed at more than $5000 there will be a tax increase of one-half of one per cent for each $5000 of additional assessed valuation.

9. A constitutional amendment providing for a State land tax upon unimproved building land and agricultural land which is not under cultivation. The first $1000 of assessed valuation to be exempt, and the tax to be graduated according to the value of land held by the individual. Provision to be made for a state building loan fund for those who wish to erect homes.

10. A law providing for the payment of a pension of $50 per month to every needy person over sixty years of age who has lived in the

State of California three years prior to the date of the coming into effect of the law.

11. A law providing for the payment of $50 per month to all persons who are blind, or who by medical examination are proved to be physically unable to earn a living; these persons also having been residents of the State for three years.

12. A pension of $50 per month to all widowed women who have dependent children; if the children are more than two in number, the pension to be increased by $25 per month for each additional child. These also to have been residents three years in the State.

FATHER CHARLES E. COUGHLIN

The National Union for Social Justice

November 11, 1934

As Upton Sinclair was preparing to wage his gubernatorial campaign in California, he visited Father Charles E. Coughlin in Royal Oak, Michigan, just outside Detroit, and reported, "He [Coughlin] agreed fully that the unemployed must be put at productive labor for their own benefit." At the time, Father Coughlin's Sunday morning radio sermons, like the one reprinted here, were attracting more than ten million listeners, and the "radio priest" was preparing to form the National Union for Social Justice to lobby in behalf of his economic program. Many of his proposals were quite vague — he favored guaranteeing all workers "a just, living, annual wage," for example, and "nationalizing those public resources which by their very nature are too important to be held in the control of private individuals"— but they proved highly attractive to those who still faced hard times. Originally an FDR supporter, Coughlin had grown increasingly disillusioned with the New Deal. In 1936 he said that the president, "Franklin doublecrossing Roosevelt," was "flirting with Communistic tendencies." Coughlin helped form the Union party and nominated William Lemke of North Dakota for

Charles E. Coughlin, *A Series of Lectures on Social Justice* (Royal Oak, Mich.: The Radio League of the Little Flower, 1935), 15–19.

president in an ultimately unsuccessful effort to deprive FDR of a second term in the White House.

My friends, the outworn creed of capitalism is done for. The clarion call of communism has been sounded. I can support one as easily as the other. They are both rotten! But it is not necessary to suffer any longer the slings and arrows of modern capitalism any more than it is to surrender our rights to life, to liberty and to the cherished bonds of family to communism.

The high priests of capitalism bid us beware of the radical and call upon us to expel him from our midst. There will be no expulsion of radicals until the causes which breed radicals will first be destroyed!

The apostles of Lenin and Trotzky bid us forsake all rights to private ownership and ask us to surrender our liberty for that mess of pottage labeled "prosperity," while it summons us to worship at the altar where a dictator of flesh and blood is enthroned as our god and the citizens are branded as his slaves.

Away with both of them! But never into the discard with the liberties which we have already won and the economic liberty which we are about to win — or die in the attempt!

My friends, I have spent many hours during these past two weeks — hours, far into the night, reading thousands of letters which have come to my office from the young folks and the old folks of this nation. I believe that in them I possess the greatest human document written within our times.

I am not boasting when I say to you that I know the pulse of the people. I know it better than all your newspaper men. I know it better than do all your industrialists with your paid-for advice. I am not exaggerating when I tell you of their demand for social justice which, like a tidal wave, is sweeping over this nation.

Nor am I happy to think that, through my broadcasts, I have placed myself today in a position to accept the challenge which these letters carry to me — a challenge for me to organize these men and women of all classes, not for the protection of property rights as does the American Liberty League; not for the protection of political spoils as do the henchmen of the Republican or Democratic parties. Away with them too!

But, happy or unhappy as I am in my position, I accept the challenge to organize for obtaining, for securing and for protecting the principles of social justice.

To organize for action, if you will! To organize for social united action which will be founded on God-given social truths which belong to Catholic and Protestant, to Jew and Gentile, to black and white, to rich and poor, to industrialist and to laborer.

I realize that I am more or less a voice crying in the wilderness. I realize that the doctrine which I preach is disliked and condemned by the princes of wealth. What care I for that! And, more than all else, I deeply appreciate how limited are my qualifications to launch this organization which shall be known as the NATIONAL UNION FOR SOCIAL JUSTICE.

But the die is cast! The word has been spoken! And by it I am prepared either to stand or to fall; to fall, if needs be, and thus, to be remembered as an arrant upstart who succeeded in doing nothing more than stirring up the people.

How shall we organize? To what principles of social justice shall we pledge ourselves? What action shall we take? These are practical questions which I ask myself as I recognize the fact that this NATIONAL UNION FOR SOCIAL JUSTICE must be established in every county and city and town in these United States of America.

It is for the youth of the nation. It is for the brains of the nation. It is for the farmers of the nation. It is for everyone in the nation.

Establishing my principles upon this preamble, namely, that we are creatures of a beneficent God, made to love and to serve Him in this world and to enjoy Him forever in the next; that all this world's wealth of field, of forest, of mine and of river has been bestowed upon us by a kind Father, therefore I believe that wealth, as we know it, originates from natural resources and from the labor which the children of God expend upon these resources. It is all ours except for the harsh, cruel and grasping ways of wicked men who first concentrated wealth into the hands of a few, then dominated states, and finally commenced to pit state against state in the frightful catastrophes of commercial warfare.

Following this preamble, these shall be the principles of social justice towards the realization of which we must strive:

1. I believe in liberty of conscience and liberty of education, not permitting the state to dictate either my worship to my God or my chosen avocation in life.

2. I believe that every citizen willing to work and capable of working shall receive a just, living, annual wage which will enable him both to maintain and educate his family according to the standards of American decency.

3. I believe in nationalizing those public resources which by their very nature are too important to be held in the control of private individuals.

4. I believe in private ownership of all other property.

5. I believe in upholding the right to private property but in controlling it for the public good.

6. I believe in the abolition of the privately owned Federal Reserve Banking system and in the establishment of a Government owned Central Bank.

7. I believe in rescuing from the hands of private owners the right to coin and regulate the value of money, which right must be restored to Congress where it belongs.

8. I believe that one of the chief duties of this Government owned Central Bank is to maintain the cost of living on an even keel and arrange for the repayment of dollar debts with equal value dollars.

9. I believe in the cost of production plus a fair profit for the farmer.

10. I believe not only in the right of the laboring man to organize in unions but also in the duty of the Government, which that laboring man supports, to protect these organizations against the vested interests of wealth and of intellect.

11. I believe in the recall of all non-productive bonds and therefore in the alleviation of taxation.

12. I believe in the abolition of tax-exempt bonds.

13. I believe in broadening the base of taxation according to the principles of ownership and the capacity to pay.

14. I believe in the simplification of government and the further lifting of crushing taxation from the slender revenues of the laboring class.

15. I believe that, in the event of a war for the defense of our nation and its liberties, there shall be a conscription of wealth as well as a conscription of men.

16. I believe in preferring the sanctity of human rights to the sanctity of property rights; for the chief concern of government shall be for the poor because, as it is witnessed, the rich have ample means of their own to care for themselves.

These are my beliefs. These are the fundamentals of the organization which I present to you under the name of the NATIONAL UNION FOR SOCIAL JUSTICE. It is your privilege to reject or to accept my beliefs; to follow me or to repudiate me.

Hitherto you have been merely an audience. Today, in accepting the challenge of your letters, I call upon every one of you who is weary of drinking the bitter vinegar of sordid capitalism and upon everyone who is fearsome of being nailed to the cross of communism to join this Union which, if it is to succeed, must rise above the concept of an audience and

become a living, vibrant, united, active organization, superior to politics
and politicians in principle, and independent of them in power.

This work cannot be accomplished in one week or two weeks or in
three months, perchance. But it must begin today, at this moment. It
shall be a Union for the employed and the unemployed, for the old and
the young, for the rich and the poor, independent of race, color or creed.
It is my answer to the challenge received from the youth of the nation;
my answer to those who have dared me to act! . . .

This is the new call to arms — not to become cannon fodder for the
greedy system of an outworn capitalism nor factory fodder for the slave
whip of communism.

This is the new call to arms for the establishment of social justice!
God wills it! Do you?

HUEY P. LONG

Share Our Wealth

May 23, 1935

*The Union party also had the support of two other administration critics:
Dr. Francis E. Townsend, author of a plan to provide monthly pensions of
two hundred dollars to everyone over the age of sixty, and Gerald L. K.
Smith, who had taken control of the Share Our Wealth movement after its
founder, Huey P. Long, was assassinated in September 1935. In Long's brief
but meteoric political career — he was elected governor of Louisiana in
1928 and senator in 1930 — he battled relentlessly against entrenched interests and eventually assumed dictatorial power in the state. He dominated the legislature, curbed the press, and built a disciplined political
machine, but he also instituted programs to benefit his constituents. He
provided free school textbooks; built new roads, bridges, and highways; and
eliminated the poll tax and property taxes on the poor. His Share Our
Wealth Society claimed to have 4.7 million members, attracted by Long's
promise, excerpted here, to redistribute the wealth in such a way as to ensure that there were "none too poor and none too rich."*

Congressional Record, 74th Cong., 1st sess., Vol. 79, 8040–43.

(The Share Our Wealth Society proposes to enforce the traditions on which this country was founded, rather than to have them harmed; we aim to carry out the guaranties of our immortal Declaration of Independence and our Constitution of the United States, as interpreted by our forefathers who wrote them and who gave them to us; we will make the works and compacts of the Pilgrim fathers, taken from the Laws of God, from which we were warned never to depart, breathe into our Government again that spirit of liberty, justice, and mercy which they inspired in our founders in the days when they gave life and hope to our country. God has beckoned fullness and peace to our land; our forefathers have set the guide stakes so that none need fail to share in this abundance. Will we now have our generation, and the generations which are to come, cheated of such heritage because of the greed and control of wealth and opportunity by 600 families?)

To members and well-wishers of the Share Our Wealth Society:

For 20 years I have been in the battle to provide that, so long as America has, or can produce, an abundance of the things which make life comfortable and happy, that none should own so much of the things which he does not need and cannot use as to deprive the balance of the people of a reasonable proportion of the necessities and conveniences of life. The whole line of my political thought has always been that America must face the time when the whole country would shoulder the obligation which it owes to every child born on earth — that is, a fair chance to life, liberty, and happiness. . . .

It is not out of place for me to say that the support which I brought to Mr. Roosevelt to secure his nomination and election as President — and without which it was hardly probable he would ever have been nominated — was on the assurances which I had that he would take the proper stand for the redistribution of wealth in the campaign. He did that much in the campaign; but after his election, what then? I need not tell you the story. We have not time to cry over our disappointments, over promises which others did not keep, and over pledges which were broken. . . .

It is impossible for the United States to preserve itself as a republic or as a democracy when 600 families own more of this Nation's wealth — in fact, twice as much — as all the balance of the people put together. Ninety-six percent of our people live below the poverty line, while 4 percent own 87 percent of the wealth. America can have enough for all to live in comfort and still permit millionaires to own more than they can ever spend and to have more than they can ever use; but America cannot allow the multimillionaires and the billionaires, a mere handful of them, to own everything unless we are willing to inflict starvation upon 125,000,000 people.

We looked upon the year 1929 as the year when too much was produced for the people to consume. We were told, and we believed, that the farmers raised too much cotton and wool for the people to wear and too much food for the people to eat. Therefore, much of it went to waste, some rotted, and much of it was burned or thrown into the river or into the ocean. But, when we picked up the bulletin of the Department of Agriculture for that year 1929, we found that, according to the diet which they said everyone should eat in order to be healthy, multiplying it by 120,000,000, the number of people we had in 1929, had all of our people had the things which the Government said they should eat in order to live well, we did not have enough even in 1929 to feed the people. In fact, these statistics show that in some instances we had from one-third to one-half less than the people needed, particularly of milk, eggs, butter, and dried fruits.

But why in the year 1929 did it appear we had too much? Because the people could not buy the things they wanted to eat, and needed to eat. That showed the need for and duty of the Government then and there, to have forced a sharing of our wealth, and a redistribution, and Roosevelt was elected on the pledge to do that very thing.

But what was done? Cotton was plowed under the ground. Hogs and cattle were burned by the millions. The same was done to wheat and corn, and farmers were paid starvation money not to raise and not to plant because of the fact that we did not want so much because of people having no money with which to buy. Less and less was produced, when already there was less produced than the people needed if they ate what the Government said they needed to sustain life. God forgive those rulers who burned hogs, threw milk in the river, and plowed under cotton while little children cried for meat and milk and something to put on their naked backs!

But the good God who placed this race on earth did not leave us without an understanding of how to meet such problems; nor did the Pilgrim fathers who landed at Plymouth in 1620 fail to set an example as to how a country and a nation of people should act under such circumstances, and our great statesmen like Thomas Jefferson, Daniel Webster, Abraham Lincoln, Theodore Roosevelt, and Ralph Waldo Emerson did not fail to explain the need and necessity for following the precedents and purposes, which are necessary, even in a land of abundance, if all the people are to share the fruits produced therein. God's law commanded that the wealth of the country should be redistributed ever so often, so that none should become too rich and none should become too poor; it commanded that debts should be canceled and released ever so often, so that the human race would not be loaded with a burden which it could never pay. When the Pilgrims landed at Plymouth in 1620, they established their law by compact, signed by everyone who was on board the *Mayflower,* and it provided that at the end of every 7 years the finances of their newly founded country would be readjusted and that all debts would be released and property redistributed, so that none should starve in the land of plenty, and none should have an abundance of more than he needed. These principles were preserved in the Declaration of Independence, signed in 1776, and in our Constitution. Our great statesmen, such men as James Madison, who wrote the Constitution of the United States, and Daniel Webster, its greatest exponent, admonished the generations of America to come that they must never forget to require the redistribution of wealth if they desire that their Republic should live.

And, now, what of America? Will we allow the political sports, the high heelers, the wiseacres, and those who ridicule us in our misery and poverty to keep us from organizing these societies in every hamlet so that they may bring back to life this law and custom of God and of this country? Is there a man or woman with a child born on the earth, or who expects ever to have a child born on earth, who is willing to have it raised under the present-day practices of piracy, where it comes into life burdened with debt, condemned to a system of slavery by which the sweat of its brow throughout its existence must go to satisfy the vanity and the luxury of a leisurely few, who can never be made to see that they are destroying the root and branch of the greatest country ever to have risen? Our country is calling; the laws of the Lord are calling; the graves of our forefathers would open today if their occupants could see the bloom and flower of their creation withering and dying because the greed of the financial masters of this country has starved and withheld from mankind those things produced by his own labor. To hell with the ridicule of the wise street-corner politician. Pay no attention to any newspaper or magazine that has sold its columns to perpetuate this crime against the people of America. Save this country. Save mankind. Who can be wrong in such a work, and who cares what consequences may come following the mandates of the Lord, of the Pilgrims, of Jefferson, Webster, and Lincoln? He who falls in this fight falls in the radiance of the future. Better to make this fight and lose than to be a party to a system that strangles humanity.

It took the genius of labor and the lives of all Americans to produce the wealth of this land. If any man, or 100 men, wind up with all that has been produced by 120,000,000 people, that does not mean that those 100 men produced the wealth of the country; it means that those 100 men stole, directly or indirectly, what 125,000,000 people produced. Let no one tell you that the money masters made this country. They did no such thing. Very few of them ever hewed the forest; very few ever hacked a crosstie; very few ever nailed a board; fewer of them ever laid a brick. Their fortunes came from manipulated finance, control of government, rigging of markets, the spider webs that have grabbed all businesses; they grab the fruits of the land, the conveniences and the luxuries that are intended for 125,000,000 people, and run their heelers to our meetings to set up the cry, "We earned it honestly." The Lord says they did no such thing. The voices of our forefathers say they did no such thing. In this land of abundance, they have no right to impose starvation, misery, and pestilence for the purpose of vaunting their own pride and greed. . . .

Here is the whole sum and substance of the share-our-wealth movement:

1. Every family to be furnished by the Government a homestead allowance, free of debt, of not less than one-third the average family wealth of the country, which means, at the lowest, that every family shall have the reasonable comforts of life up to a value of from $5,000 to $6,000. No person to have a fortune of more than 100 to 300 times the average family fortune, which means that the limit to fortunes is between $1,500,000 and $5,000,000, with annual capital levy taxes imposed on all above $1,000,000.

2. The yearly income of every family shall be not less than one-third of the average family income, which means that, according to the estimates of the statisticians of the United States Government and Wall Street, no family's annual income would be less than from $2,000 to $2,500. No yearly income shall be allowed to any person larger than from 100 to 300 times the size of the average family income, which means that no person would be allowed to earn in any year more than from $600,000 to $1,800,000, all to be subject to present income-tax laws.

3. To limit or regulate the hours of work to such an extent as to prevent overproduction; the most modern and efficient machinery would be encouraged, so that as much would be produced as possible so as to satisfy all demands of the people, but to also allow the maximum time to the workers for recreation, convenience, education, and luxuries of life.

4. An old-age pension to the persons over 60.

5. To balance agricultural production with what can be consumed according to the laws of God, which includes the preserving and storage of

surplus commodities to be paid for and held by the Government for the emergencies when such are needed. Please bear in mind, however, that when the people of America have had money to buy things they needed, we have never had a surplus of any commodity. This plan of God does not call for destroying any of the things raised to eat or wear, nor does it countenance wholesale destruction of hogs, cattle, or milk.

6. To pay the veterans of our wars what we owe them and to care for their disabled.

7. Education and training for all children to be equal in opportunity in all schools, colleges, universities, and other institutions for training in the professions and vocations of life; to be regulated on the capacity of children to learn, and not on the ability of parents to pay the costs. Training for life's work to be as much universal and thorough for all walks in life as has been the training in the arts of killing.

8. The raising of revenue and taxes for the support of this program to come from the reduction of swollen fortunes from the top, as well as for the support of public works to give employment whenever there may be any slackening necessary in private enterprise.

I now ask those who read this circular to help us at once in this work of giving life and happiness to our people — not a starvation dole upon which someone may live in misery from week to week. Before this miserable system of wreckage has destroyed the life germ of respect and culture in our American people let us save what was here, merely by having none too poor and none too rich. The theory of the Share Our Wealth Society is to have enough for all, but not to have one with so much that less than enough remains for the balance of the people.

Please, therefore, let me ask you who read this document — please help this work before it is too late for us to be of help to our people. We ask you now, (1) help to get your neighbor into the work of this society and (2) help get other Share Our Wealth societies started in your county and in adjoining counties and get them to go out to organize other societies.

To print and mail out this circular costs about 60 cents per hundred, or $6 per thousand. Anyone who reads this who wants more circulars of this kind to use in the work, can get them for that price by sending the money to me, and I will pay the printer for him. Better still, if you can have this circular reprinted in your own town or city.

Let everyone who feels he wishes to help in our work start right out and go ahead. One man or woman is as important as any other. Take up the fight! Do not wait for someone else to tell you what to do. There are no high lights in this effort. We have no State managers and no city managers. Everyone can take up the work, and as many societies can be organized as there are people to organize them. One is the same as another. The reward and compensation is the salvation of humanity. Fear no opposition. "He who falls in this fight falls in the radiance of the future!"

Yours sincerely,

HUEY P. LONG,
United States Senator, Washington, D.C.

6
Race, Ethnicity, and Reform

Although New Deal policies were chiefly concerned with economic recovery and reform, they could not ignore issues of race and ethnicity. The population of the United States, numbering about 130 million in the 1930s, was marked by extraordinary diversity. Foreign-born whites, their children, and their grandchildren constituted a little more than one-fourth of the total population. The largest number of European immigrants had come from Italy (1.6 million); Russia, Lithuania, and Romania (1.3 million); Germany (1.2 million); Poland (993,000); Denmark, Norway, and Sweden (845,000); Ireland (678,000); and Greece (163,000). The experiences of three other groups that had historically suffered from particularly harsh forms of deprivation and discrimination — Mexican Americans, African Americans, and Native Americans — illustrate the dilemmas involved in reforming a society in which class, race, and ethnicity were so closely intertwined.

Songs of the Mexican Migration: Deported [Deportados]
1933

More than a million first- and second-generation Mexican immigrants resided in the United States during the 1930s. By and large, they worked at low-paying, backbreaking jobs in the fruit, vegetable, and cotton fields of California, Texas, and the Southwest, often scraping by on less than three hundred dollars a year. Even so, the shortage of work during the Depres-

Paul S. Taylor, "Songs of the Mexican Migration," in *Puro Mexicano,* ed. J. Frank Dobie (Austin: Texas Folk-Lore Society, 1935), 225–27.

sion and a desire to cut expenditures for relief led to a determined effort to displace them. Immigration was sharply curtailed by withholding visas and beefing up border patrols. From 1931 to 1939, only 16,000 Mexicans arrived legally in the United States, compared, for example, with 58,000 in 1928. California, Arizona, and other states also barred the hiring of aliens on public works projects. Finally, Mexicans were badgered, cajoled, and threatened into returning to their native land, and sometimes they were actually deported, taking with them their American-born children. Precisely how many Mexicans were forced to leave remains unknown; estimates range from 200,000 to 400,000. The songs they wrote, such as "Deportados," describe their reactions. The economist Paul S. Taylor, who collected the songs and translated them, found no exact English equivalent for the word camellar, *which, he explained, means "to work like a beast of burden, humped over like a camel."*

DEPORTADOS

Voy á contarles, señores,
voy á contarles, señores,
todo lo que yo sufrí,
cuando dejé yo á mi Patria,
cuando dejé yo á mi Patria,
por venir á ese País.

Serían las diez de la noche,
serían las diez de la noche
comenzó un tren á silvar;
oí que dijo mi madre
hay viene ese tren ingrato
que á mi hijo se va á llevar.

Por fin sonó la campana,
por fin sonó la campana;
vámonos de la estación,
no quiero ver á mi madre
llorar por su hijo querido,
por su hijo del corazón.

Cuando á Chihuahua llegamos,
cuando á Chihuahua llegamos,
se notó gran confusión,
los empleados de la aduana,
los empleados de la aduana
que pasaban revisión.

DEPORTED

I am going to sing to you, señores,
I am going to tell you, señores,
all about my sufferings
when I left my native land,
when I left my native land,
in order to go to that country.

It must have been ten at night,
it must have been ten at night,
when a train began to whistle;
I heard my mother say,
"Here comes that hateful train
to take my son away."

Finally they rang the bell,
finally they rang the bell.
"Let's go on out of the station;
I'd rather not see my mother
weeping for her dear son,
the darling of her heart."

When we reached Chihuahua,
when we reached Chihuahua,
there was great confusion:
the customs house employees,
the customs house employees,
were having an inspection.

Llegamos por fin á Juárez,
llegamos por fin á Juárez
ahí fué mi apuración
que dónde va, que dónde viene
cuánto dinero tiene
para entrar á esta nación.

Señores, traigo dinero,
señores, traigo dinero
para poder emigrar,
su dinero nada vale,
su dinero nada vale,
te tenemos que bañar.

Los güeros son muy maloras,
los gringos son muy maloras,
se valen de la ocasión,
y á todos los mexicanos,
y á todos los mexicanos,
nos tratan sin compasión.

Hoy traen la gran polvadera,
hoy traen la gran polvadera
y sin consideración,
mujeres niños y ancianos
los llevan á la frontera
los echan de esa nación.

Adiós, paisanos queridos,
adiós, paisanos queridos,
ya nos van á deportar
pero no somos bandidos
pero no somos bandidos
venimos á camellar.

Los espero allá en mi tierra,
los espero allá en mi tierra,
ya no hay más revolución;
vamonos cuates queridos
seremos bien recibidos
en nuestra bella nación.

We finally arrived at Juárez,
we finally arrived at Juárez,
where I had my inspection:
"Where are you going, where are
    you from,
how much money have you
in order to enter this country?"

"Gentlemen, I have money,
gentlemen, I have money
enough to be able to emigrate."
"Your money is worthless,
your money is worthless;
we'll have to give you a bath."

The "blondes" are very unkind;
the *gringos* are very unkind.
They take advantage of the chance
to treat all the Mexicans,
to treat all the Mexicans
without compassion.

Today they are rounding them up,
today they are rounding them up;
and without consideration
women, children, and old folks
are taken to the frontier
and expelled from that country.

So farewell, dear countrymen,
so farewell, dear countrymen;
they are going to deport us now,
but we are not bandits,
but we are not bandits,
we came to *camellar.*

I'll wait for you there in my country,
I'll wait for you there in my country
now that there is no revolution;
let us go, brothers dear,
we will be well received
in our own beautiful land.

SELDEN MENEFEE AND ORIN C. CASSMORE

The Pecan Shellers of San Antonio

1940

Not all Mexicans worked on farms or in the fields. San Antonio, Texas, for example, had a Mexican American population of 100,000, of whom more than 10,000 were pecan shellers. Exploited and poorly paid — they earned 5 or 6 cents an hour, about $2.73 for a fifty-one-hour workweek — they benefited little from even the most forward-looking New Deal measures. Either they were not eligible for unemployment insurance benefits and old-age pensions, or they received trifling amounts. Further, when the minimum wage was set at 25 cents an hour following passage of the Fair Labor Standards Act of 1938, pecan-shelling plants were rapidly mechanized, and thousands of workers lost their jobs. Federal housing legislation provided funding for new projects and slum clearance, but the new apartments rented for $6.75 a month, considerably more than most pecan shellers could afford. This study of Mexican pecan shellers, prepared by Selden Menefee and Orin C. Cassmore under the auspices of the Works Progress Administration (WPA), explains why certain forms of endemic poverty were beyond the reach of federal programs and also reveals the long-range effects of that poverty on the workers' children.

Unemployment compensation had been of some assistance to the Mexicans, but under the provisions of the Texas system Mexican pecan workers were handicapped in several ways.

First, an employer, to come under the law, must have employed 8 or more individuals for 20 or more weeks out of the year. This provision excluded many small pecan-shelling contractors who operated only 3 or 4 months each year at the season's peak, or who employed only a few workers. Second, the "covered" industries in which the minimum qualifying amount of $72 could be earned specifically excluded agriculture, in which many of the pecan shellers worked during approximately half of the year. Third, family earnings were not counted as a unit under the law; and many individual pecan shellers under the old handwork sys-

Selden Menefee and Orin C. Cassmore, *The Pecan Shellers of San Antonio* (Washington, D.C.: Works Progress Administration, 1940), 44–51.

tem were not able to earn the necessary $72 in the 9-month qualifying period, even when working fairly steadily in shelling or other covered industries. . . .

Those pecan shellers who qualified for unemployment compensation, according to the adjuster, received total sums averaging less than $20. Pecan crackers averaged about $25 and pickers about $15, spread over a period of 3 to 6 weeks.

The old-age insurance system has had little effect in alleviating need among the Mexicans. . . . Mexican claims usually amounted to only about $10 or $12. Pecan workers as a rule received even less. The reasons for the small sums paid to Mexican laborers were, as in the case of unemployment compensation, that agricultural labor was not covered, and that wages in covered industries had in the past been very low.

The revisions in the old-age insurance program made by Congress in 1939 stood to benefit the Mexican pecan shellers, as well as other low-paid workers. . . . The date upon which regular monthly benefits were to begin was moved up to January 1, 1940, and the rate of payment was increased to 40 percent of the worker's average monthly wage (up to $50) in covered industries. But the average pecan worker in 1938, earning perhaps $10 per month, would have received only $4 per month if he had retired at 65 under these provisions. On the other hand, those who are fortunate enough to have jobs at a minimum wage of 25 or 30 cents per hour under the provisions of the Fair Labor Standards Act, for long enough to raise their average level of wages, might draw as much as $20 per month upon reaching 65.

Old-age assistance in Texas, unlike the other two Social Security programs (unemployment compensation and old-age insurance), has a citizenship requirement which has disqualified a large section of the Mexican population, particularly the older people. The program operates on a basis of need, paying maximum monthly benefits of $30. In December 1938 an average of $14.72 per person was paid out to 4,374 needy persons over 65 years of age in Bexar County. A check of names on the rolls showed that fewer than 20 percent of the recipients had Spanish names. It may be assumed that most of these were of Mexican extraction. It is apparent from this low percentage that the citizenship requirement excluded many of the Mexicans, the most needy group in the city, from the rolls.

With the growing trends toward mechanization both of agriculture and of the pecan-shelling industry, the Mexicans' need for public assistance seems likely to increase rather than to decrease in the near future. Only when private employment at living wages is available to the

Mexican worker will he be able to end his dependence upon the Government for his livelihood.

[Government Programs]

The pecan-shelling industry in San Antonio is concentrated for the most part in the West Side of the city. In this area of about 4 square miles, almost completely Spanish in its written and spoken language, live at least 65,000 of San Antonio's estimated 100,000 Mexicans. Here also is one of the most extensive slums to be found in any American city, with decrepit wooden shacks and crowded "courts" overflowing with Mexican families who are forced by poverty to live there, at rentals as low as 50 cents to a dollar per week.

HOUSING

Of the 512 families of pecan shellers who were interviewed, the average (median) number of rooms per family was only 2.2, while the average family consisted of 4.6 persons. There were 28 families, ranging from 5 to 10 persons, each of which lived in a single room.

Most of the pecan workers — 77 percent — rented their houses. The average number of rooms in the rented houses was 2.1, while the 117 who owned their homes had a median of 2.6 rooms. The average amount paid for the rented houses was $4.49 per month, or slightly over $1 per week. Over 5 percent of the renters paid no rent at all, living with relatives or in deserted or makeshift shacks. Another 8 percent paid only $1 to $2 per month rent.

Some idea of living conditions among the pecan workers may be gained from the fact that only 60, or 12 percent, had running water inside their houses. Only 9 percent had inside sanitary toilets, while 39 percent had old-fashioned "privies." The balance had outdoor toilets either of the sanitary pit type constructed in large numbers in recent years by WPA labor, or with cesspool or sewer connections.

Lighting facilities were equally primitive. Only 25 percent of the families had electric lights, the other three-fourths used kerosene lamps.

Some progress has been made in recent years toward eliminating the worst of the slums on the West Side. As a result of a campaign by the Junior Chamber of Commerce and other civic bodies, a slum clearance section was added to the city health department in 1935. Under a city ordinance which had been passed in 1915 to regulate sanitation, the city razed 1,502 of the worst slum dwellings on the West Side prior to August 1938. But this program provided no new houses to take the place of those which were destroyed.

In June 1937 the San Antonio Housing Authority was created by the city, under the terms of the United States Housing Act. It immediately made a survey of 6,723, or half, of the 13,447 Mexican families living in the West Side area. It found about 90 percent of the dwelling units inhabited by these families to be definitely below the standards set by the Authority.

The next step taken by the Housing Authority was to obtain an allocation of $3,588,000 in Federal funds for a housing project for Mexicans. Together with the city's contribution, this will allow a $4,000,000 project to be built just west of Alazan Creek. The revised plans, as of January 1939, called for an area of more than 35 acres, covering 23 square blocks of the West Side. The completed project was to contain 1,260 housing units of modernistic Spanish architecture.

The new units were to rent for $2 per room per month, including hot water but not other utilities, or about $6.75 per month for three rooms and a bath with utilities. But many Mexican families now living in the area are paying only $2 per month rent for their shacks, and will not be able to afford even the low rents contemplated for the project. Only 59 percent of the 5,213 renters who were living in substandard dwellings surveyed by the Housing Authority had incomes above the minimum annual incomes of $350 to $850 (depending on the size of the family) which were to be required of renters in the new project. Of the 512 pecan workers' families only 154, or 30 percent, had incomes above $350 in 1938, and many of these did not have the higher incomes required for families with several children.

The Housing Authority has a long-range program to provide for at least 3,000 to 5,000 new housing units to replace the worst of the slums on the Mexican West Side. In addition to the funds for the present project, $5,600,000 in Federal funds had been earmarked for housing projects in San Antonio by early in 1939.

HEALTH

San Antonio's high death and disease rates are due primarily to the extremely high rates among the Mexican people. In 1938 San Antonio had 12.5 deaths per 1,000 population, compared with a national average of approximately 10.7. There were 148 deaths from tuberculosis per 100,000 population in 1937 and 129 in 1938, compared with a national average of 54 in 1937. There were 103 infant deaths per 1,000 live births in 1937 and 81 in 1938.

On the West Side malnutrition, poor housing, lack of sanitation, and inadequate medical care take their heaviest toll. . . .

Over 72 percent of all tuberculosis deaths in San Antonio in 1938 were among Mexicans, although this group made up only 38 percent of the population. Of the tuberculosis patients from the Mexican West Side, more than 75 percent came from homes where there were unemployment, poor housing, and malnutrition. . . . In 1938 the department of health indicated that some 1,448 cases of tuberculosis were reported among children under 13 years of age. Of these cases 77 percent were Mexican children.

It is significant that the Mexican death rate from tuberculosis dropped from 1928 to 1930; then stayed about even (at a level approximately twice as high as the rate for the whole population) from 1930 to 1935; and rose again from 1935 to 1937. The fact that the death rate among the Mexicans did not rise during the worst years of the depression was due largely to the supplementary rations which they received from the Government; this gave them a more adequate diet than they had been able to obtain without Government aid prior to the depression. . . .

The Mexican infant mortality rate, 120 per 1,000 live births in 1938, is one of the highest in the Nation. Non-Mexican children have a good chance of living if they get through the first month of infancy, while the high death rate among Mexican children continues throughout the first year. Diarrhea and enteritis are extremely important causes of the high infant mortality rate among the Mexicans. These are the direct result of poor sanitation. . . .

EDUCATION

According to the 1930 Census, 7.7 percent of San Antonio's population 10 years of age and over could not read or write. Almost nine-tenths of the city's 14,462 illiterates were Mexicans, the proportion of illiteracy being 15.7 percent in this group.

Illiteracy is decreasing as the younger generation of American-born Mexicans grows up, since most of them attend school at least long enough to learn to read and write. But the proportion of youth attending school at various ages is much lower in San Antonio than in the State as a whole, or in other Texas cities. This is largely because of the inability of the Mexicans, particularly the pecan shellers and the agricultural workers who form the poorest strata of the population, to keep their children steadily in school.

Mr. Raymond Brewer, principal of Sidney Lanier High School, estimates that there are about 3,000 Mexican children of school age in San Antonio who have never entered school, and that only one-half to two-thirds of the Mexican children entering primary school finish the fifth grade. The principal reason for this is poverty. Some families cannot buy clothing for their children; or because of seasonal work, they are not able to be in town consistently enough to enter their children in school.

Of the Mexican families in San Antonio who do seasonal agricultural labor, many do not return to San Antonio and put their children in school until after the cotton and beet seasons are over, or as late as November or December in many cases; and some of them start leaving San Antonio, with their families, for the beet fields or for cotton chopping as early as April or May. Since the regular school term of 36 weeks starts in September and ends the last of May, children of the Mexican agricultural workers are severely handicapped. They tend to become retarded and to drop out of school at an early age. During the school year 1937–38, attendance at one school in the Mexican district varied from 740 at the beginning of the term to 1,499 in February.

Among the 512 pecan-shelling families studied, there were 867 children between the ages of 7 and 18. Of these, only 55 percent attended the full school term and only 62 percent attended school at all in 1938. The 217 children of migratory workers were handicapped to an even greater extent than the 650 children of families who lived in San Antonio throughout the year. In the migratory group, for example, 22 percent of the children aged 11 to 13 did not attend school in 1938, while in the non-migratory group the corresponding figure was only 11 percent. . . .

SOCIAL DISORGANIZATION AND DISCRIMINATION

Among the by-products of the depressed conditions under which the Mexicans live are delinquency and prostitution, which are concentrated in the heart of the Mexican slum area in the West Side. . . .

Mexican citizens have been unable effectively to press for a remedy for these conditions through the ballot in the past because a comparatively small number of Mexicans vote in San Antonio. In 1939, a record year for votes in the local elections, only 9,374 poll taxes were paid by Mexicans. There were two reasons for this. First, at least half of the Mexicans of voting age were not citizens. A check of 150 pecan-shelling families indicated that only about a third of the family heads were citizens. Second, the State poll tax of $1.50 per year was more than most Mexican wage earners could afford to pay. . . .

During the depression non-Mexican workers feared that the Mexicans would compete with them for jobs, forcing wages down; and businessmen objected to the large number of Mexicans who were dependent on public assistance. Both groups looked down on the Mexicans because of their race and their foreign language and customs. In some cases this feeling was so strong as to lead to demands for deporting the Mexicans.

As for the Mexicans, their reactions to this situation are most clearly shown by their objection to the use of the term "white" in such a way as to exclude Mexicans. They prefer to call whites of European extraction "Anglo-Americans" or "Anglos." The Mexicans are conscious of such Spanish blood as they may have, and are not ashamed of their predominantly Indian blood. They jealously guard against any move that would set them apart from the self-styled "white race."

The Mexican is nevertheless segregated from the rest of the community almost as effectively as the Negro. He is not kept apart from the "Anglo-Americans" in lavatories, waiting rooms, and public vehicles by law as is the Negro, but his poverty and low wages segregate him in the poorest sections of the city, in the day coaches of the railroads, in the balconies of the less pretentious theaters, and in the cheapest restaurants. These circumstances tend to perpetuate the social handicaps under which the Mexicans, and especially the pecan shellers and others of low economic status, are forced to live.

W. E. B. DU BOIS AND WALTER WHITE

The NAACP and Segregation

January–February 1934

The Depression had a devastating impact on African Americans, not only because of discrimination in hiring but also because industries (such as construction) that employed many blacks were especially hard hit. Whites began to seek jobs that African Americans had formerly held, such as service workers in hotels, restaurants, and hospitals. Although New Deal relief policies came to the rescue of many jobless African Americans, several civil rights leaders concluded that new initiatives were needed to achieve racial equality. The traditional approach, long championed by the National As-

W. E. B. Du Bois, "Segregation," *The Crisis*, January 1934, 20; W. E. B. Du Bois, "The N.A.A.C.P. and Race Segregation," *The Crisis*, February 1934, 53; Walter White, "Segregation — A Symposium," *The Crisis*, February 1934, 80–81.

sociation for the Advancement of Colored People (NAACP), emphasized a combination of political pressure and legal action to eliminate all forms of racial discrimination. But in 1934 W. E. B. Du Bois, a founder of the organization and editor of its journal, The Crisis, came out in favor of "a Negro nation within the nation." Only through "organized and deliberate self-segregation," Du Bois reasoned, could African Americans achieve economic security and cultural autonomy. His proposal sparked so much controversy that The Crisis published a symposium on segregation. Among the contributors was Walter White, the NAACP's executive secretary, who maintained that segregation was inherently evil. When the organization officially endorsed his view, Du Bois resigned.

W. E. B. Du Bois

The thinking colored people of the United States must stop being stampeded by the word segregation. The opposition to racial segregation is not or should not be any distaste or unwillingness of colored people to work with each other, to cooperate with each other, to live with each other. The opposition to segregation is an opposition to discrimination. The experience in the United States has been that usually when there is racial segregation, there is also racial discrimination.

But the two things do not necessarily go together, and there should never be an opposition to segregation pure and simple unless that segregation does involve discrimination. Not only is there no objection to colored people living beside colored people if the surroundings and treatment involve no discrimination, if streets are well lighted, if there is water, sewerage and police protection, and if anybody of any color who wishes, can live in that neighborhood. The same way in schools, there is no objection to schools attended by colored pupils and taught by colored teachers. On the contrary, colored pupils can by our own contention be as fine human beings as any other sort of children, and we certainly know that there are no teachers better than trained colored teachers. But if the existence of such a school is made reason and cause for giving it worse housing, poorer facilities, poorer equipment and poorer teachers, then we do object, and the objection is not against the color of the pupils' or teachers' skins, but against the discrimination.

In the recent endeavor of the United States government to redistribute capital so that some of the disadvantaged groups may get a chance for development, the American Negro should voluntarily and insistently demand his share. Groups of communities and farms inhabited by colored folk should be voluntarily formed. In no case should there be any discrimination against whites and blacks. But, at the same time, colored people should come forward, should organize and conduct enterprises, and their only insistence should be that the same provisions be made for the success of their enterprise that is being made for the success of any other enterprise. It must be remembered that in the last quarter of a century, the advance of the colored people has been mainly in the lines where they themselves working by and for themselves, have accomplished the greatest advance.

There is no doubt that numbers of white people, perhaps the majority of Americans, stand ready to take the most distinct advantage of voluntary segregation and cooperation among colored people. Just as soon as they get a group of black folk segregated, they use it as a point of attack and discrimination. Our counter attack should be, therefore, against this discrimination; against the refusal of the South to spend the same amount of money on the black child as on the white child for its education; against the inability of black groups to use public capital; against the monopoly of credit by white groups. But never in the world should our fight be against association with ourselves because by that very token we give up the whole argument that we are worth associating with.

Doubtless, and in the long run, the greatest human development is going to take place under experiences of widest individual contact. Nevertheless, today such individual contact is made difficult and almost impossible by petty prejudice, deliberate and almost criminal propaganda and various survivals from prehistoric heathenism. It is impossible, therefore, to wait for the millennium of free and normal intercourse before we unite, to cooperate among ourselves in groups of like-minded people and in groups of people suffering from the same disadvantages and the same hatreds.

It is the class-conscious working man uniting together who will eventually emancipate labor throughout the world. It is the race-conscious black man cooperating together in his own institutions and movements who will eventually emancipate the colored race, and the great step ahead today is for the American Negro to accomplish his economic emancipation through voluntary determined cooperative effort. . . .

. . . The N.A.A.C.P. has never officially opposed separate Negro organizations — such as churches, schools and business and cultural organizations. It has never denied the recurrent necessity of united separate action on the part of Negroes for self-defense and self-development; but it has insistently and continually pointed out that such action is in any case a necessary evil involving often a recognition from within the very color line which we are fighting without. That race pride and race loyalty, Negro ideals and Negro unity, have a place and function today, the N.A.A.C.P. never has denied and never can deny.

But all this simply touches the whole question of racial organization and initiative. No matter what we may wish or say, the vast majority of the Negroes in the United States are born in colored homes, educated in separate colored schools, attend separate colored churches, marry colored mates, and find their amusement in colored Y.M.C.A.'s and Y.W.C.A.'s. Even in their economic life, they are gradually being forced out of the place in industry which they occupied in the white world and are being compelled to seek their living among themselves. Here is segregation with a vengeance, and its problems must be met and its course guided. It would be idiotic simply to sit on the side lines and yell: "No segregation" in an increasingly segregated world.

Walter White

Numerous requests have been made of the National Association for the Advancement of Colored People for a statement of the position of the Association on editorials by Dr. Du Bois on "Segregation" in the January and February issues of *The Crisis.* It is fitting and proper that the statement of the Secretary's position should first appear in *The Crisis,* the official organ of the Association.

Various interpretations have been placed upon Dr. Du Bois's editorial, a number of them erroneous and especially the one which interprets the editorial as a statement of the position of the N.A.A.C.P. The historic position of the N.A.A.C.P. has from the date of its foundation been opposed to segregation. Dr. Du Bois's editorial is merely a personal expression on his part that the whole question of segregation should be examined and discussed anew. There can be no objection to frank and free discussion on any subject and *The Crisis* is the last place where censorship or restriction of freedom of speech should be attempted. I wish to call attention to the fact that the N.A.A.C.P. has never officially budged in its general opposition to segregation. Since Dr. Du Bois has expressed his personal opinion why this attitude might possibly have to be altered I should like to give my personal opinion why I believe we should continue to maintain the same attitude we have for nearly a quarter of a century, but I repeat that what I am about to say is merely my personal opinion just as Dr. Du Bois's editorial expressed his personal opinion.

Let us put aside for the moment the ethical and moral principles involved. It is my firm conviction, based upon observation and experience, that the truest statement in the January editorial is:

> There is no doubt that numbers of white people, perhaps the majority of Americans, stand ready to take the most distinct advantage of voluntary segregation and cooperation among colored people. Just as soon as they get a group of black folk segregated, they use it as a point of attack and discrimination.

It is for this very reason that thoughtful colored people will be opposed to following the advice that "groups of communities and farms inhabited by colored folk should be voluntarily formed" where they involve government-financed and approved arrangements like the Homestead Subsistence projects.

It is unfortunate that Dr. Du Bois's editorial has been used, we learn, by certain government officials at Washington to hold up admission of Negroes to one of the government-financed relief projects. Protests have been made to Mrs. Roosevelt and others by the N.A.A.C.P. against such exclusion. Plans to admit Negroes as a result of the protest are being delayed with the editorial in question used as an excuse for such delay.

To accept the status of separateness, which almost invariably in the case of submerged, exploited and marginal groups means inferior accommodations and a distinctly inferior position in the national and communal life, means spiritual atrophy for the group segregated. When Negroes, Jews, Catholics or Nordic white Americans voluntarily choose to live or attend church or engage in social activity together, that is their affair and no one else's. But Negroes and all other groups must without compromise and without cessation oppose in every possible fashion any attempt to impose from without the establishment of pales and ghettoes. Arbitrary segregation of this sort means almost without exception that less money will be expended for adequate sewerage, water, police and fire protection and for the building of a healthful community. It is because of this that the N.A.A.C.P. has resolutely fought such segregation, as in the case of city ordinances and state laws in the Louisville, New Orleans and Richmond segregation cases; has opposed restrictive covenants written into deeds of property, and all other forms, legal and illegal, to restrict the areas in which Negroes may buy or rent and occupy property.

This principle is especially vital where attempts are made to establish separate areas which are financed by moneys from the federal or state governments for which black people are taxed at the same rate as white.

No self-respecting Negro can afford to accept without vigorous protest any such attempt to put the stamp of federal approval upon discrimination of this character. Though separate schools do exist in the South and though for the time being little can be done towards ending the expensive and wasteful dual educational system based upon caste and color prejudice, yet no Negro who respects himself and his race can accept these segregated systems without at least inward protest. . . .

It is admittedly a longer and more difficult road to full and unrestricted admission to schools, hospitals and other public institutions, but the mere difficulty of the road should not and will not serve as a deterrent to either Negro or white people who are mindful not only of present conditions but of those to which we aspire. In a world where time and space are being demolished by science it is no longer possible to create or imagine separate racial, national or other compartments of human thought and endeavor. The Negro must, without yielding, continue the grim struggle *for* integration and *against* segregation for his own physical, moral and spiritual well-being and for that of white America and of the world at large.

A. PHILIP RANDOLPH

The March on Washington

November 1942

Another challenge to the NAACP's leadership arose in 1941, when A. Philip Randolph, head of the Brotherhood of Sleeping Car Porters, created the March on Washington Movement. Randolph called for direct action in the form of a march on the nation's capital by one hundred thousand African Americans, and he excluded white people from the organization. "Negroes are the only people who are the victims of Jim Crow," he explained, "and it is they who must take the initiative and assume the responsibility to abolish it." Randolph demanded that the president withhold defense contracts from employers who practiced discrimination and abolish segregation in federal agencies and the armed forces. Alarmed by the prospect of angry

A. Philip Randolph, "Why Should We March?" *Survey Graphic* 31 (November 1942): 488–89.

African Americans parading down Pennsylvania Avenue, Roosevelt agreed to a compromise. On June 25, 1941, he issued Executive Order 8802, which provided that government agencies, job training programs, and defense contractors put an end to discrimination. He also created the Committee on Fair Employment Practices to investigate violations. The executive order did not provide for integration of the armed forces, much less other areas of American life, and so Randolph kept the movement going in hopes of maintaining pressure on the administration to make World War II a war for democracy at home as well as abroad.

Though I have found no Negroes who want to see the United Nations lose this war, I have found many who, before the war ends, want to see the stuffing knocked out of white supremacy and of empire over subject peoples. American Negroes, involved as we are in the general issues of the conflict, are confronted not with a choice but with the challenge both to win democracy for ourselves at home and to help win the war for democracy the world over.

There is no escape from the horns of this dilemma. There ought not to be escape. For if the war for democracy is not won abroad, the fight for democracy cannot be won at home. If this war cannot be won for the white peoples, it will not be won for the darker races.

Conversely, if freedom and equality are not vouchsafed the peoples of color, the war for democracy will not be won. Unless this double-barreled thesis is accepted and applied, the darker races will never wholeheartedly fight for the victory of the United Nations. That is why those familiar with the thinking of the American Negro have sensed his lack of enthusiasm, whether among the educated or uneducated, rich or poor, professional or nonprofessional, religious or secular, rural or urban, north, south, east or west.

That is why questions are being raised by Negroes in church, labor union and fraternal society; in poolroom, barbershop, schoolroom, hospital, hair-dressing parlor; on college campus, railroad, and bus. One can hear such questions asked as these: What have Negroes to fight for? What's the difference between Hitler and that "cracker" Talmadge of Georgia? Why has a man got to be Jim-Crowed to die for democracy? If you haven't got democracy yourself, how can you carry it to somebody else?

What are the reasons for this state of mind? The answer is: discrimination, segregation, Jim Crow. Witness the navy, the army, the air corps; and also government services at Washington. In many parts of the

South, Negroes in Uncle Sam's uniform are being put upon, mobbed, sometimes even shot down by civilian and military police, and on occasion lynched. Vested political interests in race prejudice are so deeply entrenched that to them winning the war against Hitler is secondary to preventing Negroes from winning democracy for themselves. This is worth many divisions to Hitler and Hirohito. While labor, business, and farm are subjected to ceilings and floors and not allowed to carry on as usual, these interests trade in the dangerous business of race hate as usual.

When the defense program began and billions of the taxpayers' money were appropriated for guns, ships, tanks and bombs, Negroes presented themselves for work only to be given the cold shoulder. North as well as South, and despite their qualifications, Negroes were denied skilled employment. Not until their wrath and indignation took the form of a proposed protest march on Washington, scheduled for July 1, 1941, did things begin to move in the form of defense jobs for Negroes. The march was postponed by the timely issuance (June 25, 1941) of the famous Executive Order No. 8802 by President Roosevelt. But this order and the President's Committee on Fair Employment Practices, established thereunder, have as yet only scratched the surface by way of eliminating discriminations on account of race or color in war industry. Both management and labor unions in too many places and in too many ways are still drawing the color line.

It is to meet this situation squarely with direct action that the March on Washington Movement launched its present program of protest mass meetings. Twenty thousand were in attendance at Madison Square Garden, June 16; sixteen thousand in the Coliseum in Chicago, June 26; nine thousand in the City Auditorium of St. Louis, August 14. Meetings of such magnitude were unprecedented among Negroes.* The vast throngs were drawn from all walks and levels of Negro life — businessmen, teachers, laundry workers, Pullman porters, waiters, and red caps; preachers, crapshooters, and social workers; jitterbugs and Ph.D.'s. They came and sat in silence, thinking, applauding only when they considered the truth was told, when they felt strongly that something was going to be done about it.

The March on Washington Movement is essentially a movement of the people. It is all Negro and pro-Negro, but not for that reason anti-

---

*In view of charges made that they were subsidized by Nazi funds, it may not be amiss to point out that of the $8,000 expenses of the Madison Square meeting every dime was contributed by Negroes themselves, except for tickets bought by some liberal white organizations.

Program of the March on Washington Movement

1. We demand, in the interest of national unity, the abrogation of every law which makes a distinction in treatment between citizens based on religion, creed, color, or national origin. This means an end to Jim Crow in education, in housing, in transportation and in every other social, economic, and political privilege; and especially, we demand, in the capital of the nation, an end to all segregation in public places and in public institutions.

2. We demand legislation to enforce the Fifth and Fourteenth Amendments guaranteeing that no person shall be deprived of life, liberty or property without due process of law, so that the full weight of the national government may be used for the protection of life and thereby may end the disgrace of lynching.

3. We demand the enforcement of the Fourteenth and Fifteenth Amendments and the enactment of the Pepper Poll Tax bill so that all barriers in the exercise of the suffrage are eliminated.

4. We demand the abolition of segregation and discrimination in the army, navy, marine corps, air corps, and all other branches of national defense.

5. We demand an end to discrimination in jobs and job training. Further, we demand that the FEPC be made a permanent administrative agency of the U.S. Government and that it be given power to enforce its decisions based on its findings.

6. We demand that federal funds be withheld from any agency which practices discrimination in the use of such funds.

7. We demand colored and minority group representation on all administrative agencies so that these groups may have recognition of their democratic right to participate in formulating policies.

8. We demand representation for the colored and minority racial groups on all missions, political and technical, which will be sent to the peace conference so that the interests of all people everywhere may be fully recognized and justly provided for in the post-war settlement.

white or anti-Semitic, or anti-Catholic, or anti-foreign, or anti-labor. Its major weapon is the non-violent demonstration of Negro mass power. Negro leadership has united back of its drive for jobs and justice. "Whether Negroes should march on Washington, and if so, when?" will be the focus of a forthcoming national conference. For the plan of a

protest march has not been abandoned. Its purpose would be to demonstrate that American Negroes are in deadly earnest, and all out for their
full rights. No power on earth can cause them today to abandon their
fight to wipe out every vestige of second class citizenship and the dual
standards that plague them.

A community is democratic only when the humblest and weakest person can enjoy the highest civil, economic, and social rights that the
biggest and most powerful possess. To trample on these rights of both
Negroes and poor whites is such a commonplace in the South that it
takes readily to anti-social, anti-labor, anti-Semitic and anti-Catholic propaganda. It was because of laxness in enforcing the Weimar constitution
in republican Germany that Nazism made headway. Oppression of the
Negroes in the United States, like suppression of the Jews in Germany,
may open the way for a fascist dictatorship.

By fighting for their rights now, American Negroes are helping to
make America a moral and spiritual arsenal of democracy. Their fight
against the poll tax, against lynch law, segregation, and Jim Crow, their
fight for economic, political, and social equality, thus becomes part of
the global war for freedom.

JOHN COLLIER

A New Deal for American Indians

1938

*Numbering 350,000, Native Americans made up only a small percentage
of the nation's population, but the Roosevelt administration attempted to
bring about a radical change in their status. Ever since the late nineteenth
century, federal policy had endeavored to force Native Americans to assim-
ilate into white society. But FDR appointed John Collier, an activist in the
American Indian Defense Association, as commissioner of Indian affairs.
Collier wished to preserve Native American culture, in part by having Indian children attend day schools on the reservations rather than leave
home for boarding schools. He also wanted to replace the paternalistic rule
of whites with democratically elected tribal governments and to prevent the
allotment of Native American lands to whites. In 1934 Congress passed the*

Report of Commissioner of Indian Affairs, *Annual Report of the Secretary of the Interior,
1938* (Washington, D.C., 1938), 209–63.

Indian Reorganization, or Wheeler-Howard, Act, which went a long way toward fulfilling Collier's objectives, as he explains in this excerpt from his annual report for 1938.

In all our colorful American life there is no group around which there so steadfastly persists an aura compounded of glamour, suspicion and romance, as the Indian. For generations, the Indian has been, and is today, the center of an amazing series of wonderings, fears, legends, hopes.

Yet those who have worked with Indians know that they are neither the cruel, warlike, irreligious savages imagined by some, nor are they the "fortunate children of nature's bounty" described by tourists who see them for an hour at some glowing ceremonial. We find the Indians, in all the basic forces and forms of life, human beings like ourselves. The majority of them are very poor people living under severely simple conditions. We know them to be deeply religious. We know them to be possessed of all the powers, intelligence, and genius within the range of human endowment. Just as we yearn to live out our own lives in our own ways, so, too, do the Indians, in their ways.

For nearly 300 years white Americans, in our zeal to carve out a nation made to order, have dealt with the Indians on the erroneous, yet tragic, assumption that the Indians were a dying race — to be liquidated. We took away their best lands; broke treaties, promises; tossed them the most nearly worthless scraps of a continent that had once been wholly theirs. But we did not liquidate their spirit. The vital spark which kept them alive was hardy. So hardy, indeed, that we now face an astounding, heartening fact.

The Indians Are No Longer a Dying Race

Actually, the Indians, on the evidence of Federal census rolls of the past 8 years, are increasing at almost twice the rate of the population as a whole.

With this fact before us, our whole attitude toward the Indians has necessarily undergone a profound change. Dead is the centuries-old notion that the sooner we eliminated this doomed race, preferably humanely, the better. No longer can we, with even the most generous intentions, pour millions of dollars and vast reservoirs of energy, sympathy, and effort into any unproductive attempts at some single, artificial permanent solution of the Indian problem. No longer can we naively talk of or think of the "Indian problem." Our task is to help Indians meet the myriad of complex, interrelated, mutually dependent situations which develop among them, according to the very best light we can get on those happenings — much as we deal with our own perplexities and opportunities.

We, therefore, define our Indian policy somewhat as follows: So productively to use the moneys appropriated by the Congress for Indians, as to enable them, on good, adequate lands of their own, to earn decent livelihoods and lead self-respecting, organized lives in harmony with their own aims and ideals, as an integral part of American life. Under such a policy, the ideal end result will be the ultimate disappearance of any need for Government aid or supervision. This will not happen tomorrow; perhaps not in our lifetime; but with the revitalization of Indian hope due to the actions and attitudes of this Government during the last few years, that aim is a probability, and a real one. . . .

So intimately is all of Indian life tied up with the land and its utilization that to think of Indians is to think of land. The two are inseparable. Upon the land and its intelligent use depends the main future of the American Indian.

The Indian feels toward his land not a mere ownership sense but a devotion and veneration befitting what is not only a home but a refuge. At least 9 out of 10 Indians remain on or near the land. When times are good, a certain number drift away to town or city to work for wages. When times become bad, home to the reservation the Indian comes, and to the comparative security which he knows is waiting for him. The Indian still has much to learn in adjusting himself to the strains of competition amid an acquisitive society; but he long ago learned how to contend with the stresses of nature. Not only does the Indian's major source of livelihood derive from the land, but his social and political organizations are rooted in the soil.

A major aim, then, of the Indian Service is to help the Indians to keep and consolidate what lands they now have and to provide more and better lands upon which they may effectively carry on their lives. Just as important is the task of helping the Indian make such use of his land as will conserve the land, insure Indian self-support, and safeguard or build up the Indian's social life. Many subsequent chapters of this report deal with this latter task.

In 1887, the General Allotment Act was passed, providing that after a certain trust period, fee simple title to parcels of land should be given to individual Indians. Individual proprietorship meant loss — a paradox in view of the Indian's love for the land, yet an inevitable result, when it is understood that the Indian by tradition was not concerned with possession, did not worry about titles or recordings, but regarded the land as a fisherman might regard the sea, as a gift of nature, to be loved and feared, to be fought and revered, and to be drawn on by all as an inexhaustible source of life and strength.

The Indian let the ownership of his alloted lands slip from him. The job of taking the Indian's lands away, begun by the white man through military expeditions and treaty commissions, was completed by cash purchase — always of course, of the best lands which the Indian had left. In 1887, the Indian had remaining 130,000,000 acres. In 1933, the Indian had left only 49,000,000 acres, much of it waste and desert.

Since 1933, the Indian Service has made a concerted effort — an effort which is as yet but a mere beginning — to help the Indian to build back his land holdings to a point where they will provide an adequate basis for a self-sustaining economy, a self-satisfying social organization.

By the close of the fiscal year 1938, the area of the lands held in trust for the Indians by the Government had been increased to approximately 51,540,307 acres — approximately 67 percent tribally owned, and 33 percent in allotments held in trust for the benefit of individuals. . . .

Reorganization and Self-Government Activities

It is necessary to restate from time to time the historical processes underlying the administration of Indian affairs. It is necessary because repeatedly the question is raised as to why Indian lands should be tax-exempt, or why the United States should administer health, education, and other social services for the Indian population. In brief, why should the Indian be under guardianship?

WHY INDIANS' SPECIAL STATUS?

European colonizers and their descendants brought to America ideas of land ownership, morality, government, and religion which were meaningless to the native American. In time these ideas became dominant to the exclusion of Indian habits of thought. Since we were a humane Nation and were not bent on destroying the Indians, we assumed the responsibility of showing them how our ideas operated. We wanted them to learn our ways so that they could exist side by side with us. In other words, we instituted a system of Indian education which is with us today.

We took away from the Indian all but a tiny fraction of his wealth in land, water, and other resources, and even his food supply, insofar as that consisted of game and wild products; and by doing so we charged ourselves with the responsibility of keeping the Indian from starvation.

Furthermore, since the Indian's understanding of property differed from ours, it was obvious that he would not long retain the little property left him if he was not protected. That made it necessary to erect trust-barriers around him which would prevent predatory men from making off with the means by which the Indian was to be taught a new way of existing.

By placing trust-barriers around Indian property, we exempted his land from State and local taxation. In taking this action we were subjecting the Indian to possible discrimination on the part of the States which would have resulted in leaving him without health care, education, roads, or any of the services which a State renders its people. States and local communities cannot furnish services without revenue. Once again, then, it became necessary for the Federal Government to assume an obligation toward the Indian tribes whose property it was seeking to protect.

These are the factors which Congress and the courts have borne in mind when they have dealt with Indian questions. The historical process has been long and involved. A mass of rules and regulations has accumulated and is today operative in the Indian Service. It is not an inert mass, as so often is assumed. There are within it directional drives, the aim of which has always been to solve or to cure the fundamental dislocation of a people overwhelmed by a superior force.

We are now at work developing a policy which we believe to be broad enough and sound enough to achieve, if continued, the purpose for which the Indian Service has always worked — the Indian's adjustment to his new world and a termination of his "problem." That policy is based on two ideas — organization, and a fuller use of land. Out of organization will come greater participation in the management of property and domestic affairs; and out of land use, which contemplates the purchase of land for those now landless and credit to carry on operations, will come better living conditions. Fundamental to the program is a recognition of the right of Indian culture to survive and enrich the daily life of the individual and the group. Not humanitarianism alone, but a belief that human beings are at their best when they are left at peace in those matters of conscience which come closest to them, prompts this attitude. . . .

EIGHTY-TWO TRIBES ARE ORGANIZED

At the end of this fiscal year there were 82 tribes, with a population of 93,520 Indians, operating under constitutions and bylaws; and of these, 57 tribes, having a membership of 64,000 Indians, had become incorporated under Federal charters. What this means can better be understood by explaining that these tribal constitutions contain specific grants of power, as follows: The right to negotiate with the Federal, State, and local governments, and to advise and to consult with the Interior Department on all activities which may affect the tribe; to approve or veto any sale, lease or other disposition of tribal property which may be authorized or executed by the Secretary of the Interior or the Commissioner of Indian Affairs; to advise the Secretary of the Interior with regard to all appropriation estimates or Federal projects for the benefit of the tribe; to make assignments of tribal land to its members; to manage all economic affairs of the tribe, subject to the terms of a charter; to appropriate for public purposes any available tribal funds; to devise a system of taxation by which funds for tribal use may be obtained; to determine its own tribal membership; to protect and preserve wildlife and natural resources and to regulate the conduct of trade; to cultivate native arts and crafts and culture; to administer charity and to protect health and the general welfare of the tribe; to charter subordinate organizations for economic purposes; to regulate the domestic relations of its members; to regulate the procedure of the governing body. These are powers which the tribe may exercise without interference by any arm of the Federal Government.

Certain additional powers are subject to review or approval by the Secretary of the Interior, including the right to employ legal counsel, to exclude nonmembers from reservation lands, to govern the conduct of its own members and administer justice through a tribal court, to purchase for public purposes property under condemnation proceedings, and to regulate the inheritance of property other than individual allotments of land.

J. C. MORGAN

The Voice of a Navajo Indian

April 10, 1934

The Indian Reorganization Act provided that each tribe would decide whether or not to create self-governing mechanisms. Eventually, 181 tribes agreed to set up tribal governments, but much to John Collier's dismay,

Senate Committee on Indian Affairs, *To Grant Indians the Freedom to Organize: Hearings before the Committee on Indian Affairs,* 73rd Cong., 2nd sess., 1934, 405–7.

77 tribes voted in the negative. One of those tribes was the Navajo, in a June 1935 referendum, by the narrow margin of 8,197 to 7,679. The opposition to Collier was led by J. C. Morgan, a highly assimilated graduate of a boarding school, a teacher in the Indian Service, and an assistant to a Christian missionary. Morgan asserted that Collier wanted to keep Native Americans "in the blanket" by encouraging native dances, rituals, and traditions. Instead, he argued, Native Americans should be educated in modern ways, taking their rightful place in society. "Do you not think the Indians should be encouraged to emerge from the old paganistic life, that they should be given every opportunity to accept civilization and Christianity?" he asked. Morgan pressed his argument in newspaper articles, testimony before Congress, and a widely circulated address to the Navajo Indian Council on April 10, 1934, which is excerpted here.

Mr. Chairman: I am going to speak on the Wheeler-Howard bill just as I see it myself. I have no outside influence as to what to say, but I have all right to believe what I think. It is most unfortunate that we haven't any lawyers, doctors, and what is worse, we haven't any politicians; the fact is, we haven't any professionally trained men and women in the whole tribe to draw from to advise us. This suggests a question: Can a ship make its course across the sea without a pilot? Everyone agrees that that cannot be done.

We are discussing something the Navajo Indian people do not ask for; it is something they never even dreamed of, but it is something that is going to be forced upon us. How can our people help themselves when a stronger hand forces them? This bill, if we accept, will cause us pain in the days to come. I believe before doing anything or taking anything we must first be prepared for it.

It is now about 64 years since an agency and a school were first established for this tribe according to the treaty. In 60 years 9 good size boarding schools have been built by the Government which in many ways has been very beneficial to our tribe. The delegates who have been to school, who sit here in the council, and all those in the audience are the products of the boarding schools and no one can deny that. Assertions have been made continually in the papers and magazines that nothing has been done for the Indians educationally or property protection until Mr. Collier's appointment. I am free to deny this assertion for the fact of the above statement. I want to mention also that there are four good Christian schools in operation for our young men and women. I want to emphasize the word "Christian" because so many people not in sympathy with this name hate to hear or see the sight of the word

"Christian" especially concerning the mission work and the Indians. I want to say that in many ways good work is being done in these Christian schools, and I favor its continual educational work.

Now, as I understand it, some of the boarding schools where some of the Navajo children are today, that took many years to build and at a great expense to the Government, are to be reduced to nothing more than a day school. Day-school system among our people will not replace our boarding schools, but day schools will only do some good in a few localities. The question is, where will the day schools put our people; how long will a day school take to prepare a camp boy or girl for college or university? To my notion it will not get us anywhere. Reducing the boarding schools is to deprive our people from acquiring practical education. By depriving the people of education is to deprive them of the right of American citizenship.

When I went to school I learned that "cramming" is a bad thing. Especially so when dealing with the uneducated people. This is exactly what is going on now, "cramming" this long-legged bill that none of us understand. I have read the bill, but I cannot understand it, and I know no one in the council understands it.

This bill tends to isolate our Navajo people upon a reservation. My friends, a foreigner has a better chance than we have, so I say, why should we be pushed aside from something that we have a right to enjoy as well as any foreigner that comes to this country? This bill urges segregation of our Indian people and no one here can deny that. If segregation could be done, and if the Secretary of the Interior and the Commissioner of Indian Affairs have power to do that why don't they segregate all Japanese, and all Chinamen, by themselves, somewhere; why don't they segregate all the Mexicans by themselves somewhere? These people are foreigners and yet are living in all parts of the United States doing what they will under the Constitution of our country.

We, the Indians, were here before any of the ancestors of Commissioner Collier ever came to this land from across the seas. Therefore, we, the Indians, are the First Americans and by all rights are free citizens of our land. The laws of our country give us this right of citizenship. No one has any right to construct a fence around our Indians and endeavor to make them a separate nation upon a barren soil.

Listen to this: "All persons born in the United States, and subject to the jurisdiction thereof are citizens, and of the State wherein they reside." So, how can any Indian, the First American, become a respectable, law abiding citizen of this country when such right is denied him by this kind of a bill?

The Constitution of our country further provides that "No State shall make or enforce any law which shall abridge the privileges or immunities of citizens of the United States." My friends, nobody has any right to make and enforce any law on our people when we are at peace with our Government. Personally, I want my children to have the same rights and privileges in school as any child of the white citizen. Likewise, I want my people to enjoy the freedom of a citizen as well as any foreigner. The Wheeler-Howard bill now before us does not so provide, but it urges Indian self-rule when they are not ready for such step. To urge the people to accept something they do not ask for would be to wreck all future possibilities of these people. I am not speaking about myself because I can go anywhere in the United States to live, but I am now speaking for my poor people who do not know one word from the other of the English language. So, how can they know what self-rule means?

Let me finish reading the amendment to the Constitution, that I think bears heavily upon our people: "Nor shall any State deprive any person of life, liberty, or property, without due process of law; nor deny to any person within its jurisdiction the equal protection of the law." Commissioner Collier said at Fort Defiance council, "If you accept this bill, it will be your constitution, etc." Why should I accept such a bill that tends to deny me my property? If I build a home on a piece of land I naturally would want my property to go to my children as my rightful heirs, but the Wheeler-Howard bill makes a provision that the property belongs to the tribe or to the community. That would not be life and liberty to me which the Constitution of my country gives to me. I therefore object to this bill because it is unconstitutional.

The Secretary of the Interior made this statement some time ago when speaking about the Indians: "We want to encourage him (the Indian) to live his own life in his own way." Imagine what it all means, my friends, and try to analyze it. You will know how our poor people live on this great American desert, barren land. We are not exactly living, but only existing. This statement means many things as I understand it. It means that we should not have ambition for education, improvement of homes, farms and livestock, nor to have any desire to patronize hospitals, and to have no desire for church or American citizenship. It further means that we must live just as we are; a living advertisement and curio for the tourist. I object to this sentiment because it is un-American; it is abridging the privileges and immunities of the Indians becoming citizens of the United States.

Here are some members of the council and a great many in the audience that know not how to read or write but have to be told by somebody else, but even then they do not get the straight goods. That is just the trouble with the council, they are only being led to say "Amen" to somebody else's idea.

The new day-school system is to be a "hogan" style for the Navajo children. I ask this question: What is wrong with giving to our people good school buildings instead of hogans, are we so low that we are not worthy of it? In the first instance I have disapproved of one central agency idea because in many ways it is wrong. It certainly will not be of any great benefit to this large tribe. The past experiments and history covers this completely. This Navajo capital out in the lizard country will only make a good field for artists, curio hunters, and magazine writers, hence the idea that the Indian must live his own life in his own way. My friends, it is going to be a great waste of public money on such institution, while this huge sum of money ought to be used for something that will actually help the Indians and the country.

"We the people of the United States," reads the preamble, "secure the blessings of liberty to ourselves and to our posterity."

Doesn't that include every American Indian?

7

The Constitutional Revolution

The innovative, far-reaching nature of New Deal legislation eventually provoked a confrontation with the Supreme Court. Many of the Roosevelt administration's early measures were drafted so hastily and carelessly that they were unable to withstand even the most impartial judicial scrutiny, as was evident in May 1935, when the Court invalidated the National Industrial Recovery Act by a unanimous vote. But in truth the justices were anything but impartial. Four of them — Pierce Butler, James McReynolds, Willis Van Devanter, and George Sutherland — were staunch conservatives, and two others — Chief Justice Charles Evans Hughes and Owen Roberts — though more centrist in approach, were also hostile to the New Deal. The liberal justices — Benjamin N. Cardozo, Louis D. Brandeis, and Harlan Fiske Stone — were distinctly in the minority. In 1936 the conservative majority struck down the Agricultural Adjustment Act, the Bituminous Coal Conservation Act, and a New York State minimum wage law, and in so doing adopted a line of constitutional analysis that appeared to threaten other reform measures whose fate had yet to be decided: the Social Security Act, the Wagner Act, and proposed minimum wage–maximum hour legislation.

OWEN ROBERTS AND HARLAN FISKE STONE

United States v. Butler

January 6, 1936

Nothing better illustrates the gulf between the liberal and conservative viewpoints on the Court than this 6–3 decision that struck down the Agricul-

United States v. Butler, 297 US 1 (1936).

tural Adjustment Act. Designed to boost agricultural prices, the act provided for payment to farmers who reduced their output; the money to pay them was raised through a processing tax on the industries that prepared farmers' crops for market. Could Congress, using its spending power under the general welfare clause, constitutionally levy such a tax? Justice Owen Roberts, writing for the majority, thought not, because the scope of the powers delegated to Congress is limited by the powers reserved to the states. He also provided a classic assertion of the "oracular" theory of judging: Judges did not "make" law, he claimed, but merely "found" existing rules and mechanically applied them to new cases. Roberts argued that if the Court accepted the processing tax on farm products, there would be no limit to what Congress might do. This listing of purely hypothetical evils led Justice Harlan Fiske Stone to write, in his dissenting opinion, that "a tortured construction of the Constitution" could not "be justified by recourse to extreme examples."

Mr. Justice Roberts delivered the opinion of the Court.

In this case we must determine whether certain provisions of the Agricultural Adjustment Act, 1933, conflict with the Federal Constitution. . . .

The Government asserts that even if the respondents may question the propriety of the appropriation embodied in the statute their attack must fail because Article I, § 8 of the Constitution authorizes the contemplated expenditure of the funds raised by the tax. This contention presents the great and the controlling question in the case. We approach its decision with a sense of our grave responsibility to render judgment in accordance with the principles established for the governance of all three branches of the Government.

There should be no misunderstanding as to the function of this court in such a case. It is sometimes said that the court assumes a power to overrule or control the action of the people's representatives. This is a misconception. The Constitution is the supreme law of the land ordained and established by the people. All legislation must conform to the principles it lays down. When an act of Congress is appropriately challenged in the courts as not conforming to the constitutional mandate the judicial branch of the Government has only one duty—to lay the article of the Constitution which is invoked beside the statute which is challenged and to decide whether the latter squares with the former. All the court does, or can do, is to announce its considered judgment upon the question. The only power it has, if such it may be called, is the power of judgment. This court neither approves nor condemns any legislative policy.

Its delicate and difficult office is to ascertain and declare whether the legislation is in accordance with, or in contravention of, the provisions of the Constitution; and, having done that, its duty ends. . . .

We are not now required to ascertain the scope of the phrase "general welfare of the United States" or to determine whether an appropriation in aid of agriculture falls within it. Wholly apart from that question, another principle embedded in our Constitution prohibits the enforcement of the Agricultural Adjustment Act. The act invades the reserved rights of the states. It is a statutory plan to regulate and control agricultural production, a matter beyond the powers delegated to the federal government. The tax, the appropriation of the funds raised, and the direction for their disbursement, are but parts of the plan. They are but means to an unconstitutional end.

From the accepted doctrine that the United States is a government of delegated powers, it follows that those not expressly granted, or reasonably to be implied from such as are conferred, are reserved to the states or to the people. To forestall any suggestion to the contrary, the Tenth Amendment was adopted. The same proposition, otherwise stated, is that powers not granted are prohibited. None to regulate agriculture production is given, and therefore legislation by Congress for that purpose is forbidden.

It is an established principle that the attainment of a prohibited end may not be accomplished under the pretext of the exertion of powers which are granted. . . .

The power of taxation, which is expressly granted, may, of course, be adopted as a means to carry into operation another power also expressly granted. But resort to the taxing power to effectuate an end which is not legitimate, not within the scope of the Constitution, is obviously inadmissible. . . .

If the taxing power may not be used as the instrument to enforce a regulation of matters of state concern with respect to which the Congress has no authority to interfere, may it, as in the present case, be employed to raise the money necessary to purchase a compliance which the Congress is powerless to command? The Government asserts that whatever might be said against the validity of the plan if compulsory, it is constitutionally sound because the end is accomplished by voluntary cooperation. There are two sufficient answers to the contention. The regulation is not in fact voluntary. The farmer, of course, may refuse to comply, but the price of such refusal is the loss of benefits. The amount offered is intended to be sufficient to exert pressure on him to agree to the proposed regulation. The power to confer or withhold unlimited benefits is the power to coerce or destroy. If the cotton grower elects not to accept the benefits, he will receive less for his crops; those who receive payments will be able to undersell him. The result may well be financial ruin. The coercive purpose and intent of the statute is not obscured by the fact that it has not been perfectly successful. It is pointed out that, because there still remained a minority whom the rental and benefit payments were insufficient to induce to surrender their independence of action, the Congress has gone further and, in the Bankhead Cotton Act, used the taxing power in a more directly minatory fashion to compel submission. This progression only serves more fully to expose the coercive purpose of the so-called tax imposed by the present act. It is clear that the Department of Agriculture has properly described the plan as one to keep a non-cooperating minority in line. This is coercion by economic pressure. The asserted power of choice is illusory. . . .

Congress has no power to enforce its commands on the farmer to the ends sought by the Agricultural Adjustment Act. It must follow that it may not indirectly accomplish those ends by taxing and spending to purchase compliance. The Constitution and the entire plan of our government negative any such use of the power to tax and to spend as the act undertakes to authorize. It does not help to declare that local conditions throughout the nation have created a situation of national concern; for this is but to say that whenever there is a widespread similarity of local conditions, Congress may ignore constitutional limitations upon its own powers and usurp those reserved to the states. If, in lieu of compulsory regulation of subjects within the states' reserved jurisdiction, which is prohibited, the Congress could invoke the taxing and spending power as a means to accomplish the same end, clause 1 of § 8 of Article I would become the instrument for total subversion of the governmental powers reserved to the individual states.

If the act before us is a proper exercise of the federal taxing power, evidently the regulation of all industry throughout the United States may be accomplished by similar exercises of the same power. It would be possible to exact money from one branch of an industry and pay it to another branch in every field of activity which lies within the province of the states. The mere threat of such a procedure might well induce the surrender of rights and the compliance with federal regulation as the price of continuance in business. A few instances will illustrate the thought.

Let us suppose Congress should determine that the farmer, the miner or some other producer of raw materials is receiving too much for his products, with consequent depression of the processing industry and idleness of its employees. Though, by confession, there is no power vested in Congress to compel by statute a lowering of the prices of the raw material, the same result might be accomplished, if the questioned act be valid, by taxing the producer upon his output and appropriating the proceeds to the processors, either with or without conditions imposed as the consideration for payment of the subsidy. . . .

Suppose that there are too many garment workers in the large cities; that this results in dislocation of the economic balance. Upon the principle contended for an excise might be laid on the manufacture of all garments manufactured and the proceeds paid to those manufacturers who agree to remove their plants to cities having not more than a hundred thousand population. Thus, through the asserted power of taxation, the federal government, against the will of individual states, might completely redistribute the industrial population.

A possible result of sustaining the claimed federal power would be that every business group which thought itself under-privileged might demand that a tax be laid on its vendors or vendees, the proceeds to be appropriated to the redress of its deficiency of income.

These illustrations are given, not to suggest that any of the purposes mentioned are unworthy, but to demonstrate the scope of the principle for which the Government contends; to test the principle by its applications; to point out that, by the exercise of the asserted power, Congress would, in effect, under the pretext of exercising the taxing power, in reality accomplish prohibited ends. It cannot be said that they envisage improbable legislation. The supposed cases are no more improbable than would the present act have been deemed a few years ago.

Until recently no suggestion of the existence of any such power in the Federal Government has been advanced. The expressions of the framers of the Constitution, the decisions of this court interpreting that instrument, and the writings of great commentators will be searched in vain for any suggestion that there exists in the clause under discussion or elsewhere in the Constitution, the authority whereby every provision and every fair implication from that instrument may be subverted, the independence of the individual states obliterated, and the United States converted into a central government exercising uncontrolled police power in every state of the Union, superseding all local control or regulation of the affairs or concerns of the states. . . .

Mr. Justice Stone, dissenting.

I think the judgment should be reversed. . . .

The power of courts to declare a statute unconstitutional is subject to two guiding principles of decision which ought never to be absent from judicial consciousness. One is that courts are concerned only with the power to enact statutes, not with their wisdom. The other is that while unconstitutional exercise of power by the executive and legislative branches of the government is subject to judicial restraint, the only check upon our own exercise of power is our own sense of self-restraint. For the removal of unwise laws from the statute books appeal lies not to the courts but to the ballot and to the processes of democratic government. . . .

Of the assertion that the payments to farmers are coercive, it is enough to say that no such contention is pressed by the taxpayer, and no such consequences were to be anticipated or appear to have resulted from the administration of the Act. The suggestion of coercion finds no support in the record or in any data showing the actual operation of the Act. Threat of loss, not hope of gain, is the essence of economic coercion. Members of a long depressed industry have undoubtedly been tempted to curtail acreage by the hope of resulting better prices and by the proffered opportunity to obtain needed ready money. But there is nothing to indicate that those who accepted benefits were impelled by fear of lower prices if they did not accept, or that at any stage in the operation of the plan a farmer could say whether, apart from the certainty of cash payments at specified times, the advantage would lie with curtailment of production plus compensation, rather than with the same or increased acreage plus the expected rise in prices which actually occurred. . . . The presumption of constitutionality of a statute is not to be overturned by an assertion of its coercive effect which rests on nothing more substantial than groundless speculation.

It is upon the contention that state power is infringed by purchased regulation of agricultural production that chief reliance is placed. It is insisted that, while the Constitution gives to Congress, in specific and unambiguous terms, the power to tax and spend, the power is subject to limitations which do not find their origin in any express provision of the Constitution and to which other expressly delegated powers are not subject.

The Constitution requires that public funds shall be spent for a defined purpose, the promotion of the general welfare. Their expenditure usually involves payment on terms which will insure use by the selected recipients within the limits of the constitutional purpose. Expenditures would fail of their purpose and thus lose their constitutional sanction if the terms of payment were not such that by their influence on the action of the recipients the permitted end would be attained. The power of Congress to spend is inseparable from persuasion to action over which Congress has no legislative control. Congress may not command that the science of agriculture be taught in state universities. But if it would aid the teaching of that science by grants to state institutions, it is appropriate, if not necessary, that the grant be on the condition, incorporated in the Morrill Act, 12 Stat. 503, 26 Stat. 417, that it be used for the intended purpose. Similarly it would seem to be compliance with the Constitution, not violation of it, for the government to take and the university to give a contract that the grant would be so used. It makes no difference that there is a promise to do an act which the condition is calculated to induce. Condition and promise are alike valid since both are in furtherance of the national purpose for which the money is appropriated. . . .

The spending power of Congress is in addition to the legislative power and not subordinate to it. This independent grant of the power of the purse, and its very nature, involving in its exercise the duty to insure expenditure within the granted power, presuppose freedom of selection among divers ends and aims, and the capacity to impose such conditions as will render the choice effective. It is a contradiction in terms to say that there is power to spend for the national welfare, while rejecting any power to impose conditions reasonably adapted to the attainment of the end which alone would justify the expenditure.

The limitation now sanctioned must lead to absurd consequences. The government may give seeds to farmers, but may not condition the gift upon their being planted in places where they are most needed or even planted at all. The government may give money to the unemployed, but may not ask that those who get it shall give labor in return, or even use it to support their families. It may give money to sufferers from earthquake, fire, tornado, pestilence or flood, but may not impose conditions — health precautions designed to prevent the spread of disease, or induce the movement of population to safer or more sanitary areas. All that, because it is purchased regulation infringing state powers, must be left for the states, who are unable or unwilling to supply the necessary relief. The government may spend its money for vocational rehabilitation, 48 Stat. 389, but it may not, with the consent of all concerned, supervise the process which it undertakes to aid. It may spend its money for the suppression of the boll weevil, but may not compensate the farmers for suspending the growth of cotton in the infected areas. It may aid state reforestation and forest fire prevention agencies, 43 Stat. 653, but may not be permitted to supervise their conduct. It may support rural schools, . . . but may not condition its grant by the requirement that certain standards be maintained. It may appropriate moneys to be expended by the Reconstruction Finance Corporation "to aid in financing agriculture, commerce and industry," and to facilitate "the exportation of agricultural and other products." Do all its activities collapse because, in order to effect the permissible purpose, in myriad ways the money is paid out upon terms and conditions which influence action of the recipients within the states, which Congress cannot command? The answer would seem plain. If the expenditure is for a national public purpose, that purpose will not be thwarted because payment is on condition which will advance that purpose. The action which Congress induces by payments of money to promote the general welfare, but which it does not command or coerce, is but an incident to a specifically granted power, but a permissible means to a legitimate end. If appropriation in aid of a program of curtailment of agricultural production is constitutional, and it is not denied that it is, payment to farmers on condition that they reduce their crop acreage is constitutional. It is not any the less so because the farmer at his own option promises to fulfill the condition.

That the governmental power of the purse is a great one is not now for the first time announced. Every student of the history of government and economics is aware of its magnitude and of its existence in every civilized government. . . .

The suggestion that it must now be curtailed by judicial fiat because it may be abused by unwise use hardly rises to the dignity of argument. So may judicial power be abused. "The power to tax is the power to destroy," but we do not, for that reason, doubt its existence, or hold that its efficacy is to be restricted by its incidental or collateral effects upon the states. . . .

The power to tax and spend is not without constitutional restraints. One restriction is that the purpose must be truly national. Another is that it may not be used to coerce action left to state control. Another is the conscience and patriotism of Congress and the Executive. "It must be remembered that legislators are the ultimate guardians of the liberties and welfare of the people in quite as great a degree as the courts." Justice Holmes, in *Missouri, Kansas & Texas Ry. Co. v. May,* 194 U.S. 267, 270.

A tortured construction of the Constitution is not to be justified by recourse to extreme examples of reckless congressional spending which might occur if courts could not prevent — expenditures which, even if they could be thought to effect any national purpose, would be possible only by action of a legislature lost to all sense of public responsibility. Such suppositions are addressed to the mind accustomed to believe that it is the business of courts to sit in judgment on the wisdom of legislative action. Courts are not the only agency of government that must be assumed to have capacity to govern. Congress and the courts both unhappily may falter or be mistaken in the performance of their constitutional

duty. But interpretation of our great charter of government which proceeds on any assumption that the responsibility for the preservation of
our institutions is the exclusive concern of any one of the three branches
of government, or that it alone can save them from destruction is far
more likely, in the long run, "to obliterate the constituent members" of
"an indestructible union of indestructible states" than the frank recognition that language, even of a constitution, may mean what it says: that the
power to tax and spend includes the power to relieve a nationwide economic maladjustment by conditional gifts of money.

ROBERT M. LA FOLLETTE JR.

Unpacking the Court

February 13, 1937

*President Roosevelt surely knew that his proposal to enlarge the Supreme
Court would outrage his conservative opponents, but he could not have anticipated how severely it would divide his liberal supporters. That division
is illustrated by the contrasting responses to the plan in this and the next selection. Robert M. La Follette, Jr., represented Wisconsin in the U.S. Senate. His father, who had also served in the Senate, had run for president in
1924 on the Progressive party platform, which called for a constitutional
amendment permitting Congress to override a judicial veto and providing
for the election of all federal judges for ten-year terms. Although some backers of Roosevelt's proposal conceded its shortcomings — The Nation, for example, admitted that "it can be used as effectively by a reactionary President as by a liberal, and ultimately it may produce simply a benchful of
younger reactionaries"— "Young Bob" La Follette offered unqualified support in the speech reprinted here.*

The Founding Fathers, the generations who built the spiritual and material foundations of this country, were opposed to judicial usurpation and

Robert M. La Follette Jr., "Unpacking the Court," *Congressional Quarterly,* March 1937,
84–85.

refused to regard the Supreme Court as sacrosanct. The views of those who framed the Constitution about the proper exercise of judicial power have been maintained throughout our history by liberal leaders including Jefferson, Jackson, Lincoln, Theodore Roosevelt, and my father.

A remoulding of the doctrine of judicial supremacy to restore the balance of power among the three coordinate branches of government will be a return to rather than a departure from fundamental constitutional principles. The Supreme Court, like the Congress, should reign under and not over the Constitution.

I believe in a government of laws and not of men. But when the validity of our laws depends upon the whim and caprice of five out of nine fallible men, when a majority of the Court is accused by Justice Stone, joined by other minority members equally devoted to the Constitution, of adopting "a tortured construction of the Constitution," of reading their own "personal economic predilection" in the fundamental law of the land, government by the judiciary becomes government of men and not of laws.

Thus, it is not the Constitution but the decisions of a majority of the Justices which stand in the way of necessary legislation regarding labor, agriculture, finance, and the conservation of our human and material resources.

Congress, no less than the Court, is charged with the duty of protecting and defending the Constitution. If it is the judgment of the Congress that the powers should be given to the Congress not already conferred upon it, the Congress must seek those powers by amendment. But if in the solemn judgment of the Congress those powers are already vested in it by the Constitution, it is the constitutional duty of the Congress, as a coordinate and independent branch of the Government, to take such steps as may be within its competence to exercise those powers. Congress cannot disturb a decision of the Supreme Court in a particular case, but Congress is not bound to submit to interpretations of the Constitution which deny to Congress its constitutional rights.

The Founding Fathers provided checks upon the executive and checks upon the Congress, and it cannot be assumed that the judiciary was to be free from all restraint. Impeachment is not the sole check.

No jurist has ever questioned the expressed constitutional right of the Congress to determine the number of Justices who shall make up the Supreme Court of the United States. That is the check of joint Congressional and Presidential action which the constitutional fathers with almost prophetic foresight provided to prevent the arbitrary obstruction of the popular will by a judiciary which has lost touch with the needs and aspirations of the people. The time and manner of the exercise of that check is a matter to be determined by the Congress responsible to the people of the United States.

The proposal of the President is nothing more nor less than a call to Congress to exercise its power under the Constitution to prevent the majority of the Supreme Court from thwarting the popular will.

Those who are opposing the President in this struggle rise to sanctimonious heights and brand as irreverent any attack on the Supreme Court. Our Founding Fathers never intended the Supreme Court to be the dictator of this nation. Not a word in the Constitution sanctions it. But when the Court substitutes for the will of the people of this country its own will; when it supplants the prevailing economic theory with its own smug theory of days gone by; when it decrees that it is beyond the power of the people to meet the national needs — then it has become a dictator and we have succumbed to a Fascist system of control which is inconsistent with fundamental principles upon which our government is founded. If it is irreverent to attack that dictatorship, then I am irreverent and every citizen who believes in true democracy should be irreverent.

There is a lot of talk of the President "packing" the Court. Let's not be misled by a red herring. The Court has been "packed" for years — "packed" in the interests of Economic Royalists, "packed" for the benefit of the Liberty Leaguers, "packed" in the cause of reaction and laissez-faire.

Let's be frank about this matter. The vested interests have for years prevailed in selection of judges. Under our form of government the will of the majority should prevail. If the majority of the people want progress, they should have it.

November 3rd last made it clear and unmistakable where the vast majority of the people stand. They want to be free from the shackles of vested interests. They have rejected the Economic Royalists. In the words of Lincoln, they want a government of the people, by the people and for the people. They cannot have it if the Supreme Court places itself above the Constitution and arrogates to itself legislative functions. One clear way in which they can have their will of last November expressed is to have the Congress "unpack" a Court which has long been "packed" by the forces of reaction.

A Congress which fails to "unpack" the Court has a short memory and is unresponsive to the voice of the majority. A Congress which fails to "unpack" the Court is allowing the Economic Royalists to rule this country with a Court "packed" against the people. This condition is intolerable. So long as the Court is "packed" against the people, the will of the majority cannot prevail. We then have not democracy but the worst form of dictatorship.

The President's proposals are certainly moderate and reasonable. Had such proposals been made by a Harding, a Coolidge, or a Hoover, their motives would not be suspect. But the reactionaries contend that President Roosevelt has an evil motive and a sinister purpose in this as in everything else he has proposed for the good of the people. These critics deliberately conceal the fact that even if none of the Justices resigns and none is obliged to resign, President Roosevelt would appoint only six out of fifteen Justices and the new Justices would still form only a minority of the Court. There would still be nine Justices, seven of whom were nominated by Republican Presidents and two by a former Democratic President. Those who say these proposals would make the Court subservient to the wishes of President Roosevelt are really questioning the integrity and independence of Justice Brandeis, Justice Stone and Justice Cardozo.

Beware of those who declaim so vehemently about an independent judiciary, for they are really concerned in having a judiciary subservient to their own ideas. And don't be fooled by the crocodile tears of those who point to the careers of Justice Holmes and Justice Brandeis as reasons against the President's proposal; check back on those weepers and you will find that they cursed the opinions of Holmes while he lived and fought the confirmation of Brandeis to the last ditch.

Most of those who are urging or who are paying for propaganda to urge constitutional amendment as the only way of meeting these difficulties are those who before last November were talking about the sacredness of the Constitution and the sinfulness of amending it. Driven from that first trench by the vote of 27 million people in November, they are now back in their second trench urging amendment rather than the quicker means of bringing justice to the people which are unquestionably available to the Congress and the President under the terms of that same Constitution.

The Constitution requires that an amendment be ratified by three-quarters of the states — each state having one vote. But never forget that the twelve smallest states in the nation — enough to block or delay amendment — can do this with only ten percent of the population of the nation. You can be sure that the Economic Royalists are not forgetting the usefulness of that ten percent.

I have no doubt as to the wisdom of the substance of the President's proposals. He has pointed out the only way in which the popular will may be translated into effective legislative action during the next four years.

Progressives who hesitate or divide upon this issue must assume full responsibility if the mandate registered by the overwhelming majority of the voters at the last election is thwarted.

For the long future I am in favor of the submission by this Congress to the people of an amendment which would give the Congress power to override a decision of the Court declaring any act of Congress unconstitutional so as to provide in future years a more certain mechanism of restraining arbitrary judicial action.

But that amendment must be *in addition to* the President's proposal for immediate action by statute. While an amendment is taking its long and laborious course no man or woman who values the continuity of our democratic and legal traditions — no man or woman who realizes the desperate necessity of making democracy work and work now — can stand idle and submit to the chaos of judicial usurpation which it is within the constitutional power of the Congress to remedy.

HERBERT H. LEHMAN

A Greatly Dangerous Precedent

July 19, 1937

Herbert H. Lehman, who succeeded FDR as governor of New York, was one of the New Deal's most dedicated supporters. Yet in February 1937, he privately informed FDR that he could not support Court reform, writing, in part, "I feel that the end which you desire to attain does not justify the means which you recommend." It came as an especially unwelcome shock to the president when Lehman made his views public in the form of an open letter to Senator Robert F. Wagner that was released to the New York Times. *A few days earlier, FDR's last chance to obtain a compromise Court bill, which would have permitted the appointment of one additional justice a year for each member of the Court who was seventy-five years of age, had suffered a fatal setback. To hold the support of wavering senators, Roosevelt had let it be known that he would name Senate majority leader Joseph Robinson of Arkansas to the first vacant seat on the Court. But on July 14, Robinson died of a heart attack. After learning of Lehman's letter to Senator Wagner, Republican senator Arthur H. Vandenberg of Michigan, said, referring to the Court bill, "All that remains to be done is to call the coroner."*

My dear Senator Wagner:

I am writing to you as a citizen of the State of New York, which you represent in the United States Senate, to voice my opposition to the Court Bill and to express the hope that you will vote against it.

The President is already familiar with my views with regard to the bill. Several months ago I wrote to him that I believe its enactment would not be in the best interest of the country. In the months that have passed since then my convictions have become strengthened.

Like many others I have frequently felt keen disappointment that important legislative measures have been declared unconstitutional by a slim and unconvincing margin in the Supreme Court. And yet I believe that the orderly and deliberate processes of government should not be sacrificed merely to meet an immediate situation.

From the broad standpoint of the public interest whatever immediate gain might be achieved through the proposed change in the court would, in my opinion, be far more than offset by a loss of confidence in the independence of the courts and in governmental procedure.

I have whole-heartedly supported most of the President's social program both while he was Governor of New York and since he became President of the United States. His program taken as a whole has in my opinion represented the greatest step forward in social reform that any nation has undertaken for many years. I look forward to the opportunity of continuing to support his courageous leadership in matters that are in the interest of the social well-being of our people.

This bill, however, I believe to be contrary to their interest. Its enactment would create a greatly dangerous precedent which could be availed of by future less well-intentioned administrations for the purpose of oppression or for the curtailment of the constitutional rights of our citizens.

Very sincerely yours,
HERBERT H. LEHMAN

CHARLES EVANS HUGHES
AND GEORGE SUTHERLAND

West Coast Hotel v. Parrish

March 29, 1937

The justices did their part to bury Roosevelt's Court-packing plan by changing their position on crucial issues. The key ruling came in West Coast Hotel v. Parrish, *when Justice Owen Roberts cast the deciding fifth vote to uphold a Washington State minimum wage law. Passed in 1913, the act made it unlawful to employ women or minors "at wages which are not adequate for their maintenance"; standards were to be set by a state commission. The justices handed down their decision on March 29, 1937, at the height of the Court-packing controversy, although the vote had been taken in conference on December 19, 1936, before FDR announced his plan. Speaking for the majority, Chief Justice Charles Evans Hughes asserted that reasonable regulation, adopted in the interests of the community, by definition fulfilled the Fourteenth Amendment's due process requirements. The Court thereby reversed its 1923 holding in* Adkins v. Children's Hospital. *It was not surprising that Justice George Sutherland, who had written the majority opinion in* Adkins, *dissented in* Parrish, *maintaining that "the meaning of the Constitution does not change with the ebb and flow of economic events."*

Mr. Chief Justice Hughes delivered the opinion of the Court.

This case presents the question of the constitutional validity of the minimum wage law of the State of Washington. . . .

The appellant conducts a hotel. The appellee Elsie Parrish was employed as a chambermaid and (with her husband) brought this suit to recover the difference between the wages paid her and the minimum wage fixed pursuant to the state law. The minimum wage was $14.50 per week of 48 hours. The appellant challenged the act as repugnant to the due process clause of the Fourteenth Amendment of the Constitution of the United States. The Supreme Court of the State, reversing the trial court, sustained the statute and directed judgment for the plaintiffs.

West Coast Hotel v. Parrish, 300 US 379 (1937).

Parrish v. West Coast Hotel Co., 185 Wash. 581; 55 P. (2d) 1083. The case is here on appeal.

The appellant relies upon the decision of this Court in *Adkins v. Children's Hospital,* 261 U.S. 525, which held invalid the District of Columbia Minimum Wage Act, which was attacked under the due process clause of the Fifth Amendment. On the argument at bar, counsel for the appellees attempted to distinguish the *Adkins* case upon the ground that the appellee was employed in a hotel and that the business of an innkeeper was affected with a public interest. That effort at distinction is obviously futile, as it appears that in one of the cases ruled by the *Adkins* opinion the employee was a woman employed as an elevator operator in a hotel. . . .

The Supreme Court of Washington has upheld the minimum wage statute of that State. It has decided that the statute is a reasonable exercise of the police power of the State. In reaching that conclusion the state court has invoked principles long established by this Court in the application of the Fourteenth Amendment. The state court has refused to regard the decision in the *Adkins* case as determinative and has pointed to our decisions both before and since that case as justifying its position. We are of the opinion that this ruling of the state court demands on our part a reexamination of the *Adkins* case. The importance of the question, in which many States having similar laws are concerned, the close division by which the decision in the *Adkins* case was reached, and the economic conditions which have supervened, and in the light of which the reasonableness of the exercise of the protective power of the State must be considered, make it not only appropriate, but we think imperative, that in deciding the present case the subject should receive fresh consideration. . . .

The principle which must control our decision is not in doubt. The constitutional provision invoked is the due process clause of the Fourteenth Amendment governing the States, as the due process clause invoked in the *Adkins* case governed Congress. In each case the violation alleged by those attacking minimum wage regulation for women is deprivation of freedom of contract. What is this freedom? The Constitution does not speak of freedom of contract. It speaks of liberty and prohibits the deprivation of liberty without due process of law. In prohibiting that deprivation the Constitution does not recognize an absolute and uncontrollable liberty. Liberty in each of its phases has its history and connotation. But the liberty safeguarded is liberty in a social organization which requires the protection of law against the evils which menace the health, safety, morals and welfare of the people. Liberty under the Constitution is thus necessarily subject to the restraints of due process, and regulation which is reasonable in relation to its subject and is adopted in the interests of the community is due process. . . .

What can be closer to the public interest than the health of women and their protection from unscrupulous and overreaching employers? And if the protection of women is a legitimate end of the exercise of state power, how can it be said that the requirement of the payment of a minimum wage fairly fixed in order to meet the very necessities of existence is not an admissible means to that end? The legislature of the State was clearly entitled to consider the situation of women in employment, the fact that they are in the class receiving the least pay, that their bargaining power is relatively weak, and that they are the ready victims of those who would take advantage of their necessitous circumstances. The legislature was entitled to adopt measures to reduce the evils of the "sweating system," the exploiting of workers at wages so low as to be insufficient to meet the bare cost of living, thus making their very helplessness the occasion of a most injurious competition. The legislature had the right to consider that its minimum wage requirements would be an important aid in carrying out its policy of protection. The adoption of similar requirements by many States evidences a deep-seated conviction both as to the presence of the evil and as to the means adopted to check it. Legislative response to that conviction cannot be regarded as arbitrary or capricious, and that is all we have to decide. Even if the wisdom of the policy be regarded as debatable and its effects uncertain, still the legislature is entitled to its judgment.

There is an additional and compelling consideration which recent economic experience has brought into a strong light. The exploitation of a class of workers who are in an unequal position with respect to bargaining power and are thus relatively defenceless against the denial of a living wage is not only detrimental to their health and well being but casts a direct burden for their support upon the community. What these workers lose in wages the taxpayers are called upon to pay. The bare cost of living must be met. We may take judicial notice of the unparalleled demands for relief which arose during the recent period of depression and still continue to an alarming extent despite the degree of economic recovery which has been achieved. It is unnecessary to cite official statistics to establish what is of common knowledge through the length and breadth of the land. While in the instant case no factual brief has been presented, there is no reason to doubt that the State of Washington has encountered the same social problem that is present elsewhere. The community is not bound to provide what is in effect a

subsidy for unconscionable employers. The community may direct its
law-making power to correct the abuse which springs from their selfish
disregard of the public interest. The argument that the legislation in
question constitutes an arbitrary discrimination, because it does not extend to men, is unavailing. This Court has frequently held that the legislative authority, acting within its proper field, is not bound to extend
its regulation to all cases which it might possibly reach. The legislature "is free to recognize degrees of harm and it may confine its restrictions to those classes of cases where the need is deemed to be clearest."
If "the law presumably hits the evil where it is most felt, it is not to be
overthrown because there are other instances to which it might have
been applied." There is no "doctrinaire requirement" that the legislation
should be couched in all embracing terms. . . .

This familiar principle has repeatedly been applied to legislation
which singles out women, and particular classes of women, in the exercise of the State's protective power. . . . Their relative need in the presence of the evil, no less than the existence of the evil itself, is a matter for
the legislative judgment.

Our conclusion is that the case of *Adkins v. Children's Hospital, supra,*
should be, and it is, overruled. The judgment of the Supreme Court of
the State of Washington is

Affirmed.

Mr. Justice Sutherland, dissenting:

Mr. Justice Van Devanter, Mr. Justice McReynolds, Mr. Justice Butler
and I think the judgment of the court below should be reversed. . . .

The suggestion that the only check upon the exercise of the judicial
power, when properly invoked, to declare a constitutional right superior
to an unconstitutional statute is the judge's own faculty of self-restraint,
is both ill considered and mischievous. Self-restraint belongs in the do-
main of will and not of judgment. The check upon the judge is that imposed by his oath of office, by the Constitution and by his own conscientious and informed convictions; and since he has the duty to make up
his own mind and adjudge accordingly, it is hard to see how there could
be any other restraint. This court acts as a unit. It cannot act in any other
way; and the majority (whether a bare majority or a majority of all but
one of its members), therefore, establishes the controlling rule as the
decision of the court, binding, so long as it remains unchanged, equally
upon those who disagree and upon those who subscribe to it. Otherwise,
orderly administration of justice would cease. But it is the right of those

in the minority to disagree, and sometimes, in matters of grave importance, their imperative duty to voice their disagreement at such length as the occasion demands — always, of course, in terms which, however forceful, do not offend the proprieties or impugn the good faith of those who think otherwise.

It is urged that the question involved should now receive fresh consideration, among other reasons, because of "the economic conditions which have supervened"; but the meaning of the Constitution does not change with the ebb and flow of economic events. We frequently are told in more general words that the Constitution must be construed in the light of the present. If by that it is meant that the Constitution is made up of living words that apply to every new condition which they include, the statement is quite true. But to say, if that be intended, that the words of the Constitution mean today what they did not mean when written — that is, that they do not apply to a situation now to which they would have applied then — is to rob that instrument of the essential element which continues it in force as the people have made it until they, and not their official agents, have made it otherwise. . . .

The judicial function is that of interpretation; it does not include the power of amendment under the guise of interpretation. To miss the point of difference between the two is to miss all that the phrase "supreme law of the land" stands for and to convert what was intended as inescapable and enduring mandates into mere moral reflections.

If the Constitution, intelligently and reasonably construed in the light of these principles, stands in the way of desirable legislation, the blame must rest upon that instrument, and not upon the court for enforcing it according to its terms. The remedy in that situation — and the only true remedy — is to amend the Constitution. . . .

Coming, then, to a consideration of the Washington statute, it first is to be observed that it is in every substantial respect identical with the statute involved in the *Adkins* case. Such vices as existed in the latter are present in the former. And if the *Adkins* case was properly decided, as we who join in this opinion think it was, it necessarily follows that the Washington statute is invalid.

In support of minimum-wage legislation it has been urged, on the one hand, that great benefits will result in favor of underpaid labor, and, on the other hand, that the danger of such legislation is that the minimum will tend to become the maximum and thus bring down the earnings of the more efficient toward the level of the less-efficient employees. But with these speculations we have nothing to do. We are concerned only with the question of constitutionality. . . .

The Washington statute, like the one for the District of Columbia, fixes minimum wages for adult women. Adult men and their employers are left free to bargain as they please; and it is a significant and an important fact that all state statutes to which our attention has been called are of like character. The common-law rules restricting the power of women to make contracts have, under our system, long since practically disappeared. Women today stand upon a legal and political equality with men. There is no longer any reason why they should be put in different classes in respect of their legal right to make contracts; nor should they be denied, in effect, the right to compete with men for work paying lower wages which men may be willing to accept. And it is an arbitrary exercise of the legislative power to do so. . . .

An appeal to the principle that the legislature is free to recognize degrees of harm and confine its restrictions accordingly, is but to beg the question, which is — since the contractual rights of men and women are the same, does the legislation here involved, by restricting only the rights of women to make contracts as to wages, create an arbitrary discrimination? We think it does. Difference of sex affords no reasonable ground for making a restriction applicable to the wage contracts of all working women from which like contracts of all working men are left free. Certainly a suggestion that the bargaining ability of the average woman is not equal to that of the average man would lack substance. The ability to make a fair bargain, as everyone knows, does not depend upon sex.

BENJAMIN N. CARDOZO

Helvering v. Davis

May 24, 1937

Of all the members of the Court, Benjamin N. Cardozo was the most sympathetic to the broad social objectives of the New Deal. So it was appropriate that he would write the opinion sustaining the Social Security Act. In a case involving the unemployment insurance provisions of the act (Steward Machine Co. v. Davis), *he noted that because unemployment had become*

Helvering v. Davis, 301 US 619 (1937).

a national problem, "there was need of help from the nation if the people were not to starve." In the case of Helvering v. Davis, *which upheld the act's old-age pension provisions, Cardozo affirmed three principles underlying the constitutional revolution of 1937. First, the original intent of the Founding Fathers was not necessarily binding on the present because "what is critical or urgent changes with the times." Second, Congress had an obligation, in enacting legislation, to look facts squarely in the face — to respond, that is, to the real needs of actual people. Third, the Court's function was not to determine whether Congress had acted wisely but only whether it had acted constitutionally. The justices, he thought, must respect the choice made by Congress "unless the choice is clearly wrong, a display of arbitrary power, not an exercise of judgment."*

. . . The scheme of benefits created by the provisions of Title II is not in contravention of the limitations of the Tenth Amendment.

Congress may spend money in aid of the "general welfare." . . . Yet difficulties are left when the power is conceded. The line must still be drawn between one welfare and another, between particular and general. Where this shall be placed cannot be known through a formula in advance of the event. There is a middle ground or certainly a penumbra in which discretion is at large. The discretion, however, is not confided to the courts. The discretion belongs to Congress, unless the choice is clearly wrong, a display of arbitrary power, not an exercise of judgment. This is now familiar law.

. . . Nor is the concept of the general welfare static. Needs that were narrow or parochial a century ago may be interwoven in our day with the well-being of the Nation. What is critical or urgent changes with the times.

The purge of nation-wide calamity that began in 1929 has taught us many lessons. Not the least is the solidarity of interests that may once have seemed to be divided. Unemployment spreads from State to State, the hinterland now settled that in pioneer days gave an avenue of escape. *Home Building & Loan Assn. v. Blaisdell,* 290 U.S. 398, 442. Spreading from State to State, unemployment is an ill not particular but general, which may be checked, if Congress so determines, by the resources of the Nation. If this can have been doubtful until now, our ruling today in the case of the *Steward Machine Co., supra,* has set the doubt at rest. But the ill is all one, or at least not greatly different, whether men are thrown out of work because there is no longer work to do or because the disabilities of age make them incapable of doing it. Rescue becomes necessary irrespective of the cause. The hope behind this statute is to save men and women from the rigors of the poor house as well as from the haunting fear that such a lot awaits them when journey's end is near.

Congress did not improvise a judgment when it found that the award of old age benefits would be conducive to the general welfare. The President's Committee on Economic Security made an investigation and report, aided by a research staff of Government officers and employees, and by an Advisory Council and seven other advisory groups. Extensive hearings followed before the House Committee on Ways and Means, and the Senate Committee on Finance. A great mass of evidence was brought together supporting the policy which finds expression in the act. Among the relevant facts are these: The number of persons in the United States 65 years of age or over is increasing proportionately as well as absolutely. What is even more important the number of such persons unable to take care of themselves is growing at a threatening pace. More and more our population is becoming urban and industrial instead of rural and agricultural. The evidence is impressive that among industrial workers the younger men and women are preferred over the older. In times of retrenchment the older are commonly the first to go, and even if retained, their wages are likely to be lowered. The plight of men and women at so low an age as 40 is hard, almost hopeless, when they are driven to seek for reemployment. Statistics are in the brief. A few illustrations will be chosen from many there collected. In 1930, out of 224 American factories investigated, 71, or almost one third, had fixed maximum hiring age limits; in 4 plants the limit was under 40; in 41 it was under 46. In the other 153 plants there were no fixed limits, but in practice few were hired if they were over 50 years of age. With the loss of savings inevitable in periods of idleness, the fate of workers over 65, when thrown out of work, is little less than desperate. A recent study of the Social Security Board informs us that "one-fifth of the aged in the United States were receiving old-age assistance, emergency relief, institutional care, employment under the works program, or some other form of aid from public or private funds; two-fifths to one-half were dependent on friends and relatives, one-eighth had some income from earnings; and possibly one-sixth had some savings or property. Approximately three out of four persons 65 or over were probably dependent wholly or partially on others for support." . . .

The problem is plainly national in area and dimensions. Moreover, laws of the separate states cannot deal with it effectively. Congress, at least, had a basis for that belief. States and local governments are often lacking in the resources that are necessary to finance an adequate program of security for the aged. This is brought out with a wealth of illustration in recent studies of the problem. Apart from the failure of resources, states and local governments are at times reluctant to increase so heavily the burden of taxation to be borne by their residents for fear of placing themselves in a position of economic disadvantage as compared with neighbors or competitors. We have seen this in our study of the problem of unemployment compensation. *Steward Machine Co. v. Davis, supra.* A system of old age pensions has special dangers of its own, if put in force in one state and rejected in another. The existence of such a system is a bait to the needy and dependent elsewhere, encouraging them to migrate and seek a haven of repose. Only a power that is national can serve the interests of all.

Whether wisdom or unwisdom resides in the scheme of benefits set forth in Title II, it is not for us to say. The answer to such inquiries must come from Congress, not the courts. Our concern here, as often, is with power, not with wisdom. Counsel for respondent has recalled to us the virtues of self-reliance and frugality. There is a possibility, he says, that aid from a paternal government may sap those sturdy virtues and breed a race of weaklings. If Massachusetts so believes and shapes her laws in that conviction, must her breed of sons be changed, he asks, because some other philosophy of government finds favor in the halls of Congress? But the answer is not doubtful. One might ask with equal reason whether the system of protective tariffs is to be set aside at will in one state or another whenever local policy prefers the rule of *laissez faire.* The issue is a closed one. It was fought out long ago. When money is spent to promote the general welfare, the concept of welfare or the opposite is shaped by Congress, not the states. So the concept be not arbitrary, the locality must yield. Constitution, Art. VI, Par. 2.

8

Morale in Wartime:
A Portfolio of Propaganda Posters

During World War II, the government exploited every available form of publicity to win support for its policies. The Treasury Department sponsored a radio show to promote the sale of war bonds. The Office of War Information set up a Bureau of Motion Pictures to review film scripts with a view toward ensuring that they would contribute to "a unified, fully mobilized America." Businesses were encouraged to employ war-related themes in their advertising campaigns — to exhort potential customers, for example, to accept the sacrifices demanded by wartime mobilization. Posters, prepared by federal agencies and war contractors, were tacked up everywhere: on factory gates, office bulletin boards, and roadside billboards. Sometimes posters evoked feelings of pride in the American way of life; sometimes they aroused feelings of hatred toward the Axis Powers. Ever-present visual reminders of the war effort, they were designed, in either case, to boost civilian morale.

"United We Win," prepared by the War Manpower Commission, was intended to foster interracial harmony by showing a black man and a white man working side by side against the backdrop of the Stars and Stripes. That image, however, was overly idealized. Although African Americans won significant gains in defense industries (making up more than 8 percent of workers in those industries in 1945, compared with only 3 percent in 1942), patterns of occupational discrimination persisted. Even worse, the advances African Americans made sometimes triggered white animosity, as in Mobile, Alabama, where white shipyard workers rioted when African Americans were promoted to jobs as welders. Ironically, the poster implicitly recognized the existence of hierarchical patterns of employment: The African American figure is positioned below the white figure, is wearing a more recognizably blue-collar shirt and cap, and is using a simpler tool rather than the more sophisticated power drill. In that sense, the poster's unstated message accurately portrays the reality of the wartime workplace.

U.S. War Manpower Commission, *United We Win, 1943*
(National Archives)

U.S. Employment Service, *Do the Job HE Left Behind, 1943[?]*
(National Archives)

Like African Americans, women benefited from the virtually limitless need for workers in national defense. Six million women joined the labor force between 1940 and 1945, and the percentage of women holding jobs rose from 28 percent to 37 percent. And yet the war also reinforced gender segregation in the workplace: Women invariably did different kinds of work than men. Moreover, the same public relations campaigns that urged women to take war-related jobs also called on them to preserve their identities as wives, mothers, and homemakers, since they would resume these traditional roles when the war was over. This dual message was apparent in the U.S. Employment Service poster here reprinted, "Do the Job HE Left Behind." Although women were urgently needed as riveters on ships and planes, the poster suggests that they need not sacrifice their femininity to take these jobs, presenting a figure with long eyelashes, sensuous lips, and rather dainty work gloves. It was, after all, HIS job, not hers.

War always involves the dehumanization, or even demonization, of the enemy, and World War II was no exception. With respect to Germany and Italy, public hatred was directed chiefly against Adolf Hitler and Benito Mussolini. In the case of Japan, however, it was aimed at the Japanese people. As historian John Dower has shown in *War without Mercy,* the Japanese were depicted as subhuman, primitive, and inherently inferior; as monkeys, baboons, gorillas, dogs, rats, rattlesnakes, cockroaches, and vermin. "Lookout Monks!" portrays both Germans and Japanese as apelike, but with apparent differences: The German face is recognizably human, a caricature of Hitler, but the Japanese face is a racial stereotype with buckteeth and thick glasses. Moreover, the German is armed with a revolver, suggesting some measure of technological achievement, while the Japanese figure grasps a more primitive weapon, a bloodstained knife, representing the "stab in the back" at Pearl Harbor.

Posters were frequently used to promote the sale of war bonds, or "Victory Bonds." In all, the Treasury Department launched seven bond drives, which raised a total of $135 billion. Although most of the securities were purchased by banks, insurance companies, and corporations, about twenty-five million workers bought low-denomination bonds through payroll savings plans. A famous poster publicizing the seventh bond drive showed U.S. Marines raising the American flag on Mount Suribachi after the Battle of Iwo Jima. An earlier one, shown here, perfectly illustrates the widely held view that the war was a religious crusade, in which, as one congressman said, "the forces of Christian peace

Packer Aircraft, *Lookout Monks! Here's Your Plane Warning! 1942*
(National Archives)

U.S. Treasury Department, *Buy Victory Bonds, 1945*
(National Archives)

and freedom and justice and decency and morality are arrayed against the evil pagan forces of strife, injustice, treachery, immorality, and slavery." In this poster, a benign President Roosevelt looks down, on a worshipful family as if from on high, his words rendered in Gothic lettering framed by a cross and a beam of heavenly light.

9

The "Good War"?

Studs Terkel called his best-selling oral history of World War II *"The Good War,"* purposely using quotation marks because he considered it "incongruous" to attach the adjective *good* to the noun *war.* Yet in the minds of most Americans who remember the war, there is nothing incongruous about the connection. The war is generally thought to have been a just war, fought to combat the menace of fascism by a united people who willingly made sacrifices for the common good and who managed to overcome ethnic divisions and religious differences. The war, moreover, brought prosperity to a nation still bogged down in the Depression, and the resulting full employment benefited African Americans and women, who found new job opportunities in national defense, the civil service, and the military. The war did not produce the harsh curtailment of civil liberties that many had feared. Freedom of speech, press, and assembly were protected, and there was no public hysteria or mob violence. As one woman interviewed by Terkel explained, "The war was fun for America."

WESTERN DEFENSE COMMAND

Instructions to All Persons of Japanese Ancestry
April 30, 1942

The interpretation of World War II as "the good war," though not without merit, is overstated. Nothing better illustrates the war's manifestly less appealing side than the relocation and incarceration of Japanese Americans. In the spring of 1942, more than 110,000 Japanese Americans were forced to leave their homes on the West Coast. (See poster on pp. 192–93.) About

WESTERN DEFENSE COMMAND AND FOURTH ARMY
WARTIME CIVIL CONTROL ADMINISTRATION
Presidio of San Francisco, California

INSTRUCTIONS

TO ALL PERSONS OF

JAPANESE

ANCESTRY

LIVING IN THE FOLLOWING AREA:

All of that portion of the County of Alameda, State of California, within that boundary beginning at the point at which the southerly limits of the City of Berkeley meet San Francisco Bay; thence easterly and following the southerly limits of said city to College Avenue; thence southerly on College Avenue to Broadway; thence southerly on Broadway to the southerly limits of the City of Oakland; thence following the limits of said city westerly and northerly, and following the shoreline of San Francisco Bay to the point of beginning.

Pursuant to the provisions of Civilian Exclusion Order No. 27, this Headquarters, dated April 30, 1942, all persons of Japanese ancestry, both alien and non-alien, will be evacuated from the above area by 12 o'clock noon, P.W.T., Thursday May 7, 1942.

No Japanese person living in the above area will be permitted to change residence after 12 o'clock noon, P.W.T., Thursday, April 30, 1942, without obtaining special permission from the representative of the Commanding General, Northern California Sector, at the Civil Control Station located at:

530 Eighteenth Street,
Oakland, California.

Such permits will only be granted for the purpose of uniting members of a family, or in cases of grave emergency.

The Civil Control Station is equipped to assist the Japanese population affected by this evacuation in the following ways:

1. Give advice and instructions on the evacuation.

2. Provide services with respect to the management, leasing, sale, storage or other disposition of most kinds of property, such as real estate, business and professional equipment, household goods, boats, automobiles and livestock.

3. Provide temporary residence elsewhere for all Japanese in family groups.

4. Transport persons and a limited amount of clothing and equipment to their new residence.

U.S. Army, Western Defense Command, *Final Report, Japanese Evacuation from the West Coast, 1942* (Washington, D.C., 1943), 99–100.

THE FOLLOWING INSTRUCTIONS MUST BE OBSERVED:

1. A responsible member of each family, preferably the head of the family, or the person in whose name most of the property is held, and each individual living alone, will report to the Civil Control Station to receive further instructions. This must be done between 8:00 A. M. and 5:00 P. M. on Friday, May 1, 1942, or between 8:00 A. M. and 5:00 P. M. on Saturday, May 2, 1942.

2. Evacuees must carry with them on departure for the Assembly Center, the following property:

   (a) Bedding and linens (no mattress) for each member of the family;

   (b) Toilet articles for each member of the family;

   (c) Extra clothing for each member of the family;

   (d) Sufficient knives, forks, spoons, plates, bowls and cups for each member of the family;

   (e) Essential personal effects for each member of the family.

All items carried will be securely packaged, tied and plainly marked with the name of the owner and numbered in accordance with instructions obtained at the Civil Control Station. The size and number of packages is limited to that which can be carried by the individual or family group.

3. No pets of any kind will be permitted.

4. No personal items and no household goods will be shipped to the Assembly Center.

5. The United States Government through its agencies will provide for the storage at the sole risk of the owner of the more substantial household items, such as iceboxes, washing machines, pianos and other heavy furniture. Cooking utensils and other small items will be accepted for storage if crated, packed and plainly marked with the name and address of the owner. Only one name and address will be used by a given family.

6. Each family, and individual living alone will be furnished transportation to the Assembly Center or will be authorized to travel by private automobile in a supervised group. All instructions pertaining to the movement will be obtained at the Civil Control Station.

Go to the Civil Control Station between the hours of 8:00 A. M. and 5:00 P. M., Friday, May 1, 1942, or between the hours of 8:00 A. M. and 5:00 P. M., Saturday, May 2, 1942, to receive further instructions.

J. L. DeWitt
Lieutenant General, U. S. Army
Commanding

April 30, 1942

*two-thirds of the evacuees were American citizens. None had been charged
with any crime. Attempts were made to justify relocation on the grounds of
military necessity, but it was really motivated by racial prejudice — by the
view, expressed by General John L. DeWitt of the Western Defense Command, that "the Japanese race is an enemy race." The poster, one of many
notifying Japanese Americans that they were to be sent to assembly centers,
unintentionally reveals the policy's underlying racism. The evacuees are
first referred to, accurately, as "persons of Japanese ancestry," but later they
are termed "Japanese person[s]," "the Japanese population," and "all Japanese." The word "non-alien" was apparently more palatable than "citizen."
Under the circumstances, the government's offer to store personal property
"at the sole risk of the owner" was not taken seriously.*

Footprints: Poetry of the American Relocation Camp Experience

ca. 1942–1944

*Since the assembly centers were constructed at stockyards and racetracks,
the evacuees were temporarily housed in cattle stalls or even pigpens hastily
converted for human occupancy — hence the reference to a horse stable in
the poem by Hakujaku. By the fall of 1942, however, nearly all Japanese
Americans had moved to one of ten newly built relocation camps located in
seven western states. Housed in wooden barracks, families were furnished
with army cots and blankets and shared communal sanitary, bathing, laundry, and dining facilities. In February 1943, many of the evacuees faced
a dilemma eloquently described by another poet, Sunada Toshu. The government distributed a loyalty questionnaire (originally designed for male
evacuees of draft age) to all adults — men and women, citizens and aliens
— asking them to swear "unqualified allegiance" to the United States and
to renounce any obedience to the emperor of Japan. Of the 75,000 who responded, 8,700 either refused to forswear allegiance to the emperor or qualified their answers. Many were first-generation immigrants who were*

"Footprints: Poetry of the American Relocation Camp Experience," trans. and comp. Con-
stance Hayashi and Keiho Yamanaka, *Amerasia Journal* (1976): 115–17.

barred from acquiring American citizenship and who justifiably feared that they would be left with no nationality if they answered affirmatively. Even so, the government took their responses as proof of their disloyalty and segregated them in one camp, Tule Lake, California.

Kutsuato no
  tenten to shite
  yuki no michi — Muin

1. Footprints,
   dots being made
   path of snow

Yuki no yama
  ji o negurushii
  fu ressha — Hibutsu

2. Snow in mountain pass
   unable to sleep
   the prison train

Shashin daite nete
  yume mite samete
  Mizora samui
    yo yuki no kaze — Sasabune

3. Falling asleep with
   a photograph,
   awakened by a dream,
   cold snowy wind of
   Missoula

Samete no
  koe seshi mago no
  kage o oi — Oshio

4. Awakened again
   by a voice
   chasing the shadows of
     my grandchild

Tachinoki no
  shirase o nigiru
  haru no yo ni
    haha no mite toru
      tsuma omoinu — Sojin

5. Notice of evacuation
   one spring night
   the image of my wife
   holding the hands of my mother

Zaibei no
  sanjunen wa
  yume to nari — Sasabune

6. Thirty years
   in America
   just empty dreams

Tsuma wa izuko
  ko wa izuretomo
  shiranami no
    taiheiyo engan wa
      jigoku emaki — Hibutsu

7. Where is my wife
   where is my child
   white waves on the
     Pacific coast
   a picture of hell

Kondo wakare rya
  aware mo sumai
  nakoka tomodomo
    namida no tane ga
      tsukite kawaite
        nakenumade — Sasabune

8. If we part this time
   we might never meet again
   so shall we cry together?
   until the seeds of our tears
   dry away
   and we can cry no more

Hiroi sora da
  Nipponjin no
    homu ga nai — Sunada Toshu

Chu fuchu
  hito moshi kikaba
    nanto kotaen — Sunada Toshu

Saku no naka nu
  sunde torikau
    hitogokoro — Nikaido Gensui

Sekitan no
  yama mo kodomo mo
    asobi basho — Yamanaka Keiho

Umagoya mo
  sumeba miyako no
    kaze ga fuki — Hakujaku

Gaman shite
  gaman shite iru
    hifu no iro — Sanada Kikyo

Tatakai ni
  kentaiki ari
    wahei setsu — Katsuki Sukyo

Kangetsu o
  funde yakei no
    mawari kinu — Muin

Iminshi wa
  owareri akikaze
    mata samishi — Sanada Kikyo

9. With such a wide sky
   the Japanese
   have no home

10. Loyalty, disloyalty,
    if asked,
    what should I answer?

11. Birds,
    living in a cage,
    the human spirit

12. Even a mountain
    of coal becomes
    a children's playground

13. If you live in a
    horse stable
    the wind of cities
    blow through

14. Endure!
    We are enduring
    by the color of our skin

15. Weary
    of war,
    rumors of peace

16. While making rounds
    the night sentry
    steps on the Winter moon

17. Immigrant's story
    has ended, lonely again
    is the Autumn wind

HUGO BLACK AND FRANK MURPHY

Korematsu v. United States

December 18, 1944

The Supreme Court eventually sanctioned the policy of evacuation and relocation. In June 1943, in Hirabayashi v. *United States, the justices unanimously decided that a curfew order affecting only Japanese Americans did not violate their constitutional rights. In December 1944, in* Korematsu v. *United States, the Court sanctioned the order providing for the exclusion of Japanese Americans from the West Coast. But in this case the justices were sharply divided, as the opinions below demonstrate. Writing for the majority, Justice Hugo Black asserted that "Korematsu was not excluded from the Military Area because of hostility to him or his race." Three members of the Court — Robert Jackson, Owen Roberts, and Frank Murphy — filed dissents. Justice Murphy, who had reluctantly joined the majority in* Hirabayashi, *now explained why he thought the majority opinion amounted to a "legalization of racism." In a companion case,* ex parte Endo, *the Court ruled that although temporary detention was permissible, once a person's loyalty had been established, the government could not detain that person in a relocation center. The decision was handed down the day after the government revoked the relocation order.*

Mr. Justice Black delivered the opinion of the Court.

The petitioner, an American citizen of Japanese descent, was convicted in a federal district court for remaining in San Leandro, California, a "Military Area," contrary to Civilian Exclusion Order No. 34 of the Commanding General of the Western Command, U.S. Army, which directed that after May 9, 1942, all persons of Japanese ancestry should be excluded from that area. No question was raised as to petitioner's loyalty to the United States. The Circuit Court of Appeals affirmed, and the importance of the constitutional question involved caused us to grant certiorari.

It should be noted, to begin with, that all legal restrictions which curtail the civil rights of a single racial group are immediately suspect. That is not to say that all such restrictions are unconstitutional. It is to say that

---

Korematsu v. United States, 323 US 214 (1944).

courts must subject them to the most rigid scrutiny. Pressing public necessity may sometimes justify the existence of such restrictions; racial antagonism never can. . . .

Exclusion Order No. 34, which the petitioner knowingly and admittedly violated, was one of a number of military orders and proclamations, all of which were substantially based upon Executive Order No. 9066, 7 Fed. Reg. 1407. That order, issued after we were at war with Japan, declared that "the successful prosecution of the war requires every possible protection against espionage and against sabotage to national-defense material, national-defense premises, and national-defense utilities. . . ."

One of the series of orders and proclamations, a curfew order, which like the exclusion order here was promulgated pursuant to Executive Order 9066, subjected all persons of Japanese ancestry in prescribed West Coast military areas to remain in their residences from 8 p.m. to 6 a.m. As is the case with the exclusion order here, that prior curfew order was designed as a "protection against espionage and against sabotage." In *Hirabayashi v. United States,* 320 U.S. 81, we sustained a conviction obtained for violation of the curfew order. The Hirabayashi conviction and this one thus rest on the same 1942 Congressional Act and the same basic executive and military orders, all of which orders were aimed at the twin dangers of espionage and sabotage.

The 1942 Act was attacked in the *Hirabayashi* case as an unconstitutional delegation of power; it was contended that the curfew order and other orders on which it rested were beyond the war powers of the Congress, the military authorities and of the President, as Commander in Chief of the Army; and finally that to apply the curfew order against none but citizens of Japanese ancestry amounted to a constitutionally prohibited discrimination solely on account of race. To these questions, we gave the serious consideration which their importance justified. We upheld the curfew order as an exercise of the power of the government to take steps necessary to prevent espionage and sabotage in an area threatened by Japanese attack.

In the light of the principles we announced in the *Hirabayashi* case, we are unable to conclude that it was beyond the war power of Congress and the Executive to exclude those of Japanese ancestry from the West Coast war area at the time they did. True, exclusion from the area in which one's home is located is a far greater deprivation than constant confinement to the home from 8 p.m. to 6 a.m. Nothing short of apprehension by the proper military authorities of the gravest imminent danger to the public safety can constitutionally justify either. But exclusion from a threatened area, no less than curfew, has a definite and close relationship to the prevention of espionage and sabotage. The military authorities, charged with the primary responsibility of defending our shores, concluded that curfew provided inadequate protection and ordered exclusion. They did so, as pointed out in our *Hirabayashi* opinion, in accordance with Congressional authority to the military to say who should, and who should not, remain in the threatened areas.

In this case the petitioner challenges the assumptions upon which we rested our conclusions in the *Hirabayashi* case. He also urges that by May 1942, when Order No. 34 was promulgated, all danger of Japanese invasion of the West Coast had disappeared. After careful consideration of these contentions we are compelled to reject them.

Here, as in the *Hirabayashi* case, *supra,* at p. 99, ". . . we cannot reject as unfounded the judgment of the military authorities and of Congress that there were disloyal members of that population, whose number and strength could not be precisely and quickly ascertained. We cannot say that the war-making branches of the Government did not have ground for believing that in a critical hour such persons could not readily be isolated and separately dealt with, and constituted a menace to the national defense and safety, which demanded that prompt and adequate measures be taken to guard against it."

Like curfew, exclusion of those of Japanese origin was deemed necessary because of the presence of an unascertained number of disloyal members of the group, most of whom we have no doubt were loyal to this country. It was because we could not reject the finding of the military authorities that it was impossible to bring about an immediate segregation of the disloyal from the loyal that we sustained the validity of the curfew order as applying to the whole group. In the instant case, temporary exclusion of the entire group was rested by the military on the same ground. The judgment that exclusion of the whole group was for the same reason a military imperative answers the contention that the exclusion was in the nature of group punishment based on antagonism to those of Japanese origin. That there were members of the group who retained loyalties to Japan has been confirmed by investigations made subsequent to the exclusion. Approximately five thousand American citizens of Japanese ancestry refused to swear unqualified allegiance to the United States and to renounce allegiance to the Japanese Emperor, and several thousand evacuees requested repatriation to Japan.

We uphold the exclusion order as of the time it was made and when the petitioner violated it. . . . In doing so, we are not unmindful of the hardships imposed by it upon a large group of American citizens. . . . But hardships are part of war, and war is an aggregation of hardships. All citizens alike, both in and out of uniform, feel the impact of war in greater or lesser measure. Citizenship has its responsibilities as well as its privileges, and in time of war the burden is always heavier. Compulsory exclusion of large groups of citizens from their homes, except under circumstances of direst emergency and peril, is inconsistent with our basic governmental institutions. But when under conditions of modern warfare our shores are threatened by hostile forces, the power to protect must be commensurate with the threatened danger. . . .

It is said that we are dealing here with the case of imprisonment of a citizen in a concentration camp solely because of his ancestry, without evidence or inquiry concerning his loyalty and good disposition towards the United States. Our task would be simple, our duty clear, were this a case involving the imprisonment of a loyal citizen in a concentration camp because of racial prejudice. Regardless of the true nature of the assembly and relocation centers — and we deem it unjustifiable to call them concentration camps with all the ugly connotations that term implies — we are dealing specifically with nothing but an exclusion order. To cast this case into outlines of racial prejudice, without reference to the real military dangers which were presented, merely confuses the issue. Korematsu was not excluded from the Military Area because of hostility to him or his race. He *was* excluded because we are at war with the Japanese Empire, because the properly constituted military authorities feared an invasion of our West Coast and felt constrained to take proper security measures, because they decided that the military urgency of the situation demanded that all citizens of Japanese ancestry be segregated from the West Coast temporarily, and finally, because Congress, reposing its confidence in this time of war in our military leaders — as inevitably it must — determined that they should have the power to do just this. There was evidence of disloyalty on the part of some, the military authorities considered that the need for action was great, and time was short. We cannot — by availing ourselves of the calm perspective of hindsight — now say that at that time these actions were unjustified.

Affirmed.

Mr. Justice Murphy, dissenting.

This exclusion of "all persons of Japanese ancestry, both alien and non-alien," from the Pacific Coast area on a plea of military necessity in the absence of martial law ought not to be approved. Such exclusion goes over "the very brink of constitutional power" and falls into the ugly abyss of racism.

In dealing with matters relating to the prosecution and progress of a war, we must accord great respect and consideration to the judgments of the military authorities who are on the scene and who have full knowledge of the military facts. The scope of their discretion must, as a matter of necessity and common sense, be wide. And their judgments ought not to be overruled lightly by those whose training and duties ill-equip them to deal intelligently with matters so vital to the physical security of the nation.

At the same time, however, it is essential that there be definite limits to military discretion, especially where martial law has not been declared. Individuals must not be left impoverished of their constitutional rights on a plea of military necessity that has neither substance nor support. Thus, like other claims conflicting with the asserted constitutional rights of the individual, the military claim must subject itself to the judicial process of having its reasonableness determined and its conflicts with other interests reconciled. . . .

The judicial test of whether the Government, on a plea of military necessity, can validly deprive an individual of any of his constitutional rights is whether the deprivation is reasonably related to a public danger that is so "immediate, imminent, and impending" as not to admit of delay and not to permit the intervention of ordinary constitutional processes to alleviate the danger. . . . Civilian Exclusion Order No. 34, banishing from a prescribed area of the Pacific Coast "all persons of Japanese ancestry, both alien and non-alien," clearly does not meet that test. Being an obvious racial discrimination, the order deprives all those within its scope of the equal protection of the laws as guaranteed by the Fifth Amendment. It further deprives these individuals of their constitutional rights to live and work where they will, to establish a home where they choose and to move about freely. In excommunicating them without benefit of hearings, this order also deprives them of all their constitutional rights to procedural due process. Yet no reasonable relation to an "immediate, imminent, and impending" public danger is evident to support this racial restriction which is one of the most sweeping and complete deprivations of constitutional rights in the history of this nation in the absence of martial law.

It must be conceded that the military and naval situation in the spring of 1942 was such as to generate a very real fear of invasion of the Pacific Coast, accompanied by fears of sabotage and espionage in that area. The military command was therefore justified in adopting all reasonable means necessary to combat these dangers. In adjudging the military action taken in light of the then apparent dangers, we must not erect too high or too meticulous standards; it is necessary only that the action have some reasonable relation to the removal of the dangers of invasion, sabotage and espionage. But the exclusion, either temporarily or permanently, of all persons with Japanese blood in their veins has no such reasonable relation. And that relation is lacking because the exclusion order necessarily must rely for its reasonableness upon the assumption that *all* persons of Japanese ancestry may have a dangerous tendency to commit sabotage and espionage and to aid our Japanese enemy in other ways. It is difficult to believe that reason, logic or experience could be marshalled in support of such an assumption.

That this forced exclusion was the result in good measure of this erroneous assumption of racial guilt rather than bona fide military necessity is evidenced by the Commanding General's Final Report on the evacuation from the Pacific Coast area. In it he refers to all individuals of Japanese descent as "subversive," as belonging to "an enemy race" whose "racial strains are undiluted," and as constituting "over 112,000 potential enemies . . . at large today" along the Pacific Coast. In support of this blanket condemnation of all persons of Japanese descent, however, no reliable evidence is cited to show that such individuals were generally disloyal, or had generally so conducted themselves in this area as to constitute a special menace to defense installations or war industries, or had otherwise by their behavior furnished reasonable ground for their exclusion as a group.

Justification for the exclusion is sought, instead, mainly upon questionable racial and sociological grounds not ordinarily within the realm of expert military judgment, supplemented by certain semi-military conclusions drawn from an unwarranted use of circumstantial evidence. . . .

The main reasons relied upon by those responsible for the forced evacuation, therefore, do not prove a reasonable relation between the group characteristics of Japanese Americans and the dangers of invasion, sabotage and espionage. The reasons appear, instead, to be largely an accumulation of much of the misinformation, half-truths and insinuations that for years have been directed against Japanese Americans by people with racial and economic prejudices — the same people who have been among the foremost advocates of the evacuation. A military judgment based upon such racial and sociological considerations is not entitled to the great weight ordinarily given the judgments based upon strictly military considerations. Especially is this so when every charge relative to race, religion, culture, geographical location, and legal and economic status has been substantially discredited by independent studies made by experts in these matters.

The military necessity which is essential to the validity of the evacuation order thus resolves itself into a few intimations that certain individuals actively aided the enemy, from which it is inferred that the entire group of Japanese Americans could not be trusted to be or remain loyal to the United States. No one denies, of course, that there were some disloyal persons of Japanese descent on the Pacific Coast who did all in their power to aid their ancestral land. Similar disloyal activities have been engaged in by many persons of German, Italian and even more pioneer stock in our country. But to infer that examples of individual disloyalty prove group disloyalty and justify discriminatory action against the entire group is to deny that under our system of law individual guilt is the sole basis for deprivation of rights. Moreover, this inference, which is at the very heart of the evacuation orders, has been used in support of the abhorrent and despicable treatment of minority groups by the dictatorial tyrannies which this nation is now pledged to destroy. To give constitutional sanction to that inference in this case, however well-intentioned may have been the military command on the Pacific Coast, is to adopt one of the cruelest of the rationales used by our enemies to destroy the dignity of the individual and to encourage and open the door to discriminatory actions against other minority groups in the passions of tomorrow.

No adequate reason is given for the failure to treat these Japanese Americans on an individual basis by holding investigations and hearings to separate the loyal from the disloyal, as was done in the case of persons of German and Italian ancestry. See House Report No. 2124 (77th Cong., 2d Sess.) 247–52. It is asserted merely that the loyalties of this group "were unknown and time was of the essence." Yet nearly four months elapsed after Pearl Harbor before the first exclusion order was issued; nearly eight months went by until the last order was issued; and the last of these "subversive" persons was not actually removed until almost eleven months had elapsed. Leisure and deliberation seem to have been more of the essence than speed. And the fact that conditions were not such as to warrant a declaration of martial law adds strength to the belief that the factors of time and military necessity were not as urgent as they have been represented to be.

Moreover, there was no adequate proof that the Federal Bureau of Investigation and the military and naval intelligence services did not have the espionage and sabotage situation well in hand during this long period. Nor is there any denial of the fact that not one person of Japanese ancestry was accused or convicted of espionage or sabotage after Pearl Harbor while they were still free, a fact which is some evidence of the loyalty of the vast majority of these individuals and of the effectiveness of the established methods of combatting these evils. It seems incredible that under these circumstances it would have been impossible to hold loyalty hearings for the mere 112,000 persons involved — or at least for the 70,000 American citizens — especially when a large part of this number represented children and elderly men and women. Any inconvenience that may have accompanied an attempt to conform to procedural due process cannot be said to justify violations of constitutional rights of individuals.

I dissent, therefore, from this legalization of racism. Racial discrimination in any form and in any degree has no justifiable part whatever in our democratic way of life. It is unattractive in any setting but it is utterly revolting among a free people who have embraced the principles set forth in the Constitution of the United States. All residents of this nation are kin in some way by blood or culture to a foreign land. Yet they are primarily and necessarily a part of the new and distinct civilization of the United States. They must accordingly be treated at all times as the heirs of the American experiment and as entitled to all the rights and freedoms guaranteed by the Constitution.

PEARL S. BUCK AND A. LEONARD ALLEN

Debate about the Repeal of the Chinese Exclusion Acts
May 20, 1943

The importance attached to race was evident in the debate over the repeal of the Chinese Exclusion Acts. Passed in 1882 to bar the immigration of laborers, the acts were later amended to keep out "all persons of the Chinese race." But as sympathy for China, a wartime ally, steadily rose, so did sentiment for eliminating these highly discriminatory provisions. Their repeal, President Roosevelt said, would "silence the distorted Japanese propaganda." When congressional hearings were held in May 1943, the following exchange took place between Pearl S. Buck and Democratic congressman A. Leonard Allen of Louisiana. A renowned author, Buck had received the Pulitzer Prize for The Good Earth *(1931), a novel about Chi-*

House Committee on Immigration and Naturalization, *Repeal of the Chinese Exclusion Acts: Hearings before the Committee on Immigration and Naturalization,* 78th Cong., 1st sess., 1943, 68–78.

nese life, and had been awarded the Nobel Prize for literature in 1938. Her arguments failed to convince Allen, who feared that repeal would be the opening wedge in a broad drive for racial equality. In the fall of 1943, Congress repealed the exclusion acts and granted Chinese immigrants the right to become naturalized citizens. Yet the new law did not entirely repudiate the racist assumptions on which the older policy had rested. An annual admission quota of 105 was established for all "persons of the Chinese race" no matter where they were born, and the Chinese wives and children of American citizens were barred from entering the United States even though the relatives of other immigrants were permitted to enter on a nonquota basis.

Miss Buck: Mr. Chairman, I cannot go back quite as far as I wish I could, though I go back increasingly far each year. I can only say that four-fifths of my life — and I am now 50 years old — have been spent in China, and it is as an American who has had all those years in China that I must speak today, particularly on a matter of the importance of this repeal as a war measure.

I should just like to say this: Those many years in China have given me this advantage, I know the Chinese people, I know how they live. . . .

I could speak with some feeling, I can assure you, on the way the Chinese feel, as our allies in this war, when they are not allowed to enter our country on a quota, as is allowed to the peoples of Europe and Africa.

The Japanese have not failed to taunt them with the friendliness of our words and the unfriendliness of our deeds. The Chinese have heard this propaganda and while they have not heeded it much, it has nevertheless been true. As a war measure, it would simply be the wisest thing we could do to make it impossible for Japan to use this sort of propaganda any more, by making it untrue.

But I shall leave this aspect of the subject to others because I want to talk about that which I am best fitted to talk about from my own experience — what the effect of the Exclusion Act is from an American point of view.

I do this because I know that American boys are going to have to be in China, sooner or later, in large numbers. . . .

China is nearer to Japan than any other country except Russia. Russia has offered us no bases for attack upon Japan and China has offered us everything — you will remember that Generalissimo

Chiang Kai-shek cabled to President Roosevelt after Pearl Harbor, offering, as he said, "All we are and all we have." That offer, not yet accepted, will one day have to be accepted if Japan is to be attacked on the scale which we all expect. When that day comes, many Americans will be upon Chinese soil.

They will be welcome there, for in spite of very shabby treatment from us, the Chinese still feel friendly to us.

Our help to China has been very small indeed. I do not even count a few millions of dollars of relief money. Millions have been collected for other countries. Very little of our lend-lease promises to China have been fulfilled. The reason why the Chinese accept our little help without open complaint or even feeling is that they traditionally do not base friendship upon material gifts. They make every allowance for us, and continue to regard us as the people with whom they would rather be friends than anyone else.

What really hurts them is not this lack of material help which they can excuse because of the many demands on us, so much as our continued attitude toward them expressed in total exclusion acts which until this war broke out, made it actually harder for a Chinese to enter this country than a Japanese.

Now, unless these unjust total exclusion acts are repealed, it is going to be very hard for our men, when they go to China, to feel like friends and act like friends to Chinese. The wall of this injustice is going to rise higher and higher between our two peoples. Our men will be continually embarrassed by the Chinese questions. "Why," the Chinese will ask, "why are we altogether excluded from your country if you are our friends and our allies?"

"Oh," our men will have to say, "those are old laws, obsolete now, because conditions have altogether changed."

"Then," the Chinese questioners will ask, "if they are obsolete, if conditions have changed, why not repeal the laws?"

What will our men answer then? Do not imagine that Chinese don't know what the facts are. I tell you all Chinese know about the total exclusion of Chinese from our country. All Chinese know that they are allowed no quota. All Chinese know of the ugly and inexcusable humiliation which Chinese suffer even when they are coming in on a visitor's visa, or are citizens of this country coming home again.

The Chinese people know these things very well, and how do I know they know? Because I have been an American in China. Because I have myself suffered the sort of embarrassment I would have our men spared. Time after time I have cringed when the Chinese put questions to me and as an American I had no answer.

I have tried to explain that these exclusion acts were made at a time when Chinese themselves were being exploited by ruthless Americans who enticed them to this country in droves, combing the streets of over-crowded Chinese cities for cheap labor in American mines and on American railroads.

But I had to confess time and again, that these conditions existed no more. I had to confess that there was no reason at all for the total exclusion of Chinese from the United States. I had to confess that the Chinese we have here are among our best citizens — they do not go on relief; their crime record is very low; they are honest and industrious and friendly.

"Then why are we excluded?" This was always the next question. I parried it as best I could. I tried to laugh and say, "Why do you care? It would only be a hundred-odd who could go in. You have a great and beautiful country of your own."

"No," they said, that was not the point. "Whether one went in or a hundred was not the point." The Chinese wholly understood the need for restricted immigration. They did not want or expect to enter the United States in large numbers. Some day, in fact, China, too, might have restricted immigration when industry there had developed far enough to be an attraction to other peoples.

No, the point was this, that China's friendly feelings were hurt by the total exclusion which implied that Chinese were an inferior people to all others — to Mexicans, and to South Americans, to the peoples of Germany and Italy, and Spain, and all Europe.

Literate Chinese, great scholars, brilliant young men and women, famous Chinese citizens, were all held inferior to the most illiterate peasant of Europe so long as the total exclusion of Chinese was continued.

How could I answer this? It was true. We have excluded not only Chinese coolies; we have excluded Chinese of the highest quality and attainment by our total exclusion laws. It is the injustice of the total exclusion that hurts the Chinese, the humiliation it puts upon them as a people, and now as our ally, and this hurt is what is difficult for the American in China to bear. He is ashamed of being unable, as an American, to meet this accusation of injustice.

It is more than injustice. It is a denial of our democratic ideals, and this makes the American on Chinese soil ashamed. And being ashamed, he is angry at having to bear upon himself and in himself the effects of the injustice and the lack of democracy of his nation. There is a wall between him and the kindly Chinese people. He knows that they are right and he is wrong, and that is hard to bear.

I do most earnestly hope, therefore, that as a war measure, if for nothing else, the exclusion acts against the Chinese may now be repealed and that China may be put on a quota basis, on an equality with other nations, in order that when our men go to China, as they will inevitably go, that they will not have to endure the stigma and the shame of carrying with them the burden of their country's injustice toward our ally China.

If this burden is not removed and wrong made right before they go, the enemy Japanese will renew their strong propaganda on this very point, and will taunt the Chinese more than ever with the fact that they are still totally excluded from our country and so are held in a lower position than any of our other allies. . . .

Mr. Allen: Miss Buck, I was greatly interested in your statement in chief this morning.

In considering a question like this, the members of this committee and the Congress have to try to consider the thing that will grow out from this ultimately. We have to look at it in the broadest aspect and see what the probabilities would be in the future, and that brings up the question of dealing with the Oriental question as a whole.

In other words, it is not quite so simple as dealing with the Chinese alone. We all feel very kindly toward the Chinese; I do myself and so far as bringing in a hundred Chinese, if that were the end of it and if it never got beyond that, no one would seriously object.

We feel that we should do everything we can to help the Chinese; they are a great people.

Now, there are two serious phases of this, to me. One is the question of breaking down our policy which we have had in this country for more than 60 years, and it is a very serious question.

And the other question is whether or not it is best to bring this up and air it at this time.

Frankly, I have felt that it was a bad thing to do at this time because it brings a reflection of opinion pro and con, and it gets into the newspapers, it gets back to Japan, it gets back to China, and I say to you very frankly I am afraid that no good will come of that.

I hope that you will believe that I am sincere in that.

Now, the other question is the question of policy of our country dealing with these Orientals.

Do you feel that we should take this step with reference to the Chinese and not with other Orientals?

Miss Buck: Is that the question?

Mr. Allen: That is one question.

Miss Buck: I think that if I understand what we are talking about today, it is the repeal of those laws which discriminate against the Chinese, not against other Oriental peoples. There are 14 laws which mention the Chinese by name and put the Chinese in a position inferior to other Oriental peoples, and it is those laws I think I was told we were discussing today; so I should think it would be better to put our Allies on equal basis with the Japanese and the Hindus and the other Oriental people.

That was the first question.

The second question is, is it a good time now?

Unfortunately our enemies have already aired this question, Mr. Allen. If we could have kept it quiet, if we could have sat on the lid, you know; in fact, many Americans have wanted to bring it up before now, and I personally have been in the position of sitting on that lid until I found how thoroughly the lid was off the shoe, until I found how it is being aired from the enemy point of view.

I have put the question to the Chinese, "Suppose the thing is turned down and it is aired unfavorably, would it not be very bad?"

And they have said, "Since the thing is discussed completely unfavorably over most of the world anyway, it is better to have it out, and for our own sakes, we would like to know where we are with the American people."

So it was when the Chinese said that they, themselves, would welcome it being brought up, though unfavorably acted upon, that I finally consented to come here today.

Mr. Allen: Well, I appreciate your sincerity on this question; I give you credit for that.

Now, I would like to know the frame of your mind with respect to the broader aspect, and we members here, Miss Buck, must face that.

In other words, we cannot take this step and expect it to stop there. Further demands will come. We are obliged to look at the broader aspect.

In other words, this committee, in the past, has been confronted with bills to grant citizenship to Hindus and Koreans, and perhaps others, and we have consistently said no.

Now, I think I am warranted in saying that other groups are watching this and if this passes, then before this very session is over, we are going to be confronted with the same demand for the 400,000,000 Hindus or Indians, or whatever you please to call them, and other groups.

Now, what would you do with these?

Miss Buck: Well, my frame of mind on that is that if this Immigration Committee wishes to pass those bills and allow those people to come in, I would feel it was all right.

Mr. Allen: You would feel that they should be granted the same?

Miss Buck: If you wanted to, but that is not what I am here for today. It is up to you.

Mr. Allen: I know, my dear lady, but you are giving an expression of your opinion, are you not? I understood that you are giving an expression of your opinion, based upon your experience. Now I simply want your opinion also with reference to the other things.

Miss Buck: Well, I have been in China a long time. I have never lived in India or Korea. I think I would leave it up to this committee, really.

Mr. Allen: You would?

Miss Buck: Yes.

Mr. Allen: That is what we would all like to do, leave it up to the committee.

Miss Buck: That is what you think your Government is for, really.

Mr. Allen: Miss Buck. Let me ask you this further question to ascertain the frame of your mind in testifying on this great question — and it is a great question — let me ask you if it is not a fact that you believe in full social equality among all the races?

Miss Buck: Are you asking me that?

Mr. Allen: Yes, I am asking you that.

Miss Buck: Well, I tell you, I do not think that is very important now, because this is wartime, and this is a war measure. I do not think social equality has one thing to do, at this moment, with war.

I think repeal of these acts has a lot to do with war measures.

Mr. Allen: I ask you again, Miss Buck, if you would not be so kind as to tell me what your opinion is along that line, and if it is not a fact that you do believe in social equality among all the races.

Miss Buck: What do you mean by social equality, exactly?

Mr. Allen: Well, I think I have heard the gentlelady over the radio, and I think I have read some of the things that she has written with reference to the status of colored people in the United States, and especially in the South, in which I understood her philosophy to be that she believed that there ought to be full and complete social equality among Negroes and whites, and all other groups.

Miss Buck: Well, I tell you, I thought the Negro immigration question was finished.

Did we not pass a law in 1870 allowing colored people to come in from Africa?

Mr. Allen: I am not asking you about the question of immigration; I am asking you about social equality among races.

Miss Buck: I do not think that that has anything to do with the meeting today.

Mr. Allen: You do not want to answer that, Miss Buck?

Miss Buck: Yes. Let us talk about it afterward, shall we?

Mr. Allen: I want it in the record.

Mr. Gossett: I do not like to take up all the time debating whether social equality is good, bad, or indifferent. I think it is immaterial before this committee. If Mr. Allen is going to ask every witness whether they believe in social equality, that is injecting a lot of foreign material.

Mr. Allen: I do not think my good friend from Texas could convince his friends down in Texas that the question of social equality is immaterial.

Mr. Gossett: But that does not have anything to do with the bill.

ROBERT JACKSON AND FELIX FRANKFURTER

West Virginia State Board of Education v. Barnette
June 14, 1943

A notable victory for individual freedom in time of war came in a set of cases involving the Jehovah's Witnesses, a religious group whose adherents refused to salute the American flag because of the biblical injunction not to "bow down thyself" before any "graven image." Since public schools in eighteen states required the flag salute, the children of Jehovah's Witnesses were placed in a difficult position: To salute the flag would violate their consciences, but not to do so would result in their expulsion from school. In 1940, in the Gobitis *decision, the Supreme Court ruled by an 8–1 margin that a compulsory flag salute did not violate the First Amendment's free exercise of religion clause. Speaking for the majority, Justice Felix Frankfurter asserted that "national unity is the basis of national security." In the years that followed, however, a number of justices changed their minds, and two new Court appointees, one of them Robert Jackson, also thought* Gobitis *had been wrongly decided. In this decision,* West Virginia State Board

---

West Virginia State Board of Education v. Barnette, 319 US 614 (1943).

of Education v. Barnette, *the Court reversed itself by a 6–3 vote. In Jackson's striking language, "compulsory unification of opinion achieves only the unanimity of the graveyard." The dissent by Justice Frankfurter reflects his anger at the repudiation of his position in* Gobitis *as well as his belief that the justices should refrain from writing their "private notions of policy into the Constitution."*

Mr. Justice Jackson delivered the opinion of the Court.

Following the decision by this Court on June 3, 1940, in *Minersville School District v. Gobitis,* 310 U.S. 586, the West Virginia legislature amended its statutes to require all schools therein to conduct courses of instruction in history, civics, and in the Constitutions of the United States and of the State "for the purpose of teaching, fostering and perpetuating the ideals, principles and spirit of Americanism, and increasing the knowledge of the organization and machinery of the government." . . .

The Board of Education on January 9, 1942, adopted a resolution containing recitals taken largely from the Court's *Gobitis* opinion and ordering that the salute to the flag become "a regular part of the program of activities in the public schools," that all teachers and pupils "shall be required to participate in the salute honoring the Nation represented by the Flag; provided, however, that refusal to salute the Flag be regarded as an act of insubordination, and shall be dealt with accordingly."

The resolution originally required the "commonly accepted salute to the Flag" which it defined. Objections to the salute as "being too much like Hitler's" were raised by the Parent and Teachers Association, the Boy and Girl Scouts, the Red Cross, and the Federation of Women's Clubs. Some modification appears to have been made in deference to these objections, but no concession was made to Jehovah's Witnesses. What is now required is the "stiff-arm" salute, the saluter to keep the right hand raised with palm turned up while the following is repeated: "I pledge allegiance to the Flag of the United States of America and to the Republic for which it stands; one Nation, indivisible, with liberty and and justice for all."

Failure to conform is "insubordination" dealt with by expulsion. Readmission is denied by statute until compliance. Meanwhile the expelled child is "unlawfully absent" and may be proceeded against as a delinquent. His parents or guardians are liable to prosecution, and if convicted are subject to fine not exceeding $50 and jail term not exceeding thirty days.

Appellees, citizens of the United States and of West Virginia, brought suit in the United States District Court for themselves and others similarly situated asking its injunction to restrain enforcement of these laws and regulations against Jehovah's Witnesses. The Witnesses are an unincorporated body teaching that the obligation imposed by law of God is superior to that of laws enacted by temporal government. Their religious beliefs include a literal version of Exodus, Chapter 20, verses 4 and 5, which says: "Thou shalt not make unto thee any graven image, or any likeness of anything that is in heaven above, or that is in the earth beneath, or that is in the water under the earth; thou shalt not bow down thyself to them nor serve them." They consider that the flag is an "image" within this command. For this reason they refuse to salute it.

Children of this faith have been expelled from school and are threatened with exclusion for no other cause. Officials threaten to send them to reformatories maintained for criminally inclined juveniles. Parents of such children have been prosecuted and are threatened with prosecutions for causing delinquency. . . .

This case calls upon us to reconsider a precedent decision, as the Court throughout its history often has been required to do. Before turning to the *Gobitis* case, however, it is desirable to notice certain characteristics by which this controversy is distinguished.

The freedom asserted by these respondents does not bring them into collision with rights asserted by any other individual. It is such conflicts which most frequently require intervention of the State to determine where the rights of one end and those of another begin. But the refusal of these persons to participate in the ceremony does not interfere with or deny rights of others to do so. Nor is there any question in this case that their behavior is peaceable and orderly. The sole conflict is between authority and rights of the individual. The State asserts power to condition access to public education on making a prescribed sign and profession and at the same time to coerce attendance by punishing both parent and child. The latter stand on a right of self-determination in matters that touch individual opinion and personal attitude.

As the present Chief Justice said in dissent in the *Gobitis* case, the State may "require teaching by instruction and study of all in our history and in the structure and organization of our government, including the guaranties of civil liberty, which tend to inspire patriotism and love of country." 310 U.S. at 604. Here, however, we are dealing with a compulsion of students to declare a belief. They are not merely made acquainted with the flag salute so that they may be informed as to what it is or even what it means. The issue here is whether this slow and easily neglected route to aroused loyalties constitutionally may be shortcut by substituting a compulsory salute and slogan. . . .

It is also to be noted that the compulsory flag salute and pledge requires affirmation of a belief and an attitude of mind. It is not clear whether the regulation contemplates that pupils forego any contrary convictions of their own and become unwilling converts to the prescribed ceremony or whether it will be acceptable if they simulate assent by words without belief and by a gesture barren of meaning. It is now a commonplace that censorship or suppression of expression of opinion is tolerated by our Constitution only when the expression presents a clear and present danger of action of a kind the State is empowered to prevent and punish. It would seem that involuntary affirmation could be commanded only on even more immediate and urgent grounds than silence. But here the power of compulsion is invoked without any allegation that remaining passive during a flag salute ritual creates a clear and present danger that would justify an effort even to muffle expression. To sustain the compulsory flag salute we are required to say that a Bill of Rights which guards the individual's right to speak his own mind, left it open to public authorities to compel him to utter what is not in his mind. . . .

Government of limited power need not be anemic government. Assurance that rights are secure tends to diminish fear and jealousy of strong government, and by making us feel safe to live under it makes for its better support. Without promise of a limiting Bill of Rights it is doubtful if our Constitution could have mustered enough strength to enable its ratification. To enforce those rights today is not to choose weak government over strong government. It is only to adhere as a means of strength to individual freedom of mind in preference to officially disciplined uniformity for which history indicates a disappointing and disastrous end.

The subject now before us exemplifies this principle. Free public education, if faithful to the ideal of secular instruction and political neutrality, will not be partisan or enemy of any class, creed, party, or faction. If it is to impose any ideological discipline, however, each party or denomination must seek to control, or failing that, to weaken the influence of the educational system. Observance of the limitations of the Constitution will not weaken government in the field appropriate for its exercise. . . .

The very purpose of a Bill of Rights was to withdraw certain subjects from the vicissitudes of political controversy, to place them beyond the reach of majorities and officials and to establish them as legal principles to be applied by the courts. One's right to life, liberty, and property, to free speech, a free press, freedom of worship and assembly, and other fundamental rights may not be submitted to vote; they depend on the outcome of no elections. . . .

National unity as an end which officials may foster by persuasion and example is not in question. The problem is whether under our Constitution compulsion as here employed is a permissible means for its achievement.

Struggles to coerce uniformity of sentiment in support of some end thought essential to their time and country have been waged by many good as well as by evil men. Nationalism is a relatively recent phenomenon but at other times and places the ends have been racial or territorial security, support of a dynasty or regime, and particular plans for saving souls. As first and moderate methods to attain unity have failed, those bent on its accomplishment must resort to an ever-increasing severity. As governmental pressure toward unity becomes greater, so strife becomes more bitter as to whose unity it shall be. Probably no deeper division of our people could proceed from any provocation than from finding it necessary to choose what doctrine and whose program public educational officials shall compel youth to unite in embracing. Ultimate futility of such attempts to compel coherence is the lesson of every such effort from the Roman drive to stamp out Christianity as a disturber of its pagan unity, the Inquisition, as a means to religious and dynastic unity, the Siberian exiles as a means to Russian unity, down to the fast failing efforts of our present totalitarian enemies. Those who begin coercive elimination of dissent soon find themselves exterminating dissenters. Compulsory unification of opinion achieves only the unanimity of the graveyard.

It seems trite but necessary to say that the First Amendment to our Constitution was designed to avoid these ends by avoiding these beginnings. There is no mysticism in the American concept of the State or of the nature or origin of its authority. We set up government by consent of the governed, and the Bill of Rights denies those in power any legal opportunity to coerce that consent. Authority here is to be controlled by public opinion, not public opinion by authority.

The case is made difficult not because the principles of its decision are obscure but because the flag involved is our own. Nevertheless, we apply the limitations of the Constitution with no fear that freedom to be intellectually and spiritually diverse or even contrary will disintegrate the social organization. To believe that patriotism will not flourish if patriotic ceremonies are voluntary and spontaneous instead of a compulsory routine is to make an unflattering estimate of the appeal of our institutions to free minds. We can have intellectual individualism and the rich cultural diversities that we owe to exceptional minds only at the price of occasional eccentricity and abnormal attitudes. When they are so harmless to others or to the State as those we deal with here, the price is not too great. But freedom to differ is not limited to things that do not matter much. That would be a mere shadow of freedom. The test of its substance is the right to differ as to things that touch the heart of the existing order.

If there is any fixed star in our constitutional constellation, it is that no official, high or petty, can prescribe what shall be orthodox in politics, nationalism, religion, or other matters of opinion or force citizens to confess by word or act their faith therein. If there are any circumstances which permit an exception, they do not now occur to us.

We think the action of the local authorities in compelling the flag salute and pledge transcends constitutional limitations on their power and invades the sphere of intellect and spirit which it is the purpose of the First Amendment to our Constitution to reserve from all official control.

The decision of this Court in *Minersville School District v. Gobitis* and the holdings of those few *per curiam* decisions which preceded and foreshadowed it are overruled, and the judgment enjoining enforcement of the West Virginia Regulation is

Affirmed.

Mr. Justice Frankfurter, dissenting.

One who belongs to the most vilified and persecuted minority in history is not likely to be insensible to the freedoms guaranteed by our Constitution. Were my purely personal attitude relevant I should wholeheartedly associate myself with the general libertarian views in the Court's opinion, representing as they do the thought and action of a lifetime. But as judges we are neither Jew nor Gentile, neither Catholic nor agnostic. We owe equal attachment to the Constitution and are equally bound by our judicial obligations whether we derive our citizenship from the earliest or the latest immigrants to these shores. As a member of this Court I am not justified in writing my private notions of policy into the Constitution, no matter how deeply I may cherish them or how mischievous I may deem their disregard. The duty of a judge who must decide which of two claims before the Court shall prevail, that of a State to enact and enforce laws within its general competence or that of an individual to refuse obedience because of the demands of his conscience, is not that of the ordinary person. It can never be emphasized too much that one's own opinion about the wisdom or evil of a law should be excluded altogether when one is doing one's duty on the bench. The only opinion of our own even looking in that direction that is material is our opinion whether legislators could in reason have enacted such a law. In the light of all the circumstances, including the history of this question in this Court, it would require more daring than I possess to deny that reasonable legislators could have taken the action which is before us for review. Most unwillingly, therefore, I must differ from my brethren with regard to legislation like this. I cannot bring my mind to believe that the "liberty" secured by the Due Process Clause gives this Court authority to deny to the State of West Virginia the attainment of that which we all recognize as a legitimate legislative end, namely, the promotion of good citizenship, by employment of the means here chosen. . . .

Under our constitutional system the legislature is charged solely with civil concerns of society. If the avowed or intrinsic legislative purpose is either to promote or to discourage some religious community or creed, it is clearly within the constitutional restrictions imposed on legislatures and cannot stand. But it by no means follows that legislative power is wanting whenever a general non-discriminatory civil regulation in fact touches conscientious scruples or religious beliefs of an individual or a group. Regard for such scruples or beliefs undoubtedly presents one of the most reasonable claims for the exertion of legislative accommodation. It is, of course, beyond our power to rewrite the State's requirement, by providing exemptions for those who do not wish to participate in the flag salute or by making some other accommodations to meet their scruples. That wisdom might suggest the making of such accommodations and that school administration would not find it too difficult to make them and yet maintain the ceremony for those not refusing to conform, is outside our province to suggest. Tact, respect, and generosity toward variant views will always commend themselves to those charged with the duties of legislation so as to achieve a maximum of good will and to require a minimum of unwilling submission to a general law. But the real question is, who is to make such accommodations, the courts or the legislature? . . .

We are told that a flag salute is a doubtful substitute for adequate understanding of our institutions. The states that require such a school exercise do not have to justify it as the only means for promoting good citizenship in children, but merely as one of diverse means for accomplishing a worthy end. We may deem it a foolish measure, but the point is that this Court is not the organ of government to resolve doubts as to whether it will fulfil its purpose. Only if there be no doubt that any reasonable mind could entertain can we deny to the states the right to resolve doubts their way and not ours.

That which to the majority may seem essential for the welfare of the state may offend the consciences of a minority. But, so long as no inroads are made upon the actual exercise of religion by the minority, to deny the political power of the majority to enact laws concerned with civil matters, simply because they may offend the consciences of a minority, really means that the consciences of a minority are more sacred and more enshrined in the Constitution than the consciences of a majority. . . .

Of course patriotism cannot be enforced by the flag salute. But neither can the liberal spirit be enforced by judicial invalidation of illiberal legislation. Our constant preoccupation with the constitutionality of legislation rather than with its wisdom tends to preoccupation of the American mind with a false value. The tendency of focussing attention on constitutionality is to make constitutionality synonymous with wisdom, to regard a law as all right if it is constitutional. Such an attitude is a great enemy of liberalism. Particularly in legislation affecting freedom of thought and freedom of speech much which should offend a free-spirited society is constitutional. Reliance for the most precious interests of civilization, therefore, must be found outside of their vindication in courts of law. Only a persistent positive translation of the faith of a free society into the convictions and habits and actions of a community is the ultimate reliance against unabated temptations to fetter the human spirit.

RANDOLPH PAUL

Report to the Secretary [of the Treasury] on the Acquiescence of This Government in the Murder of the Jews

January 13, 1944

In the summer of 1942, American officials learned of the Nazi program to exterminate European Jews, but beyond issuing a statement asserting that those who perpetrated war crimes would face retribution after the Allied victory, the Roosevelt administration did nothing to rescue victims of the Holocaust. By the end of 1943, Jewish groups had become highly critical of the State Department's dilatory response to the crisis, and so had officials in the Treasury Department. This memorandum was prepared for Secretary of the Treasury Henry Morgenthau by an aide, Randolph Paul. It bluntly states the case for shifting the responsibility for rescue plans from the State Department to a more sympathetic agency. When Morgenthau met with FDR on January 16, 1944, he took along a summary of Paul's memorandum, which concluded, "The matter of rescuing the Jews from extermination is a trust too great to remain in the hands of men who are indifferent, callous, and perhaps even hostile." On January 22, less than a week later, FDR created the War Refugee Board.

One of the greatest crimes in history, the slaughter of the Jewish people in Europe, is continuing unabated.

This Government has for a long time maintained that its policy is to work out programs to save those Jews of Europe who could be saved.

I am convinced on the basis of the information which is available to me that certain officials in our State Department, which is charged with carrying out this policy, have been guilty not only of gross procrastination and wilful failure to act, but even of wilful attempts to prevent action from being taken to rescue Jews from Hitler.

I fully recognize the graveness of this statement and I make it only after having most carefully weighed the shocking facts which have come to my attention during the last several months.

Henry Morgenthau Diaries, Franklin D. Roosevelt Library.

Unless remedial steps of a drastic nature are taken, and taken immediately, I am certain that no effective action will be taken by this Government to prevent the complete extermination of the Jews in German controlled Europe, and that this Government will have to share for all time responsibility for this extermination.

The tragic history of this Government's handling of this matter reveals that certain State Department officials are guilty of the following:

(1) They have not only failed to use the Governmental machinery at their disposal to rescue Jews from Hitler, but have even gone so far as to use this Government machinery to prevent the rescue of these Jews.

(2) They have not only failed to cooperate with private organizations in the efforts of these organizations to work out individual programs of their own, but have taken steps designed to prevent these programs from being put into effect.

(3) They not only have failed to facilitate the obtaining of information concerning Hitler's plans to exterminate the Jews of Europe but in their official capacity have gone so far as to surreptitiously attempt to stop the obtaining of information concerning the murder of the Jewish population of Europe.

(4) They have tried to cover up their guilt by:
    (a) concealing and misrepresentation;
    (b) the giving of false and misleading explanations for their failures to act and their attempts to prevent action; and
    (c) the issuance of false and misleading statements concerning the "action" which they have taken to date.

Although only part of the facts relating to the activities of the State Department in this field are available to us, sufficient facts have come to my attention from various sources during the last several months to fully support the conclusions at which I have arrived. . . .

JOHN W. PEHLE AND JOHN J. McCLOY

Debate about the Bombing of Auschwitz
July–November 1944

The War Refugee Board (WRB) arranged to remove some Jews from Axis territory, to find safe havens for them, and to send shipments of food and other supplies to concentration camp inmates. In all, according to historian David Wyman, the WRB helped to save approximately two hundred thousand Jews. In the summer of 1944, WRB director John H. Pehle urged the War Department to consider bombing the gas chambers, crematoriums, and railroad lines at Auschwitz. American planes were then flying bombing missions within a few miles of the concentration camp. As the following exchange of letters shows, Assistant Secretary of War John J. McCloy rejected the proposal. In November, after receiving a horrifying report from two escapees, Pehle made a more urgent plea, pointing out that there were also industrial sites at Auschwitz, so bombing would be of decided military advantage. Once again, McCloy rejected the suggestion. In late November, the Nazis began dismantling the gas chambers at Auschwitz. The camp was liberated by the Russian army on January 27, 1945.

PEHLE TO McCLOY, JUNE 29, 1944

In connection with my recent conversation with you, I am attaching a copy of a cable just received from our representative in Bern, Switzerland. I wish to direct your attention particularly to the paragraphs concerning the railway lines being used for the deportation of Jews from Hungary to Poland and the proposal of various agencies that vital sections of these lines be bombed.

McCLOY TO PEHLE, JULY 4, 1944

The War Department is of the opinion that the suggested air operation is impracticable. It could be executed only by the diversion of considerable air support essential to the success of our forces now engaged in decisive operations and would in any case be of such very doubtful efficacy that it would not amount to a practical project.

War Refugee Board Records, Franklin D. Roosevelt Library.

The War Department fully appreciates the humanitarian motives which prompted the suggested operation but for the reasons stated above the operation suggested does not appear justified.

PEHLE TO McCLOY, NOVEMBER 8, 1944

I send you herewith copies of two eye-witness descriptions of the notorious German concentration and extermination camps of Auschwitz and Birkenau in Upper Silesia, which have just been received from the Board's Special Representative in Bern, Switzerland, Roswell McClelland, whom we have borrowed from the American Friends Service Committee. No report of Nazi atrocities received by the Board has quite caught the gruesome brutality of what is taking place in these camps of horror as have these sober, factual accounts of conditions in Auschwitz and Birkenau. I earnestly hope that you will read these reports.

The destruction of large numbers of people apparently is not a simple process. The Germans have been forced to devote considerable technological ingenuity and administrative know-how in order to carry out murder on a mass production basis, as the attached reports will testify. If the elaborate murder installations at Birkenau were destroyed, it seems clear that the Germans could not reconstruct them for some time.

Until now, despite pressure from many sources, I have been hesitant to urge the destruction of these camps by direct, military action. But I am convinced that the point has now been reached where such action is justifiable if it is deemed feasible by competent military authorities. I strongly recommend that the War Department give serious consideration to the possibility of destroying the execution chambers and crematories in Birkenau through direct bombing action. It may be observed that there would be other advantages of a military nature to such an attack. The Krupp and Siemens factories, where among other things cases for hand grenades are made, and a Buna plant [synthetic rubber], all within Auschwitz, would be destroyed. The destruction of the German barracks and guardhouses and the killing of German soldiers in the area would also be accomplished. The morale of underground groups might be considerably strengthened by such a dramatic exhibition of Allied air support and a number of the people confined in Auschwitz and Birkenau might be liberated in the confusion resulting from the bombing. That the effecting of a prison break by such methods is not without precedent is indicated by the description in the enclosed copy of a recent *New York Times* article of the liberation from Amiens prison of 100 French patriots by the RAF.

Obviously, the War Refugee Board is in no position to determine whether the foregoing proposal is feasible from a military standpoint.

Nevertheless in view of the urgency of the situation, we feel justified in making the suggestion. I would appreciate having the views of the War Department as soon as possible.

McCLOY TO PEHLE, NOVEMBER 18, 1944

I refer to your letter of November 8th, in which you forwarded the report of two eye-witnesses on the notorious German concentration and extermination camps of Auschwitz and Birkenau in Upper Silesia.

The Operations Staff of the War Department has given careful consideration to your suggestion that the bombing of these camps be undertaken. In consideration of this proposal the following points were brought out:

a. Positive destruction of these camps would necessitate precision bombing, employing heavy or medium bombardment, or attack by low flying or dive bombing aircraft, preferably the latter.

b. The target is beyond the maximum range of medium bombardment, dive bombers and fighter bombers located in United Kingdom, France, or Italy.

c. Use of heavy bombardment from United Kingdom bases would necessitate a hazardous round trip flight unescorted of approximately 2000 miles over enemy territory.

d. At the present critical stage of the war in Europe, our strategic air forces are engaged in the destruction of industrial target systems vital to the dwindling war potential of the enemy, from which they should not be diverted. The positive solution to this problem is the earliest possible victory over Germany, to which end we should exert our entire means.

This case does not at all parallel the Amiens mission because of the location of the concentration and extermination camps and the resulting difficulties encountered in attempting to carry out the proposed bombing.

Based on the above, as well as the most uncertain, if not dangerous effect such a bombing would have on the object to be attained, the War Department has felt that it should not, at least for the present, undertake these operations.

I know that you have been reluctant to press this activity on the War Department. We have been pressed strongly from other quarters, however, and have taken the best military opinion on its feasibility, and we believe the above conclusion is a sound one.

ELEANOR ROOSEVELT

Race, Religion, and Prejudice
May 11, 1942

World War II dramatically transformed American liberalism and, eventually, the agenda of American politics. The war, Alan Brinkley has maintained, "was a critical moment . . . in the movement of liberals toward a commitment to racial justice." No one voiced that commitment or defined its nature, extent, and limitations more clearly than Eleanor Roosevelt, whose outspoken belief in equality had, over the years, earned her great admiration in the African American community. Calling for legal, political, and economic equality for African Americans in this article in The New Republic, *a leading liberal periodical, she argued that all forms of discrimination were incompatible with the antitotalitarian character of the war. At the same time, she counseled the need for gradualism, or, as she put it, "tact and patience," an outlook that would characterize the liberal approach to eliminating segregated schools and other areas of American life for two decades after the war.*

. . . One of the phases of this war that we have to face is the question of race discrimination.

We have had a definite policy toward the Chinese and Japanese who wished to enter our country for many years, and I doubt very much if after this war is over we can differentiate between the peoples of Europe, the Near East and the Far East.

Perhaps the simplest way of facing the problem in the future is to say that we are fighting for freedom, and one of the freedoms we must establish is freedom from discrimination among the peoples of the world, either because of race, or of color, or of religion.

The people of the world have suddenly begun to stir and they seem to feel that in the future we should look upon each other as fellow human beings, judged by our acts, by our abilities, by our development, and not by any less fundamental differences.

Here in our own country we have any number of attitudes which have become habits and which constitute our approach to the Jewish people,

Eleanor Roosevelt, "Race, Religion, and Prejudice," *The New Republic,* May 11, 1942, 630.

the Japanese and Chinese people, the Italian people, and above all, to the Negro people in our midst.

Perhaps because the Negroes are our largest minority, our attitude towards them will have to be faced first of all. I keep on repeating that the way to face this situation is by being completely realistic. We cannot force people to accept friends for whom they have no liking, but living in a democracy it is entirely reasonable to demand that every citizen of that democracy enjoy the fundamental rights of a citizen.

Over and over again, I have stressed the rights of every citizen:

Equality before the law.
Equality of education.
Equality to hold a job according to his ability.
Equality of participation through the ballot in the government.

These are inherent rights in a democracy, and I do not see how we can fight this war and deny these rights to any citizen in our own land.

The other relationships will gradually settle themselves once these major things are part of our accepted philosophy.

It seems trite to say to the Negro, you must have patience, when he has had patience so long; you must not expect miracles overnight, when he can look back to the years of slavery and say — how many nights! he has waited for justice. Nevertheless, it is what we must continue to say in the interests of our government as a whole and of the Negro people; but that does not mean that we must sit idle and do nothing. We must keep moving forward steadily, removing restrictions which have no sense, and fighting prejudice. If we are wise we will do this where it is easiest to do it first, and watch it spread gradually to places where the old prejudices are slow to disappear.

There is now a great group of educated Negroes who can become leaders among their people, who can teach them the value of things of the mind and who qualify as the best in any field of endeavor. With these men and women it is impossible to think of any barriers of inferiority, but differences there are and always will be, and that is why on both sides there must be tact and patience and an effort at real understanding. Above everything else, no action must be taken which can cause so much bitterness that the whole liberalizing effort may be set back over a period of many years.

FRANKLIN D. ROOSEVELT

An Economic Bill of Rights

January 11, 1944

In this 1944 State of the Union message, Franklin D. Roosevelt spoke of overcoming distinctions based on race or creed. But FDR was chiefly concerned with an "Economic Bill of Rights"—that is, with proposals for an expanded welfare state. Drawing on a report submitted to him earlier by the National Resources Planning Board, titled Security, Work, and Relief Policies, *the president emphasized the importance of education, health care, and housing. Individual liberty required not only protection from government, he asserted, but also protection by government. According to biographer James MacGregor Burns, FDR overcame the false dichotomy between liberty and security, between freedom and equality: "Now Roosevelt was asserting that individual political liberty and collective welfare were not only compatible, but they were mutually fortifying." The president considered his proposals so vital that he repeated his address as a fireside chat that same evening.*

It is our duty now to begin to lay the plans and determine the strategy for the winning of a lasting peace and the establishment of an American standard of living higher than ever before known. We cannot be content, no matter how high that general standard of living may be, if some fraction of our people — whether it be one-third or one-fifth or one-tenth — is ill-fed, ill-clothed, ill-housed, and insecure.

This Republic had its beginning, and grew to its present strength, under the protection of certain inalienable political rights — among them the right of free speech, free press, free worship, trial by jury, freedom from unreasonable searches and seizures. They are our rights to life and liberty.

As our Nation has grown in size and stature, however — as our industrial economy expanded — these political rights proved inadequate to assure us equality in the pursuit of happiness.

Samual I. Rosenman, ed., *The Public Papers and Addresses of Franklin D. Roosevelt* (New York: Harper and Bros., 1950), 13:40–42.

We have come to a clear realization of the fact that true individual freedom cannot exist without economic security and independence. "Necessitous men are not free men." People who are hungry and out of a job are the stuff of which dictatorships are made.

In our day these economic truths have become accepted as self-evident. We have accepted, so to speak, a second Bill of Rights under which a new basis of security and prosperity can be established for all — regardless of station, race, or creed.

Among these are:

The right to a useful and remunerative job in the industries or shops or farms or mines of the Nation;

The right to earn enough to provide adequate food and clothing and recreation;

The right of every farmer to raise and sell his products at a return which will give him and his family a decent living;

The right of every businessman, large and small, to trade in an atmosphere of freedom from unfair competition and domination by monopolies at home or abroad;

The right of every family to a decent home;

The right to adequate medical care and the opportunity to achieve and enjoy good health;

The right to adequate protection from the economic fears of old age, sickness, accident, and unemployment;

The right to a good education.

All of these rights spell security. And after this war is won we must be prepared to move forward, in the implementation of these rights, to new goals of human happiness and well-being.

America's own rightful place in the world depends in large part upon how fully these and similar rights have been carried into practice for our citizens. For unless there is security here at home there cannot be lasting peace in the world. . . .

Chronology of Events during the Era of Franklin D. Roosevelt (1933–1945)

1933

March   FDR is inaugurated president.

March–June   "First Hundred Days" witnesses the creation of the National Recovery Administration, Agricultural Adjustment Administration, Tennessee Valley Authority, and Civilian Conservation Corps.

September   Dr. Francis E. Townsend proposes the Old Age Revolving Pension Plan.

1934

June   Congress passes the Indian Reorganization Act.

August   American Liberty League is founded.

November   Father Charles E. Coughlin creates the National Union for Social Justice.

November   Upton Sinclair's bid for governor of California, on the EPIC platform, ends in defeat.

1935

May   Supreme Court strikes down the National Recovery Administration in *A. L. A. Schechter Poultry Corp. v. United States,* the "sick chicken" case.

June–August   "Second Hundred Days" witnesses the passage of the Social Security Act and National Labor Relations Act and the creation of the Works Progress Administration.

September   Senator Huey P. Long of Louisiana is assassinated.

October   John L. Lewis leads the industrial unions comprising the Congress of Industrial Organizations (CIO) out of the American Federation of Labor.

1936

January   Supreme Court declares the Agricultural Adjustment Act unconstitutional in *United States v. Butler.*

March   Dorothea Lange takes the photograph *Migrant Mother.*

November   FDR is reelected, defeating the Republican candidate, Governor Alf Landon of Kansas.

1937

January   CIO sit-down strikes begin at General Motors plants in Flint, Michigan.

February   FDR proposes a plan to enlarge the Supreme Court.

March–May   Supreme Court upholds state minimum wage laws for women, the National Labor Relations Act, and the Social Security Act.

1938

April   FDR accepts a spending plan to combat the "Roosevelt recession."

June   Congress passes the Fair Labor Standards Act, setting minimum wages and maximum hours.

June–August   FDR fails in his attempt to "purge" conservative Democrats in party primaries.

1939

April   John Steinbeck's *The Grapes of Wrath* is published.

June   Congress eliminates the Federal Theatre Project.

September   World War II begins in Europe.

1940

July   Eleanor Roosevelt addresses the Democratic National Convention.

September   Congress passes the Selective Service Act, the nation's first peacetime draft.

November   FDR is elected to a third term, defeating Republican candidate Wendell Willkie.

1941

March   Congress enacts Lend-Lease to provide aid to the Allies.

June   A. Philip Randolph's planned March on Washington leads FDR to create the Committee on Fair Employment Practices.

December 7   Japan attacks Pearl Harbor, and the United States enters World War II.

1942

January   War Production Board is created to manage the wartime economy.

February   FDR issues Executive Order 9066 authorizing the relocation of Japanese Americans from the West Coast.

December   FDR gives the Works Progress Administration an "honorable discharge."

1943

June   Supreme Court overturns compulsory flag salute law in *West Virginia State Board of Education v. Barnette.*

July   Detroit race riot leaves thirty-four dead and seven hundred injured.

Fall   Congress repeals the Chinese Exclusion Acts.

December   FDR declares that "Dr. Win-the-War" must take over for "Dr. New Deal."

1944

January   FDR creates the War Refugee Board.

April   Supreme Court strikes down the white primary in *Smith v. Allwright.*

November   FDR is elected to his fourth term, defeating Republican Thomas E. Dewey.

1945

February   FDR meets with Churchill and Stalin at Yalta.

April 12   FDR dies at age sixty-three as the result of a cerebral hemorrhage.

Questions for Consideration

1. What changes, if any, took place in FDR's goals from 1933, when he gave his first inaugural address; to 1936, when he delivered his campaign speech at Madison Square Garden; to 1944, when he proposed an Economic Bill of Rights?

2. If a radical is "a person who advocates fundamental political, economic, and social reforms by direct and often uncompromising methods," how well does the term describe Huey Long, Father Charles E. Coughlin, and Upton Sinclair?

3. Are there important similarities in how Frances Perkins, Robert F. Wagner, and Harry Hopkins justified New Deal policies in the areas of Social Security, labor relations, and federal relief? Are there important differences?

4. Do the majority opinion in *United States v. Butler* and the minority opinion in *West Coast Hotel v. Parrish* furnish support for the arguments made by FDR and Senator Robert M. La Follette, Jr., in behalf of "packing" the Supreme Court?

5. What problems did the Roosevelt administration face in dealing with issues of racial, ethnic, and gender discrimination? How do those problems compare to the ones FDR faced in dealing with economic recovery and reform?

6. Which groups in society benefited most from the New Deal, which groups benefited least, and what accounted for the difference?

7. Of conservatives' criticisms of Roosevelt's policies, which are the most and the least persuasive?

8. What do the conflicting views expressed by the Supreme Court justices in cases involving Japanese American relocation and the flag salute controversy reveal about the process of judicial decision making?

9. How do the problems Roosevelt faced during the war compare to those he faced during the Depression?

10. What evidence best supports the view that World War II was a "good war," and what evidence best supports the contrary interpretation?

Selected Bibliography

FDR AS PRESIDENT

Franklin D. Roosevelt's early career is superbly treated in Geoffrey C. Ward's two-volume study, *Before the Trumpet: Young Franklin Roosevelt, 1882–1905* (New York: Harper & Row, 1985) and *A First-Class Temperament: The Emergence of Franklin Roosevelt, 1905–1928* (New York: Harper & Row, 1989). Frank Freidel completed four volumes of a projected biography, *Franklin D. Roosevelt* (Boston: Little, Brown, 1952–1973), which carry the story through the year 1933. Kenneth S. Davis also has published four volumes: *FDR: The Beckoning of Destiny, 1882–1928* (New York: Putnam, 1972); *The New York Years, 1928–1933* (New York: Putnam, 1985); *The New Deal Years, 1933–1937* (New York: Random House, 1986); and *Into the Storm, 1937–1940* (New York: Random House, 1993). An earlier two-volume work that remains especially useful is James MacGregor Burns, *Roosevelt: The Lion and the Fox* (New York: Harcourt Brace, 1956) and *Roosevelt: The Soldier of Freedom* (New York: Harcourt Brace Jovanovich, 1970).

Of the many shorter biographical works, three are particularly informative: Frank Freidel, *Franklin D. Roosevelt: A Rendezvous with Destiny* (Boston: Little, Brown, 1990); Patrick J. Maney, *The Roosevelt Presence: A Biography of Franklin Delano Roosevelt* (New York: Twayne, 1992); and Ted Morgan, *FDR: A Biography* (New York: Simon & Schuster, 1985). A more specialized study is Sean J. Savage, *Roosevelt: The Party Leader, 1932–1945* (Lexington: University Press of Kentucky, 1991). For FDR's use of the radio, consult the collection edited by Russell D. Buhite and David W. Levy, *FDR's Fireside Chats* (Norman: University of Oklahoma Press, 1992). For his relationship with journalists, see Betty Houchin Winfield, *FDR and the News Media* (Urbana: University of Illinois Press, 1990); and Graham White, *FDR and the Press* (Chicago: University of Chicago Press, 1979).

THE NEW DEAL

General works on the New Deal include William E. Leuchtenburg, *Franklin D. Roosevelt and the New Deal* (New York: Harper & Row, 1963); Arthur M. Schlesinger, *The Age of Roosevelt*, 3 vols. (Boston: Houghton Mifflin, 1957–1960), which covers the period through 1936; Robert S. McElvaine,

The Great Depression: America, 1929–1941, 2nd ed. (New York: Times Books, 1993); Roger Biles, *A New Deal for the American People* (DeKalb: Northern Illinois University Press, 1991); and Anthony J. Badger, *The New Deal: The Depression Years, 1933–1940* (New York: Hill and Wang, 1989). Two important collections of essays are William E. Leuchtenburg, *The FDR Years: On Roosevelt and His Legacy* (New York: Columbia University Press, 1995); and Steve Fraser and Gary Gerstle, eds., *The Rise and Fall of the New Deal Order: 1933–1980* (Princeton, N.J.: Princeton University Press, 1980).

The goals of New Dealers and the problems they faced may be approached through biographical studies. For an analysis of key policymakers, including David E. Lilienthal and Felix Frankfurter, see Jordan A. Schwarz, *The New Dealers: Power Politics in the Age of Roosevelt* (New York: Alfred A. Knopf, 1993). Other useful works include George Martin, *Madam Secretary: Frances Perkins* (Boston: Houghton Mifflin, 1976); Jeanne Nienaber Clarke, *Roosevelt's Warrior: Harold L. Ickes and the New Deal* (Baltimore: Johns Hopkins University Press, 1996); Graham J. White, *Henry A. Wallace: His Search for a New World Order* (Chapel Hill: University of North Carolina Press, 1995); George McJimsey, *Harry Hopkins: Ally of the Poor and Defender of Democracy* (Cambridge: Harvard University Press, 1987); and June Hopkins, *Harry Hopkins: Sudden Hero, Brash Reformer* (New York: St. Martin's Press, 1999).

Historians have naturally centered much of their attention on New Deal economic policy. For the influence of professional economists on FDR, see William J. Barber, *Designs within Disorder: Franklin D. Roosevelt, the Economists, and the Shaping of American Economic Policy, 1933–1945* (New York: Cambridge University Press, 1996). Early New Deal planning efforts are discussed in Robert F. Himmelberg, *The Origins of the National Recovery Administration, 1921–1933* (New York: Fordham University Press, 1976); and Ellis Hawley, *The New Deal and the Problem of Monopoly: A Study in Economic Ambivalence* (Princeton, N.J.: Princeton University Press, 1966). New Deal agricultural programs are evaluated in Sidney Baldwin, *Poverty and Politics: The Rise and Decline of the Farm Security Administration* (Chapel Hill: University of North Carolina Press, 1968); and Paul E. Mertz, *New Deal Policy and Southern Rural Poverty* (Baton Rouge: Louisiana State University Press, 1978). For experiments in conservation and planning, consult Walter L. Creese, *TVA's Public Planning: The Vision, The Reality* (Knoxville: University of Tennessee Press, 1990); Thomas McCraw, *TVA and the Power Fight, 1933–1939* (Philadelphia: J. B. Lippincott, 1971); and John Salmond, *The Civilian Conservation Corps, 1933–1942* (Durham, N.C.: Duke University Press, 1967). Edgar B. Nixon, ed., *Franklin D. Roosevelt and Conservation,* 2 vols. (Hyde Park, N.Y.: Franklin Delano Roosevelt Library, 1957), is an important collection of documents.

A revisionist interpretation of New Deal policies regarding Social Security and labor can be found in Colin Gordon, *New Deals: Business, Labor, and Politics in America, 1920–1935* (New York: Cambridge University Press,

1994). See also Linda Gordon, *Pitied but Not Entitled: Single Mothers and the History of Welfare, 1890–1935* (New York: Free Press, 1994); Gwendolyn Mink, *The Wages of Motherhood: Inequality in the Welfare State, 1917–1942* (Ithaca, N.Y.: Cornell University Press, 1995); and Lizbeth Cohen, *Making a New Deal: Industrial Workers in Chicago, 1919–1939* (Cambridge: Cambridge University Press, 1990). For a comprehensive account of FDR's labor policy, see Irving Bernstein, *A Caring Society: The New Deal, the Worker, and the Great Depression* (Boston: Houghton Mifflin, 1985), and for a biography of labor's champion in the U.S. Senate, see J. Joseph Huthmacher, *Senator Robert F. Wagner and the Rise of Urban Liberalism* (New York: Atheneum, 1968). Social welfare programs are considered in Roy Lubove, *The Struggle for Social Security, 1900–1935* (Cambridge: Harvard University Press, 1968); William W. Bremer, *Depression Winters: New York Social Workers and the New Deal* (Philadelphia: Temple University Press, 1984); Barbara Blumberg, *The New Deal and the Unemployed: The View from New York City* (Lewisburg, Pa.: Bucknell University Press, 1979); and Bonnie Fox Schwartz, *The Civil Works Administration, 1933–1934* (Princeton, N.J.: Princeton University Press, 1984). On the Federal Theatre Project, see Jane DeHart Mathews, *The Federal Theatre, 1935–1939: Plays, Relief and Politics* (Princeton, N.J.: Princeton University Press, 1967); and Joanne Bentley, *Hallie Flanagan: A Life in the American Theatre* (New York: Alfred A. Knopf, 1988).

ELEANOR ROOSEVELT AND AMERICAN WOMEN

Eleanor Roosevelt is the subject of several recent works, including Blanche Wiesen Cook, *Eleanor Roosevelt, 1884–1933* (New York: Viking Press, 1992), and *Eleanor Roosevelt, 1933–1938* (New York: Viking Press, 1999); and Allida M. Black, *Casting Her Own Shadow: Eleanor Roosevelt and the Shaping of Postwar Liberalism* (New York: Columbia University Press, 1996). See also Maureen Beasley, ed., *The White House Press Conferences of Eleanor Roosevelt* (New York: Garland Publishing, 1983). Two women who played important roles in the New Deal are treated in Susan Ware, *Partner and I: Molly Dewson, Feminism, and New Deal Politics* (New Haven, Conn.: Yale University Press, 1987); and Martha H. Swain, *Ellen S. Woodward: New Deal Advocate for Women* (Jackson: University Press of Mississippi, 1995). For the impact of the Depression and the New Deal on women generally, see Susan Ware, *Holding Their Own: American Women in the 1930s* (New York: Twayne, 1982) and *Beyond Suffrage: Women in the New Deal* (Cambridge: Harvard University Press, 1981); and Lois Scharf, *To Work or to Wed: Female Employment, Feminism, and the Great Depression* (Westport, Conn.: Greenwood Press, 1980). The way in which conceptions of gender influenced New Deal art projects is examined in Barbara Melosh, *Engendering Culture: Manhood and Womanhood in New Deal Public Art and Theater* (Washington, D.C.: Smithsonian Institution Press, 1991).

DOCUMENTING THE DEPRESSION

For an evaluation of documentary photography in the 1930s, see Milton Meltzer, *Dorothea Lange: A Photographer's Life* (New York: Farrar, Straus & Giroux, 1978); F. Jack Hurley, *Portrait of a Decade: Roy Stryker and the Development of Documentary Photography in the Thirties* (Baton Rouge: Louisiana State University Press, 1972); Gilles Mora and John T. Hill, *Walker Evans: The Hungry Eye* (New York: Harry N. Abrams, 1993); William Stott, *Documentary Expression and Thirties America* (New York: Oxford University Press, 1973); and the essays by Lawrence W. Levine and Alan Trachtenberg in Carl Fleischhauer and Beverly W. Brannan, eds., *Documenting America, 1935–1943* (Berkeley: University of California Press, 1988). Two recent specialized studies are Stephen J. Leonard, *Trials and Triumphs: A Colorado Portrait of the Great Depression, with FSA Photographs* (Niwot: University Press of Colorado, 1993); and Nicholas Natanson, *The Black Image in the New Deal: The Politics of FSA Photography* (Knoxville: University of Tennessee Press, 1992). Another valuable work is Charles Shindo, *Dust Bowl Migrants in the American Imagination* (Lawrence: University Press of Kansas, 1997).

RIGHT . . . AND LEFT . . . FACE

Conservative opposition to the New Deal is considered in George Wolfskill and John A. Hudson, *All but the People: FDR and His Critics, 1933–1939* (London: Macmillan, 1969); Donald McCoy, *Landon of Kansas* (Lincoln: University of Nebraska Press, 1966); Gary Dean Best, *Herbert Hoover: The Postpresidential Years, 1933–1964* (Stanford, Calif.: Hoover Institution Press, 1983); James T. Patterson, *Congressional Conservatism and the New Deal* (Lexington: University of Kentucky Press, 1967); and Richard Polenberg, *Reorganizing Roosevelt's Government: The Controversy over Executive Reorganization, 1936–1939* (Cambridge: Harvard University Press, 1966). For the American Liberty League, see Robert F. Burk, *The Corporate State and the Broker State: The Du Ponts and American National Politics, 1925–1940* (Cambridge: Harvard University Press, 1990); and George Wolfskill, *The Revolt of the Conservatives* (Boston: Houghton Mifflin, 1962).

Radical social movements in the 1930s have attracted a good deal of attention from historians. For the EPIC movement, see James N. Gregory's superb introduction to the reprint edition of Upton Sinclair, *I, Candidate for Governor: And How I Got Licked* (Berkeley: University of California Press, 1994); and Greg Mitchell, *The Campaign of the Century: Upton Sinclair's Race for Governor of California and the Birth of Media Politics* (New York: Random House, 1992). The careers of Huey Long and Father Charles E. Coughlin are considered in Alan Brinkley, *Voices of Protest: Huey Long, Father Coughlin and the Great Depression* (New York: Alfred A. Knopf, 1982); Donald I. Warren, *Radio Priest: Charles Coughlin, the Father of Hate Radio* (New York: Free Press, 1996); William Ivy Hair, *The Kingfish and His Realm: The Life and Times of Huey P. Long* (Baton Rouge: Louisiana State University

Press, 1991); and Richard C. Cortner, *The Kingfish and the Constitution: Huey Long, the First Amendment, and the Emergence of Modern Press Freedom in America* (Westport, Conn.: Greenwood, 1996).

The impact of radicalism on American culture in the 1930s is examined in Michael Denning, *The Cultural Front: The Laboring of American Culture in the Twentieth Century* (New York: Verso, 1996); and Laura Browder, *Rousing the Nation: Radical Culture in Depression America* (Amherst: University of Massachusetts Press, 1998). For campus radicalism, see Robert Cohen, *When the Old Left Was Young: Student Radicals and America's First Mass Student Movement, 1929–1941* (New York: Oxford University Press, 1993). Harvey Klehr provides a comprehensive study of the Communist party in *The Heyday of American Communism: The Depression Decade* (New York: Basic Books, 1984). He has also coedited two important documentary collections, *The Secret World of American Communism* (New Haven, Conn.: Yale University Press, 1995) and *The Soviet World of American Communism* (New Haven, Conn.: Yale University Press, 1998). See also the biographies of two leaders of the Communist party: Edward P. Johanningsmeier, *Forging American Communism: The Life of William Z. Foster* (Princeton, N.J.: Princeton University Press, 1994); and James G. Ryan, *Earl Browder: The Failure of American Communism* (Tuscaloosa: University of Alabama Press, 1997). For the policies of the Communist party during World War II, consult Maurice Isserman, *Which Side Were You On?* (Middletown, Conn.: Wesleyan University Press, 1982).

RACE, ETHNICITY, AND REFORM

The intersection of race, ethnicity, and reform during the Roosevelt years is covered in the relevant chapters of Richard Polenberg, *One Nation Divisible: Class, Race, and Ethnicity in the United States since 1938* (New York: Viking Press, 1980); and Ronald Takaki, *A Different Mirror: A History of Multicultural America* (Boston: Little, Brown, 1993). There are several accounts of African Americans and the New Deal, including Patricia Sullivan, *Days of Hope: Race and Democracy in the New Deal Era* (Chapel Hill: University of North Carolina Press, 1996); John B. Kirby, *Black Americans in the Roosevelt Era: Liberalism and Race* (Knoxville: University of Tennessee Press, 1980); Raymond Wolters, *Negroes and the Great Depression: The Problem of Economic Recovery* (Westport, Conn.: Greenwood Press, 1970); Harvard Sitkoff, *A New Deal for Blacks: The Emergence of Civil Rights as a National Issue* (New York: Oxford University Press, 1978); and Nancy J. Weiss, *Farewell to the Party of Lincoln: Black Politics in the Age of FDR* (Princeton, N.J.: Princeton University Press, 1984).

For more specialized studies, consult Nancy L. Grant, *TVA and Black Americans: Planning for the Status Quo* (Philadelphia: Temple University Press, 1990); Cheryl Lynn Greenberg, *"Or Does It Explode?": Black Harlem in the Great Depression* (New York: Oxford University Press, 1991); and

Robin D. G. Kelley, *Hammer and Hoe: Alabama Communists during the Great Depression* (Chapel Hill: University of North Carolina Press, 1990). Paula F. Pfeffer has written a fine biography, *A. Philip Randolph: Pioneer of the Civil Rights Movement* (Baton Rouge: Louisiana State University Press, 1990). The architect of the New Deal policy toward Native Americans is the subject of Kenneth R. Philp, *John Collier's Crusade for Indian Reform, 1920–1954* (Tucson: University of Arizona Press, 1977); and Lawrence C. Kelly, *The Assault on Assimilation: John Collier and the Origins of Indian Policy Reform* (Albuquerque: University of New Mexico Press, 1983). Another superb work is Donald L. Parman, *The Navajos and the New Deal* (New Haven, Conn.: Yale University Press, 1976). For accounts of Mexican American workers, see Devra Weber, *Dark Sweat, White Gold: California Farm Workers, Cotton, and the New Deal* (Berkeley: University of California Press, 1994); Mark Reisler, *By the Sweat of Their Brow: Mexican Immigrant Labor in the United States, 1900–1940* (Westport, Conn.: Greenwood Press, 1976); and Camille Guerin-Gonzales, *Mexican Workers and American Dreams: Immigration, Repatriation, and California Farm Labor* (New Brunswick, N.J.: Rutgers University Press, 1994). The complexity of class relationships is suggested by Richard A. Garcia, *Rise of the Mexican American Middle Class: San Antonio, 1929–1941* (College Station: Texas A&M University Press, 1991).

THE CONSTITUTIONAL REVOLUTION

For the relationship between the New Deal and the legal community, see John Henry Schlegel, *American Legal Realism and Empirical Social Science* (Chapel Hill: University of North Carolina Press, 1995); Ronen Shamir, *Managing Legal Uncertainty: Elite Lawyers in the New Deal* (Durham, N.C.: Duke University Press, 1995); and Peter H. Irons, *The New Deal Lawyers* (Princeton, N.J.: Princeton University Press, 1982). The "constitutional revolution" of 1937 is appraised from varying perspectives in William E. Leuchtenburg, *The Supreme Court Reborn: The Constitutional Revolution in the Age of Roosevelt* (New York: Oxford University Press, 1995); Barry Cushman, *Rethinking the New Deal Court: The Structure of a Constitutional Revolution* (New York: Oxford University Press, 1998); and Richard A. Maidment, *The Judicial Response to the New Deal: The U.S. Supreme Court and Economic Regulation, 1934–1936* (Manchester, England: Manchester University Press, 1991). Useful biographical studies include Hadley Arkes, *The Return of George Sutherland: Restoring a Jurisprudence of Natural Rights* (Princeton, N.J.: Princeton University Press, 1994); Michael E. Parrish, *Felix Frankfurter and His Times: The Reform Years* (New York: Free Press, 1982); Philippa Strum, *Louis D. Brandeis: Justice for the People* (Cambridge: Harvard University Press, 1984); Alpheus Thomas Mason, *Harlan Fiske Stone: Pillar of the Law*

(New York: Viking Press, 1956); Roger K. Newman, *Hugo Black: A Biography* (New York: Pantheon Books, 1994); and Richard Polenberg, *The World of Benjamin Cardozo: Personal Values and the Judicial Process* (Cambridge: Harvard University Press, 1997).

MORALE IN WARTIME

The government's efforts to shape public opinion during World War II are evaluated in George H. Roeder, Jr., *The Censored War: American Visual Experience during World War Two* (New Haven, Conn.: Yale University Press, 1993); Alan M. Winkler, *The Politics of Propaganda: The Office of War Information, 1942–1945* (New Haven, Conn.: Yale University Press, 1978); Clayton D. Laurie, *The Propaganda Warriors: America's Crusade against Nazi Germany* (Lawrence: University Press of Kansas, 1996); Holly Cowan Shulman, *The Voice of America: Propaganda and Democracy, 1941–1945* (Madison: University of Wisconsin Press, 1990); Clayton R. Koppes and Gregory D. Black, *Hollywood Goes to War: How Politics, Profits, and Propaganda Shaped World War II Movies* (New York: Free Press, 1987); and Bernard F. Dick, *The Star-Spangled Screen: The American World War II Film* (Lexington: University of Kentucky Press, 1985). Karal Ann Marling and John Wetenhall, *Iwo Jima: Monuments, Memories, and the American Hero* (Cambridge: Harvard University Press, 1991), explores the ways in which a famous photograph was mythologized for propaganda purposes.

THE "GOOD WAR"?

Wartime domestic policies are analyzed in Richard Polenberg, *War and Society: The United States, 1941–1945* (Philadelphia: J. B. Lippincott, 1972); John M. Blum, *V Was for Victory: Politics and American Culture during World War II* (New York: Harcourt Brace Jovanovich, 1976); William L. O'Neill, *A Democracy at War* (New York: Free Press, 1993); Lewis A. Ehrenberg and Susan E. Hirsch, eds., *The War in American Culture: Society and Consciousness during World War II* (Chicago: University of Chicago Press, 1996); Michael C. C. Adams, *The Best War Ever: America and World War II* (Baltimore: Johns Hopkins University Press, 1994); and Doris Kearns Goodwin, *No Ordinary Time: Franklin and Eleanor Roosevelt, the Home Front in World War II* (New York: Simon & Schuster, 1994).

The tragedy of Japanese American relocation has been explored by Roger Daniels in several works, including, most recently, *Prisoners without Trial: Japanese Americans in World War II* (New York: Hill and Wang, 1993). Other crucial works are Peter Irons, *Justice at War: The Story of the Japanese American Internment Cases* (New York: Oxford University Press, 1983); Gary Y. Okihiro, *Whispered Silences: Japanese Americans and World War II* (Seattle: University of Washington Press, 1996); and John W. Dower, *War without Mercy: Race and Power in the Pacific War* (New York: Pantheon Books, 1986). For the Supreme Court decisions in the *Hirabayashi* and *Ko-*

rematsu cases, an indispensable work is the final volume of Sidney Fine's biography of Justice Frank Murphy, *The Washington Years* (Ann Arbor: University of Michigan Press, 1984).

For the repeal of the Chinese Exclusion Acts, see two works by Ronald T. Takaki, *Strangers from a Different Shore: A History of Asian Americans* (Boston: Little, Brown, 1989) and *Democracy and Race: Asian Americans and World War II* (New York: Chelsea House, 1994). Also useful is Peter Conn, *Pearl S. Buck: A Cultural Biography* (New York: Cambridge University Press, 1996). For the Supreme Court and the flag-salute controversy, see David R. Manwaring, *Render unto Caesar: The Flag-Salute Controversy* (Chicago: University of Chicago Press, 1962); and Merlin Owen Newton, *Armed with the Constitution: Jehovah's Witnesses in Alabama and the U.S. Supreme Court, 1939–1946* (Tuscaloosa: University of Alabama Press, 1995).

First published in 1984, David Wyman's authoritative account of the Roosevelt administration's response to the Holocaust, *The Abandonment of the Jews: America and the Holocaust, 1941–1945,* has been reissued (New York: New Press, 1998). It may be supplemented with Richard Breitman and Alan Kraut, *American Refugee Policy and European Jewry, 1933–1945* (Bloomington: Indiana University Press, 1987); and Martin Gilbert, *Auschwitz and the Allies* (New York: Holt, Rinehart and Winston, 1981). For a different perspective, see William D. Rubinstein, *The Myth of Rescue: Why the Democracies Could Not Have Saved More Jews from the Nazis* (London: Routledge, 1997). Another useful work is Kai Bird, *The Chairman: John J. McCloy, the Making of the American Establishment* (New York: Simon & Schuster, 1992).

The impact of World War II on American liberalism is the subject of Alan Brinkley, *The End of Reform: New Deal Liberalism in Recession and War* (New York: Alfred A. Knopf, 1995). For the war's effect on civil liberties, see Samuel Walker, *In Defense of American Liberties: A History of the ACLU* (New York: Oxford University Press, 1990); and Richard W. Steele, *Free Speech in the Good War* (New York: St. Martin's Press, 1999). Additional information may be found in Edwin Amenta and Theda Skocpol, "Redefining the New Deal," in *The Politics of Social Policy in the United States,* ed. Margaret Weir, Ann Shola Orloff, and Theda Skocpol (Princeton, N.J.: Princeton University Press, 1988); and Richard Polenberg, "The Good War? A Reappraisal of How World War II Affected American Society," *Virginia Magazine of History and Biography,* July 1992.

Acknowledgments

Frances Perkins, "The Social Security Act," from *Vital Speeches of the Day,* I, 1935, 792–94. Vital Speech of the Day, City News Publishing Co., P. O. Box 1247, Mt. Pleasant, SC 29465.

John Steinbeck, "The Crisis in Agriculture" from the September 12, 1936, issue of *The Nation.* Copyright © 1936 by John Steinbeck. Reprinted with permission of The Nation.

Hallie Flanagan, excerpts from the introduction, from *Federal Theatre Plays* by Pierre De Rohan, introduction by Hallie Flanagan. Copyright © 1938 and renewed 1966 by Random House, Inc. Reprinted by permission of Random House, Inc.

Eleanor Roosevelt, "Women in the Labor Force" from *The Whitehouse Press Conferences of Eleanor Roosevelt,* Maureen Beasley, ed. Copyright © 1983 by Maureen Beasley. Reprinted by permission of Taylor and Francis, Inc.

Robert M. La Follette Jr., "Unpacking the Court" from *Congressional Quarterly,* March 1937, pp. 84–85. Copyright © 1937 by the Congressional Quarterly. Reprinted by permission of the Congressional Quarterly.

Eleanor Roosevelt, "Women in Politics" from *Good Housekeeping,* March 1940, pp. 45, 68, April 1940, pp. 201–203. Copyright © 1940 by the Hearst Corporation. Reprinted by permission of the Hearst Corporation.

Paul S. Taylor, "Songs of the Mexican Migration" in *Puro Mexicano,* J. Frank Dobie, ed., Publication of the Texas Folklore Society No. XII, 1935. Copyright © 1935 by the Texas Folklore Society. Reprinted by permission of the Texas Folklore Society.

W. E. B. Du Bois and Walter White, "The NAACP and Segregation" from *The Crisis,* January–February 1934. Copyright © 1934 by The Crisis Publication Co., Inc. We wish to thank The Crisis Publishing Co., Inc., the publisher of the magazine of the National Association for the Advancement of Colored People, for authorizing the use of this work.

C. Hayashi and K. Yamanaka, "Footprints: Poetry of the American Relocation Camp Experience" from *Amerasia Journal* (1976), 115–17. Copyright © 1976 by University of California Regents, Asian American Studies.

Herbert Hoover, "The Challenge to Liberty" (New York: Charles Scribner's Sons, 1934), pp. 197–204. Reprinted by permission of the Herbert Hoover Presidential Library.

Index

AAA. *See* Agricultural Adjustment Act
Adams, John, 63
Adkins v. Children's Hospital, 175, 176, 178, 179
administrative reform. *See* governmental administrative reform
African Americans
    Eleanor Roosevelt on, 224–25
    FDR's policies toward, 29–33
    impact of WWII on, 184, 191
    and March on Washington movement, 147–51
    NAACP and segregation, 142–47
Agricultural Adjustment Act (AAA), 11–12, 161–62
    Supreme Court ruling on, 12, 60, 161, 162–69
agriculture, John Steinbeck on crisis in, 77–83
agriculture reform, 11–12. *See also* farm policy
A. L. A. Schechter Poultry Corp. v. United States, 10–11
aliens
    impact of WWII on, 26–27
    See also immigrants
Allen, A. Leonard, and Chinese Exclusion Acts, 204–11
Alsberg, Henry, 89
American Indian. *See* Native Americans
American Indian Defense Association, 151
American Liberty League, 117–19
Anderson, Mary, 94–96
"Annual Message to the Congress" (Roosevelt), 47–52
Arent, Arthur, *Power,* 90
armed forces, and racial inequality, 30–32, 147–48
arms embargo, and neutrality laws, 23–24
Arts Project, 89–90
Auschwitz, debate about bombing, 221–23

Bankhead Cotton Act, 164
Berle, Adolf A., 9
Biddle, Francis, 26, 27, 29

Bill of Rights, 214–15
    FDR's economic, 24, 33, 226–27
Birkenau, 222, 223
Bituminous Coal Conservation Act, 161
Black, Allida M., 93
Black, Hugo, on *Korematsu v. United States,* 197–200
blind, aid to, 57, 73, 88
Blum, John Morton, 25
Bonneville Dam, FDR's speech at, 67
Brandeis, Louis D., 161, 172
Brinkley, Alan, 22, 25, 224
Brotherhood of Sleeping Car Porters, 31, 147
Brownlow, Louis, 17
Buck, Pearl
    and Chinese Exclusion Acts, 204–11
    The Good Earth, 204
Bureau of Internal Revenue, 74
Burns, James MacGregor, 1, 226
Butler, Pierce, 161, 178

Cahill, Holger, 90
"Campaign Address at Madison Square Garden" (Roosevelt), 53–57
Cardozo, Benjamin N., 161, 172
    on *Helvering v. Davis,* 180–83
Cassmore, Orin C., *The Pecan Shellers of San Antonio,* 136–42
censorship, during WWII, 27
Challenge to Liberty, The (Hoover), 114–17
Chandler, A. J., 78
Chiang Kai-shek, 206
Chicago Tribune, 27
child labor reform, 5, 9, 10, 19–20, 56
child welfare, 23, 73, 74
Chinese, racial hatred toward, 79
Chinese Exclusion Acts, 204–11
Churchill, Winston, 34
Civilian Conservation Corps, 13, 52, 65
    liquidation of, 25
civil liberties, impact of war on, 26–29, 191
civil rights
    FDR's policies for, 29–33
    See also African Americans; racial equality issues

245